D1521583

Making a Moral Society

Making a Moral Society

Ethics and the State in Meiji Japan

Richard M Reitan

University of Hawai'i Press

Honolulu

Library of Congress Cataloging-in-Publication Data
Reitan, Richard M.
    Making a moral society : ethics and the state in Meiji Japan / Richard M Reitan.
        p.   cm.
    Includes bibliographical references and index.
    ISBN 978-0-8248-3294-0 (hardcover : alk. paper)
    1. Ethics—Japan—History—19th century.   2. Ethics—Japan—History—20th
century.   I. Title.
    BJ970.R45 2010
    170.952'09034—dc22

                                                        2009018704

University of Hawai'i Press books are printed on acid-free
paper and meet the guidelines for permanence and
durability of the Council on Library Resources.

Designed by University of Hawai'i Production Department
Printed by The Maple-Vail Book Manufacturing Group

Contents

Acknowledgments

A work of this kind is never entirely one's own; it draws upon the suggestions and support of others. As this book took shape, many people offered their expertise and assistance and I wish to express to them my gratitude. Above all, I am sincerely grateful to Tetsuo Najita and Jim Ketelaar at the University of Chicago for their tireless support during the formative stages of this project. Through our many conversations, they challenged me to consider the issues addressed and questions raised in this work more deeply and more critically, while always allowing me to find my own way forward. I am also grateful to Satō Yasukuni at the University of Tokyo for pointing me toward helpful resource materials in Japan, for welcoming me, a historian, into his philosophically oriented *rinrigaku* study group, and above all for our long conversations on Meiji ethics and on ethics in general. Frank Reynolds at the University of Chicago offered kind encouragement as well as thoughtful guidance concerning the relationship between my analysis of Meiji Japan and contemporary moral discourse. Okuizumi Eizaburō of the University of Chicago's East Asian Library was always available with friendly assistance and bibliographic expertise.

I am indebted as well to Katsuya Hirano, Tong Lam, and Derek Wolff for their insightful suggestions, their always thoughtful and oftentimes challenging criticisms, and their friendship during our years at the University of Chicago and after; to the members of the history research group at the University of Washington; to Marjorie McIntosh, John Willis, Mithi Mukherjee, and Sanjay Gautam at the University of Colorado at Boulder; and to my colleagues at Franklin and Marshall College, both within and outside the history department, for their guidance and friendship. They have made the challenging first years at Franklin and Marshall easier to negotiate and entirely pleasant. Mei Yan Tsang has been wonderfully supportive as I brought this work to completion, always ready with encouragement, a creative perspective, and intelligent critique. I am grateful to her for sharing with me the weight of this task and, so, making it lighter.

Douglas Howland, Kevin Doak, and Harry Harootunian read through drafts of this book at various stages and provided penetrating comments and valuable criticism. I greatly appreciate and gratefully acknowledge the generous contribution of their time. Had I managed to address all of their suggestions more fully, this would have been a far stronger work. The editors at University of Hawai'i Press read the entire manuscript with meticulous care and found numerous ways to improve the book's clarity. Two readers for the press posed perceptive questions and offered invaluable suggestions for revision. For this work's insights, I am indebted to all of the above-mentioned colleagues and friends—their contributions have made this a better work. The responsibility for whatever shortcomings have remained is of course my own.

The Japan Foundation and the Woodrow Wilson Foundation provided generous financial support for this project, the former funding a year of research in Tokyo, the latter a year of writing through the Charlotte Newcombe Dissertation Writing Grant. In addition, I wish to thank the University of Chicago's Department of History and Center for East Asian Studies for travel grants allowing me to conduct much-needed follow up research in Japan, and Harvard University's Yenching Library for providing a travel grant and the generous use of their materials. An earlier version of chapter 5 appeared as "National Morality, the State, and 'Dangerous Thought': Approaching the Moral Ideal in late Meiji Japan," *Japan Studies Review* 9 (2005): 23–58.

Finally, this book is dedicated to the memory of my mother, Ann Reitan, and to my father, Ralph M. Reitan, whose own example of dedication and intellectual integrity has, time and again, led me back to my own work with renewed energy and commitment.

Introduction

Ethics and the Universal
in Meiji Japan

> For each new class which puts itself in the place of one ruling
> before it, is compelled, merely in order to carry through its aim,
> to represent its interest as the common interest of all the members
> of society, that is, expressed in ideal form: it has to give its ideas
> the form of universality, and represent them as the only rational,
> universally valid ones.
> —Karl Marx and Frederick Engels, *The German Ideology*

Moral universalism is a contentious idea. The theory of
"moral universals"—the idea that all humanity or all those of a particular
national or cultural community share certain common moral sensibilities, or
that one's own moral perspective is in fact a timeless moral truth—has in some
form long been a central feature of moral discourse. Those who accept this
theory may disagree over what "our values" are, or what foundation verifies the
truthfulness of these values, but that such values exist is widely presupposed.
But can any moral claim ever transcend its own historicity? Given that any
morality asserting its validity across time and space can make such an assertion
only through the specific language and cultural resources of a particular time
and place, moral universals do not appear to be universal at all. Rather than
timeless truths that have been revealed to us—whether through an examination
of the natural world, society, or our innermost "human nature"—moral universals appear from this historicizing standpoint to be contingent products of the
epistemological and normative context out of which they emerge.[1] It matters,
for example, whether a moral claim is put forward by a Shin Buddhist monk
in nineteenth-century Japan or by a philosopher in twentieth-century France;
knowledge and value for each will be understood differently. If moral truth is
produced rather than revealed—and this project will show that in some cases

it most certainly is—then the question of how it is produced becomes crucially important. This is a study of the process by which the good as a contingent perspective is recast as a timeless truth or universal principle. It sets aside the question "What is the good?" (a question basic to the way the discipline of ethics is conceptualized) and asks instead, "How is the good produced?"

To address this question, I inquire into the shifting epistemological conditions for moral truthfulness in Meiji Japan (1868–1912) and call attention to the role of the universal in legitimizing the moral claims of this time. That is, I examine the underlying presuppositions about nature, humanity, society, the nation-state, and culture that shaped what was possible to think and say about how one ought to think and act. Can nature tell us what is moral, or should we ground our moral claims in what we know of humanity? Should our focus be social relations in general or something more specific: the culture, traditions, and character of a given nation or "people"? Different answers to these questions held sway at different times in modern Japanese history. Moreover, those espousing moral perspectives sought legitimacy for their views by grounding them in a supposedly universal foundation: the laws of nature, natural law, the human personality, or the timeless Way of the Japanese people. Thus, universal values conveyed, in some cases, moral sensibilities common to all humanity; in others, the values of Japan's particular national or cultural community.

Morality was at the forefront of intellectual debates in late nineteenth century Japan. In the Social Darwinist "survival of the fittest" atmosphere of this time, the Japanese state sought to quell uprisings and rebellions and to overcome all manner of divisive social disruptions so as to produce national unity and defend its sovereignty against Western encroachment. Morality became a crucial means to attain these aims. Moral prescriptions for reordering the population came from all segments of society. Buddhist, Christian, and Confucian apologists, literary figures and artists, advocates of natural rights, anarchists, women defending nontraditional gender roles, and others put forward moral views designed to unify society. Each envisioned a unity grounded in its own moral perspective. It was in this tumultuous atmosphere that the academic discipline of ethics (*rinrigaku*) emerged.

The first departmental chair for ethics at a Japanese university was established at Tokyo Imperial University in 1893, thus conferring official recognition upon this newly formed discipline. But preliminary studies of morality associated with this discipline began more than a decade earlier. *A New Theory of Ethics* (*Rinri shinsetsu*, 1883), a work by philosophy professor Inoue Tetsujirō (1856–1944), marked the emergence of this discipline in the early 1880s and signaled the role *rinrigaku* was to play as an apparatus of the state. Scholars of ethics, together with state bureaucrats, pursued social unity and order through the cultivation of common moral sensibilities. At the same time, they provided philosophical justification for the oftentimes violent suppression of socially disruptive or "dangerous" thought and action that ran counter to the needs of the state. Thus, these two goals—producing moral unity and suppressing dangerous thought—were closely intertwined. Yet the more *rinrigaku* and the state struggled to produce and regulate a common hegemonic morality, the more resistance they encountered. Indeed, the pursuit of moral hegemony itself, I argue, sustained the violence and moral dissension it aimed to overcome.[2]

Rinrigaku scholars justified the state's acts of suppression by insisting on the universal status of its particular and perspectival claims concerning "the good." Seeking to position themselves as the dominant arbiters of the good, *rinrigaku* scholars projected their claims outward (attempting to universalize a particular form of socio-moral practice) and backward in time (reconfiguring the past to accord with their supposedly "universal" ethical claims in the present) so as to produce the moral unity the state demanded. The claim to universal status was thus a key strategy for overcoming the historical contingency of *rinrigaku*'s moral position and asserting its changeless quality. Marx alluded to such a strategy when he stated that each new class is compelled to represent its ideas (and this includes its values) as universal, as those of society as a whole.[3] But the "unchanging" universal ground for ethics in Meiji Japan changed with the particular historical context.

In the 1880s, for example, the discipline of ethics was central in establishing and defending an "ethics of civilization." Upheld as a universal morality common to all humanity, the ethics of civilization condemned public urination, mixed-sex bathing, and other "barbaric" practices associated with the "foolish masses." Scholars of ethics justified the suppressive "civilizing legislation" (*kaika jōrei*) of the state, which made such practices illegal, through an empiricist, scientific methodology that allowed them to make authoritative moral claims grounded in universal reason. While Japan's past became a repository of barbaric practices and foolish superstitions, the future promised ever higher levels of "civilization." Japan would take its place among the more fully civilized nations of the West provided that the irrational and now immoral beliefs and practices of the past could be suppressed and the foolish properly civilized.

By the turn of the century, as many struggled against the idea of a "hierarchy of civilization" because of the inferior position to which it assigned Japan, the discipline of ethics underwent a transition from an ethics of civilization to an ethics of spirit.[4] Scholars of ethics like Inoue Tetsujirō, Nakashima Rikizō, Fukasaku Yasubumi, and many others grew critical of empiricism, emphasizing the limitations of reason, observation, and experimentation as avenues for apprehending the good. Instead, by drawing on "national character" and *Volksgeist* (folk spirit)—conceptions originally associated with German Romanticism but now powerfully impacting Japan's intellectual landscape—*rinrigaku* scholars now posited a unitary Japanese morality informed by a common folk spirit. Japanese folk morality, according to its architects, demanded self-sacrifice and patriotic loyalty to the state. The ethics of civilization common to all humanity had been displaced by an ethics of spirit common to all "true Japanese." Thus, the universal continued to operate as a basis for moral authority, but in a circumscribed form. Those whose moral convictions ran counter to this emerging Japanese moral spirit (most notably anarchists and socialists) were condemned as dangerous; some were beaten or imprisoned, others—as in the 1911 High Treason Incident involving a plan to assassinate the emperor—executed. Thus, the pursuit of moral hegemony—in both early and late Meiji—involved efforts to strengthen the authority of the state's moral vision on the one hand and to suppress alternative moral views on the other.

The education system became the primary means for disseminating both the ethics of civilization of early Meiji and the ethics of spirit that emerged at the end of this period. While moral philosophers wrote scholarly works on ethics, they also produced, often in conjunction with Ministry of Education bureaucrats, primary school textbooks through which students pursued moral training (*shūshin*). *Shūshin* literally meant "to discipline the body" (*mi o osameru*), and this was indeed one of its key objectives, both in the classroom where this term was most often heard, and throughout society. Appropriate moral behavior was to be cultivated through the performative repetition of certain daily practices or bodily activities (the recitation of moral lessons in the classroom), through the discontinuation or prohibition of others (mixed-sex bathing, public urination), and through repeated exposure to stories or images of actions to be emulated (shouting out "Tennō heika banzai!" [Long live the emperor!] when struck down by an enemy's bullet on the battlefields of Manchuria).

Moral training, however, was not just about disciplining the body. Equally important was the disciplining of the mind, and much of the struggle that characterized Meiji moral discourse centered on questions revolving around precisely this issue. At stake here was the human interiority. What is the proper role of the state in shaping the moral lives of its citizens? Should "conscience" be regulated by the state? While religious apologists, socialists, and individualists demanded a space of autonomy for the individual free from state moral intervention, moral training, whether understood as *shūshin* or as the wide-scale moral reform of society, helped to expand the role of the state in shaping the moral interiority of the individual. Its effectiveness was tied to the level of authority *rinrigaku* scholars mustered for their moral-philosophical arguments and to the degree that the parameters of legitimate moral discourse could be widely naturalized.

Early in the Meiji period, *rinrigaku* established the terms, issues, and limits of "legitimate" moral discourse: the importance of social unity, the survival of the state, loyal self-sacrifice for the social good, fulfilling one's duties as a subject of the state, knowing one's "station" and proper role in society, preserving "our" traditional values. Debate could (and did) take place concerning how unity was to be attained, what loyalty demanded of state subjects, and which values were "traditional," but these terms were established with sufficient authority and broad interpretive potential so as to allow the state to maintain control and effectively negotiate contingent historical changes unforeseen in the early Meiji period. Such changes included the emergence of new social classes and subject positions, industrialization and rapid urbanization, and economic and social mobilization in times of war. In this sense, much of the resistance to *rinrigaku* took place within a space of discourse where prioritizing the good of the state was already accepted. With *rinrigaku*'s success in establishing authority for its own modes of moral inquiry, religious apologists, advocates of anarchism and individualism, and others found themselves with little authority to speak for "the good." I investigate how and with what success these various groups resisted the discipline of ethics and the state.

This study begins with an examination of the morality of "civilization" (out of which *rinrigaku* emerged) and that which was to be civilized—the barbaric or "foolish" thought and actions of the "masses." Civilization (*bunmeikaika*), in the sense used here, was a complex discourse on hierarchy according to which societies progress from barbarism to an enlightened stage of development epitomized by an imagined space called "the West." I argue that Inoue Tetsujirō's *New Theory of Ethics* reflects the norms of civilization and that it was the first comprehensive attempt to objectify the good in accordance with the new modes of moral inquiry that came to be called *rinrigaku*. *Rinrigaku* scholars like Inoue called for the civilizing of the "unenlightened masses," commonly referred to as the "foolish people." That civilizing was necessary, and indeed urgent, was the starting point for these scholars. Thus, although they claimed to objectively seek the foundations of "the good," they were rather constructing an ethical foundation with which to legitimize a set of values to which they (and the state) were already committed. An examination of several works of *gesaku* (literature of play) provides an example of how this discourse on civilization was contested. *Gesaku* writers satirizing the seriousness of "moral civility" subverted the authority of *rinrigaku* and the state and thus marked the limit of civilization's authority.

After an examination of the broad moral space of "civilization," I turn in the second chapter to the dominant moral theories of early Meiji and the underlying epistemology that shaped and authorized them. *Rinrigaku* scholars of the early 1880s defined "the good" in terms of state power and social order. While they claimed to speak from a value-neutral position, a position from which to inquire into and apprehend the good, their methodologies and ethical theories were invariably rooted in culturally and historically specific epistemological presuppositions. I approach *rinrigaku* as a discourse on the good emerging out of a modern epistemology. My concern here is with "modernity" not as a point in time but as having to do with a particular set of authoritative and fundamental presuppositions about knowledge and truth that (re)shaped thought, action, and (of particular concern in this work) the good. A marked opposition between subject and object, between, for example, the observer and what he or she observes, was a central presupposition that characterized this epistemology. Other presuppositions included the view of truth or the good as essential (possessing an essence that makes it what it is) and revelatory (capable of being revealed through the application of instrumental reason). This framework for knowledge, which I call an epistemology of representation, informed *rinrigaku* and—as it grew in authority and engaged with competing normative positions—other views of the good as well. An examination of this epistemology is a useful task because it helps to reveal the contingency of *rinrigaku*'s ethical claims, it facilitates our interpretation of moral texts from this period, and it allows us to explore the formation of moral subjectivity—a moral position or intellectual space shaped by, but also constituting or shaping, discourse and material practices.

In chapter 3 I focus on the fluidity of moral subjectivity (the constantly shifting nature of the norms to which we are subject and how we apprehend, resist, or practice them) by juxtaposing *rinrigaku* texts with moral writings by religious apologists. According to *rinrigaku* scholars of early Meiji, religion (*shūkyō*)—and Christianity most of all—posed a threat to social order. At this time, *rinrigaku* and religion struggled for the authority to speak on what is ethical. *Rinrigaku* academics sought to expel religion from "legitimate" ethical inquiry. In an effort to defend their views, religious apologists internalized many features of the epistemology that grounded *rinrigaku*, but changed them in the process to accord with their own theories and understandings. In the hands of defenders of religion, key terms and concepts that informed *rinrigaku*'s style of moral inquiry were transformed and redirected to new ends unforeseen by those who first insisted upon them. Buddhists, for example, linked the idea of karma with the scientific law of cause and effect, while Christian thinkers explained "evolutionary progress" as the gradual unfolding of "God's plan." But this internalization of science and progress also transformed the moral space of religion. This discursive exchange between *rinrigaku* scholars and defenders of religion reflects the way the production of the good and epistemological preconceptions were inextricably bound to one another. Moreover, despite the efforts made at this time to speak on behalf of some timeless, moral universal truth, it attests to the fluidity of moral subjectivity and the contested and indeterminate nature of its production in Meiji Japan.

By the beginning of the 1890s, moral philosophers in Japan had begun to reshape their discipline. Moving away from the empiricism and utilitarianism of the prior decade, scholars of ethics now placed "spirit" at the center of ethical inquiry. They posited the good as intuitively apprehended, not rationally verified. Thus, intuition replaced reason, metaphysics replaced empiricism, and "spirit" (whether God, individual consciousness, or the "spirit of the nation") became the basis for explaining and defining moral action. I examine this shift in my fourth chapter through the works of two thinkers, each deeply involved in the ethics of spirit: Inoue Tetsujirō, mentioned above, and moral philosopher Nakashima Rikizō (1858–1918), first to hold the chair of ethics at Tokyo Imperial University. The shift *rinrigaku* underwent was part of an effort to resist the civilizational hierarchies associated with "civilization." But this required not merely the critique of assertions of Western superiority in the realms of knowledge and virtue; it also required the destabilization of the epistemology that grounded and enabled civilization. This epistemology of representation linked truth with the observable, the rationally verifiable, and the measurable. "Spirit," the unobservable and intuitively apprehended, provided a means to contest civilization and its underlying epistemology and transformed the topography of moral thought in 1890s Japan.

In the final chapter of this volume, I examine the national morality movement (*kokumin dōtoku*), its close association with the state, and its opposition to what its proponents deemed "dangerous thought." From the 1900s, a state-sponsored national morality came to dominate moral discourse in Japan. This morality of the national folk posited as a moral ideal a morally homogeneous society of dutiful subjects all equally loyal to the state. Competing visions of the state, the individual, and the good were represented as "dangerous thought" and violently suppressed—the most vivid example being the execution of twelve anarchist activists in the High Treason Incident of 1911. I argue that the pursuit of the national morality ideal required the eradication of obstacles in its path, hence the suppression of dangerous thought. Yet, the state's violent tactics engendered violent resistance. Anarchists, for example, redefined the meaning of moral action so as to defend an "ethics of terrorism" with which to directly contest the authority of *rinrigaku* and the state. Thus, rather than producing dutiful subjects and a morally cohesive society, national morality proponents merely sustained the violent social dissension they sought to overcome. In this section, I inquire into the potential violence inherent in the pursuit of moral ideals.

Finally, in the epilogue, I seek to position this study in a longer stream of history by outlining some of the conceptual linkages between the Meiji and later periods. A conceptual vocabulary, a constellation of semantically variable terms and ideas like *kokumin*, *minzoku*, the morality of self-negation, and dangerous thought, emerged by late Meiji and prefigured many of the most pressing concerns of interwar and wartime moral discourse. The epilogue also provides a summation of the major questions raised and arguments made concerning the discipline of ethics and "the universal" in Meiji Japan by turning briefly to contemporary Japan. A particular focus here is the emergence of a new discourse on national morality. I draw attention to social critic Nishibe Susumu's recent publication, *National Morality (Kokumin no dōtoku)* and its critique. Although Nishibe's moral program differs in many respects from early twentieth century statements on national morality, his desire to resuscitate the "moral spirit" common to all Japanese carries the same potential dangers and warrants the same careful scrutiny as the national morality of the Meiji period.

CHAPTER 1

Civilization and Foolishness
Contextualizing Ethics in Early Meiji Japan

There is nothing in the world more miserable and hateful than the blind stupidity of the people.
—Fukuzawa Yukichi, *An Encouragement of Learning*

During the first decade of the Meiji period (1868–1912), Japan was plagued by intense social turmoil. In the years immediately following the 1868 revolution that toppled the Tokugawa regime, the new Meiji government contended with riots, rebellions, and civil war, while perceptions of the very real threat of colonization, posed by the growing presence of the Western powers in East Asia, intensified with the introduction of Social Darwinist thought to Japan in the early 1880s. Meanwhile, the syncretic collection of moral principles called "Neo-Confucianism" that had served to legitimize the social order of the prior Tokugawa regime had lost its authority. It was amidst such social and intellectual change that various visions for reordering Japan's post-revolution society emerged. Though not always articulated in explicitly moral terms, these competing social visions nonetheless reflected or were rooted in a particular normative orientation. Buddhist and Christian apologists, defenders of an invented Confucian "orthodoxy," natural-right advocates, and others vied with one another, sometimes violently, for the authority to speak for the good of the individual and society. For those charged with governing, such contention concerning the "proper" normative foundation on which to build social order confirmed a state of moral disorientation. Moral unity became a prerequisite for the national solidarity needed to quell internal turmoil and to defend Japan's sovereignty.

Rinrigaku, the academic discipline of ethics, emerged out of this context. The practitioners of this new discipline, immersed in the prevailing scientific epistemology of the time, presented their work as value-neutral, objective inquiry into the foundations and nature of "the good." But the moral inquiry associated with this discipline and the forms of thought and action it prescribed were anything but value-neutral. Despite claims to objectivity, writers of early *rinrigaku* texts carefully produced moral foundations that would strengthen their own value positions. During the first decades of the Meiji period, the discipline of ethics was deeply rooted in a discourse on civilization. "Civilization" as understood at this time carried an assertion of Western superiority over the merely "semi-civilized" Japan. For *rinrigaku* scholars, raising Japanese society to a higher level of civilization became a moral project. But this hierarchy was not simply Western imposed; Japan itself helped to create it. An examination of the discourse on civilization and its moral underpinnings will help to elucidate *rinrigaku*'s own normative position.

A central issue running throughout the moral discourse of 1870s and 1880s Japan was the question, "Who may speak for the good?" In order to begin to address this question, it is necessary to identify the participants in this discourse and the various enunciative positions from which they attempted to speak. Mapping out the moral landscape of this period, then, is a central task of this chapter. I attempt to situate *rinrigaku* in this early Meiji discourse on morality by examining the ways in which it was produced and legitimized in accord with civilization *(bunmeikaika)* and in opposition to the uncivilized, unenlightened people, pejoratively referred to as "the foolish masses" *(gumin)* and upon whose "blind stupidity" the "enlightenment thinker" Fukuzawa Yukichi commented in the epigraph at the beginning of this chapter. Foolishness provided a backdrop against which civilization could be conceptualized and defined.

Civilizing the foolish involved both the propagation of civilized and the suppression of uncivilized conduct. The state sought to enhance the authority of civilization by disseminating civilized knowledge and norms through newly established education and legal systems. The other side to this project was the effort to de-legitimize knowledge and social practices associated with the "foolish masses." One target of this effort to regulate civilization's foolish other was the satirical literary genre called *gesaku*, which issued playful but nevertheless serious critiques of the idea of civilization. In this sense, the discourse on civilization was at the same time a discourse on "civilizing," that is, on social control.[1] In terms of both its epistemological and normative commitments, *rinrigaku* was situated in proximity to the state. *Rinrigaku*, then, functioned from its inception as a mechanism for social control by providing philosophical justification for the suppression of "socially disruptive" thought and practices that ran counter to the needs of the state. Advocates of civilization believed that with the suppression or eradication of foolishness, moral order and unity could be attained. *Rinrigaku*'s desire to produce moral order out of moral chaos was a desire for moral hegemony—for the universalization of one normative position through the suppression of others in hopes of creating a common moral space.

Inoue Tetsujirō's New Theory of Ethics

In 1881, professor of philosophy Inoue Tetsujirō delivered a lecture at Tokyo University titled "The Great Foundation of Ethics" (Rinri no taihon), a work later published as *A New Theory of Ethics* (*Rinri shinsetsu*, 1883). Although a number of texts on morality emerged during the first decade of the Meiji period, Inoue's work was particularly important. His *New Theory of Ethics* represents the first sustained effort to objectify and inquire into the good in accordance with modern scientific principles and methodologies. Conducted in the style of the detached and impartial scholar, Inoue's *New Theory* was ostensibly an objective investigation into the foundation of the good. Yet this text should be viewed not as a work that reveals the foundation of ethics (even though this is one of its claims), but as one that constructs a foundation so as to legitimize Inoue's own normative orientation. In the preface to this text, as Inoue tells of how he became interested in the subject of ethics after a stroll into town, we find a clear statement of these values in the form of the kind of social practices Inoue hoped to proscribe or reform.

> I set aside my book and left my room. I took the road leading to the area below Surugadai until I reached the edge of Mansei Bridge. I was met by a ceaseless traffic of samurai, peasants, artisans, and merchants, rickshaw men and stablemen, all milling about in every direction. Some were shouting, others kicking up the dirt, or in a blaze of emotion over gains and losses, consumed with thoughts of luxury, starved for wealth and success, enslaved by their momentary passions. They behaved as though they were birds and beasts in a struggle for food. On the street, I alone stood still. With a sense of dejection and regret, I said to myself, "Ah! Is this indeed the way of life? What squalor and ugliness!" After returning to my room, I leaned against a table below the window. I arbitrarily took books from the shelf, wanting to know the foundation for ethics [*rinri*].[2]

The details of Inoue's theory are examined in the following chapter. But even here in his preface Inoue begins to provide an evaluative orientation for the emerging discipline of ethics. Whatever his intent in prefacing his text with this passage, it provides a kind of metaphor for the status of *rinrigaku* and how one of its practitioners sought to represent it in the early 1880s. It describes a scene of a society in disarray—the ceaseless movement, the shouting, the dirt—dominated by luxury seekers and others pursuing profit and pleasure. There is hostility here for these people who resemble the birds and the beasts.[3] And while the ethically misguided indulged themselves in "momentary passions," Inoue the scholar stood apart. Indeed, Inoue himself appears as a model of the "civilized man" who, as a scholar, is qualified to take up the investigation of "correct conduct" and speak on how these others should behave.

In the very first pages of his text, then, Inoue's moral presuppositions become clear. His preface, illustrating the "foolish people" and "foolish practice," is designed both to explain the need for the form of moral inquiry that follows (his "scientific" investigation into the good will serve as a corrective to foolish practice) and to legitimize his entire project. Finally, this text situates Inoue and his initial *rinrigaku* project within the discourse on civilization and in opposition to civilization's other: foolishness. Understanding Inoue's enunciative position, therefore, requires an examination of the norms inherent in the discourse on civilization as well as the social turmoil civilization was meant to quell.

The establishment of a new government after the Meiji Revolution of 1868 did not put an end to social turmoil. Throughout the 1870s, 1880s, and 1890s, various forms of political, economic, and social instability continued. Disgruntled *shizoku* (former members of the warrior class), deprived of their traditional class privileges under the new Meiji government, initiated rebellions throughout Japan. Between 1873—when many *shizoku* resigned from the Meiji government in connection with a dispute over whether to attack Korea—and the defeat in 1878 of Saigō Takamori's forces in the Satsuma Rebellion, thirty or more *shizoku*-initiated rebellions took place.[4] Further, in August 1878 a violent rebellion with a particularly violent outcome erupted involving 260 soldiers stationed at Takehashi barracks in Tokyo. Incensed by pay reductions and by the lack of any compensation for their efforts in putting down the Satsuma Rebellion in the previous year, these soldiers moved on Akasaka Palace, intending to set fire to it and take prisoner the high-ranking government officials there. Government authorities took swift action and quickly put down this rebellion. Within seven weeks of this uprising, known as the Takehashi Uprising, fifty-three of the participating soldiers were court-martialed and executed, and an official statement was issued barring soldiers from all manner of political activity. This was the Admonition to Soldiers and Sailors (Gunjin kyōkai). The promulgation of the Imperial Precepts to Soldiers and Sailors (Gunjin chokuyu) four years later can also be attributed to this and similar uprisings. Both documents, emphasizing obedience and loyalty to the state, represent the way state-issued moral decrees were employed as a corrective to social disruptions.

Resistance to social changes among the lower classes also resulted in conflict. The abolition of the domainal system, the emancipation of the pariah *(eta)* class, tax increases, military conscription, and compulsory education all contributed to unrest among the lower classes. During the first decade of the Meiji period, over two hundred riots or other such disturbances occurred.[5]

Moreover, debate concerning the future course for Japan's political, legal, and educational structures permeated nearly every segment of society. In terms of international relations, Japan's position was no less uncertain. From the early part of the nineteenth century, Western encroachment posed the threat of colonization, but with the introduction of the Social Darwinist notion of "survival of the fittest" in the early 1880s, the implications of this threat became more severe and the need for unity more urgent. Now, not merely Japan's sovereignty but its very survival was at stake.

In 1882, scholar and educator Katō Hiroyuki (1836–1916) published one of the first works to offer a comprehensive deliberation of Social Darwinism and its implications. "It is inevitable," Katō warned, "that sooner or later the superior races will win out completely, and the inferior ones lose, to the extent of being wiped out completely."[6] Four years later, Confucian scholar Nishimura Shigeki (1828–1902) repeated this warning, once again directing the nation's attention to the threat posed by Western expansion into Asia.

> In recent years, all the Western countries have the intention of extending their power in the Orient. Everybody has seen that France has taken Annam [Vietnam], England has overthrown Burma and seized the Komun Islands of Korea, Germany has seized the South Sea Islands, and Russia has been trying to expand her territory southward. Japan stands high out of the Eastern Sea, and since her geographical features are favorable and her products abundant, it is obvious that the Western powers have for some time been drooling over our country. It is not easy to maintain our independence being situated in such an imperiled place.... Therefore, in today's situation it is our extremely urgent duty to unite the power of the entire people in order to preserve the independence of the country.[7]

Nishimura's urgent call to "unite the power of the entire people" reflects a sense of crisis. To attain such unity, according to Nishimura, "there is no other way than the promotion of morality." Unity, here, was less about a consensus on political policy as it was about the establishment of moral unity. Many shared

Nishimura's opinion that only through the cultivation of a common moral outlook might Japan quell social disruptions and attain true social unity so as to
ensure the survival of the nation. A new moral authority was needed to fill the
void created by the collapse of the former regime together with its ideological
apparatuses for control.

Indeed, many intellectuals understood the social disarray of this period as
a consequence of the decline in prior ideologies for social order. Texts written
in the two decades that followed the Meiji Revolution of 1868 relate a sense of
moral disorientation. They present a narrative of Neo-Confucian moral principles that had provided legitimacy and order to the system of government during the Tokugawa period (1600–1868) but that had lost authority because they
were no longer able to explain the social reality of the 1880s.

Looking back on the early Meiji period some fifty years later, Inoue
Tetsujirō, the author of the aforementioned *New Theory of Ethics* and a central figure in the production of *rinrigaku,* commented on this moral disarray.
"While knowledge, learning, and education all made rapid advances, traditional
morality and religion were destroyed. With nothing to take their place, many
became as a lost child on the road of good and evil, right and wrong."[8] Others
referred to this moral disorientation as a complete "collapse of morality."[9]

While this depiction of a prevailing Neo-Confucian orthodoxy providing
moral direction and social order during the years prior to the 1868 revolution is problematic,[10] moral visions associated with Neo-Confucianism (and
Buddhism as well) had indeed suffered a decline in authority. And, as Inoue
Tetsujirō observed, there was nothing to take their place. Ethical theories associated with "Western learning" had yet to become firmly established. This was a
period, according to one thinker of the time, "when the sun has already set but
the moon has not yet risen."[11] In short, no set of authoritative moral standards
were in place to compel compliance to the needs of the state as it transformed
society on various levels. What came to fill this void was a discourse on civilization and its attendant prescriptions for and prohibitions against certain forms
of thought and action.

The Norms of Civilization

"Ah, when can our people reach the level of civilization?" Attaining civilization
was an issue of central importance for many so-called "enlightenment intellectuals," and, in this particular case, the concern of Tsuda Mamichi (1829–1903),
a student of Western legal thought. And Fukuzawa Yukichi (1835–1901), one
of the best known enlightenment thinkers of this time, described the problem

of "civilizing" Japan as "the overriding anxiety of Asian intellectuals today...to the exclusion of all others."[12] What did civilization mean to these thinkers and why was its attainment thought to be so crucially important?

Attaining civilization meant adopting the knowledge and skills of the West—its political and economic institutions, its knowledge and technology, its values, and so forth. Positing the West as the embodiment or source of civilization required an uncritical essentialization of the diverse thought, values, and institutions of the societies of Western Europe and the United States. The "West" then, functioned as a regulative idea, an imagined geographical unity that enabled the "half-civilized" and the "uncivilized" to be thought. Thus, civilization in Meiji Japan was not simply an idea imported unchanged from the West; civilization was constituted through a negotiation between Japan and its representations of the West.

Yet, although the cultural productions of Western Europe and the United States were central to the term "civilization," the discourse on civilization in early Meiji Japan was equally about change. This was a discourse on barbarism and civilization both, and on the progress (with all of the evaluative connotations this term conveys) from one to the other. Civilization, then, can be understood as a complex discourse locating the nation-state at a certain stage along a temporal progression. In the mid-1870s, for example, Fukuzawa Yukichi had already affirmed Japan's half-civilized status, locating it between the "highly civilized" countries of the West and the "barbaric countries" of Africa and Australia.[13]

Importantly, civilization—as a movement to acquire the knowledge and skills of the West and to establish distance from Japan's barbaric past—was never merely descriptive; "civilization" carried with it a definite prescriptive or normative overtone.[14] As the goal of attaining civilization came to be associated with the good, the thought and practices attributed to the "foolish masses" (i.e., that which defied or obstructed civilizing efforts) quickly came to be represented as immoral or, in many cases, illegal. Representations of such thought and action as "barbaric," "uncivilized," and "foolish" helped to legitimize their suppression.

Historian Mikiso Hane, for example, notes that the Meiji government "exhorted the people to refrain from relieving themselves on the roadside, bathing in public view, engaging in mixed bathing, or walking about in loincloths. Women were told not to sit around bare breasted or feed their babies in public."[15] Ordinary practices associated with the body became targets to be suppressed as uncivilized. Food also came under the sway of civilization. Buddhism, with its prohibitions against taking life, and Shinto, with its disdain for blood as an impurity, helped to instill a strong aversion to eating meat in Japan.

For many, the eating of meat (fowl and fish were considered outside this category) was considered vile and unclean. Proponents of civilization, struggling to change these views, proclaimed meat eating to be not merely nutritious, but civilized as well.[16] Their efforts, however, were not always taken seriously. One popular dish of the day called *kaika donburi* (civilized rice in a bowl; civilized because the rice was topped with meat) probably says more about the satirical reception of civilization than about a serious linking of meat and civilized conduct.

Western-style clothing also became something of a fad. Although the tone in figure 1 from the early 1870s is satirical, it shows that clothing could also mark, at least superficially, the civilized man. Here, from right to left, is the progress of civilization: the "uncivilized man" with the swords, topknot, and apparel of the samurai, the "semi-civilized man" wearing Western-style hat and shoes and holding an umbrella, and the "fully civilized man" dressed entirely

Figure 1. *The Stages of Civilization* by Kawanabe Kyōsai, a satirical representation of civilizational progress. This illustration appeared in Kanagaki Robun's *Journey on Foot through the West* (*Seiyō dōchū hizakurige,* 1870). Reprinted with permission from the Kawanabe Kyōsai Memorial Museum, Saitama Prefecture, Japan.

in Western clothing with top hat and cane and accompanied by a dog.[17] This satirical image itself suggests that the connections between the adornment of the body and the civilizing project had become sufficiently authoritative for a critique of this kind to make sense to those who viewed it.

Civilizers, however, were concerned not only with changes in social practices associated with the body, diet, and fashion, but also with the eradication of foolish thought—folk knowledge deemed inconsistent with the age of civilization. Sakatani Shiroshi (1822–1881), a contributor to the *Meiroku zasshi* (a journal advertising the merits of civilization), sought to abolish the "foolish beliefs" of the past. He dismissed superstition (belief in fox possession, in long-nosed, winged mountain demons called *tengu,* and in folk remedies for common ailments, for example) as the remnant of the "ignorant times of earliest antiquity." In a brief essay from 1873 titled "Doubts on Fox Stories," Sakatani wrote,

> Opinions recently received from Europe make clear that these things may all be attributed to a type of mental derangement....How can we speak of ghosts when we are moving toward the world of enlightenment? All superstitions will disappear when Heaven's Way [*tennen no michi*] and Nature's Reason [*shizen no ri*] actually prevail and when men are strong and enlightened in body and mind. The impression of outmoded customs on men's minds should indeed be fully erased.[18]

Tsuda Mamichi, also a contributor to *Meiroku zasshi,* upheld a similar view, condemning the persistent belief in *tengu.* The quiet retreats of mountain regions, he admitted, can seem to some like "the habitats of ghosts and devils." "Even brave men fear such places," he wrote, "unless they are scholars well versed in physical phenomena. How much more is this so with ignorant people!"[19] Civilized knowledge guided by reason, its proponents believed, had the power to dispel the unreasonable fears that grew out of ignorance.[20]

Concepts and beliefs associated with Confucianism and Buddhism also fell into the category of backward thought. Viewing himself as one of the few working to civilize the many, Tsuda complained that the vast majority of people in Japan continued to be swayed by anachronistic beliefs. They were foolish people unwilling or unable to abandon the customs of the past, and thus they were often misled by "groundless theories of hell, paradise, *karma,* reward and punishment, the five elements, and geomancy." For Tsuda, such people were hardly civilized and indeed could barely be called "half-enlightened."[21]

The persistence of such outmoded customs and beliefs was to blame for Japan's inferior "semi-developed" stage of civilization in comparison to the "most highly civilized" United States and countries of Europe. It was therefore necessary to reform the social practices of the foolish majority and to de-legitimize their "groundless theories" so that the civilizing project could proceed.[22]

And in a similar fashion, Sakatani drew a close connection between a nation's level of civilization and the conduct of its people. "Since the conduct of the people is the source of all matters relating to the nation, national conditions reflect whether conduct is good or bad."[23] Sakatani interpreted Japan's semicivilized status in relation to the West as a moral shortcoming, that is, in terms of social practice that was in need of moral reform. Sakatani spoke of good and evil as the "two moral ways extending through history and spreading through the universe." Only by establishing the good as the principle that guides people's actions, argued Sakatani, can morality be preserved and civilization attained. "Morality would be completely destroyed if good were not the controlling principle. This would be 'barbarism.'"[24] Here again, a lack of morality was equated with the barbaric, implying a close association between the good and "civilization." Civilization, with its demand for certain modes of thought and forms of practice and its condemnation of others, cannot be viewed as a purely descriptive term. The term "civilization" carried a definite evaluative nuance. In other words, the invocation of this term both *prescribed* and *proscribed*. The government made use of both pedagogical and legalistic strategies to disseminate and regulate the knowledge and norms of civilization. Japan's education system during the first decade of Meiji, calling for the rapid acquisition of knowledge, illustrates this prescriptive aspect of civilization, while civilizing legislation provides an example of its proscriptive side.

Throughout the 1870s, the Ministry of Education implemented an education curriculum emphasizing knowledge acquisition as a means to civilize the people. The Fundamental Code of Education of 1872 stressed learning that was useful in daily life while criticizing impractical theorizing and idle talk. And while it described learning as "the very foundation of success in life," it made no reference to moral training in education. Indeed, it implied that a lack of knowledge, rather than virtue, was the cause of moral disarray. "It is ignorance that leads man astray, makes him destitute, disrupts his family, and in the end destroys his life."[25]

The writings of Fukuzawa Yukichi express a similar prioritization of knowledge acquisition over moral education. In his 1872 *Encouragement of Learning (Gakumon no susume),* Fukuzawa underscored the importance of practical learning and explained "foolishness" as a lack of knowledge. He declared, "If a man does not study, he will have no knowledge. A man without knowledge is a fool *(gujin)*."[26] Knowledge was what distinguished the wise man from the fool. Education designed to instill the foolish with knowledge was the remedy.

In addition, such foolishness was to blame when the government resorted to suppression. "Over foolish people," stated Fukuzawa, apparently citing a Western proverb, "there is harsh government. It is not that the government wishes to be harsh; it is that foolish people bring harshness upon themselves. Therefore, if we do not wish harsh government, we must see to it that the people are educated." Moreover, if the foolish overcame their foolishness through "earnest study to acquire wide knowledge," "the government," Fukuzawa argued, "will be able to rule more easily and the people will be able to accept its rule agreeably, each finding his place and all helping to preserve the peace of the nation."[27] For Fukuzawa, then, knowledge acquisition rather than moral education was the primary solution to the problem of foolishness.

In addition, much of Fukuzawa's 1875 *Outline of a Theory of Civilization (Bunmei ron no gairyaku)* prioritizes knowledge over virtue. Arguing that without the aid of intelligence, private virtue could not serve any purpose, Fukuzawa asserted, "Ignorant morality is equivalent to no morality."[28] To a certain extent, he admitted, one individual can influence another to be virtuous. But morality, according to Fukuzawa, is the activity of one person and "ultimately the sphere in which moral encouragement can lead another to good is extremely limited." Intelligence, on the other hand, is something quite different. "Once some truth is discovered and announced to others, in no time at all it moves the minds of a whole nation."[29]

Fukuzawa's discussion of knowledge and virtue was largely based on Henry Thomas Buckle's *History of Civilization in England*.[30] In this work, Buckle expressed his conviction of "the superiority of intellectual acquisitions over moral feeling." Buckle argued that civilizational progress depends on both intellectual and moral advancement. "This double movement, moral and intellectual, is essential to the very idea of civilization, and includes the entire theory of mental progress." But for Buckle, the intellectual element clearly took precedence over the moral. Moral excellence, he asserted, is less productive of real good than intellectual excellence. "The deeper we penetrate into this question, the more clearly shall we see the superiority of intellectual acquisitions over moral feeling."[31] Fukuzawa accepted this position. The cultivation of a spirit of civilization called first and foremost for intellectual effort, for the acquisition of knowledge. But civilization not only prescribed certain thought and practice, but also proscribed, through suppressive legislation, activities deemed "uncivilized." What civilization proscribed, in fact, can help to further delineate the norms of this discourse.

"The government, through the establishment of laws and ordinances, suppresses those who are evil and protects those who are good. This is the business of government."[32] In this statement, Fukuzawa illustrated how easily the discourses on legalism and morality blended into one another. Civilizing the people, after all, called for the suppression of foolishness, and legislation was seen as an effective means to this end. Legalism helped to define the norms of civilization through the various practices that it proscribed. In other words, the discourse on legalism of the 1870s contributed to the production of the moral space out of which *rinrigaku* emerged. Further, legislation, an outgrowth of legal discourse, functioned (as did education and, later, *rinrigaku*) as a mechanism for social control.

Through a variety of edicts, regulations, and laws, the new Meiji government attempted to legislate civilization and morality. Sometimes referred to as "civilizing regulations" *(kaika jōrei),* such legislation was closely tied to the normative orientation of civilization. The legislation enacted was designed to proscribe certain forms of "uncivilized" practice, or in some cases to demand other forms (such as conscription, school attendance, etc.).

In the fourth article of state councilor Kido Kōin's final draft of the Charter Oath, a statement of the new government's national policy issued in the first year of Meiji (1868), the Meiji regime proscribed superstitious beliefs. "Evil practices of the past," this document proclaimed, "shall be discarded and social practice shall be based upon the accepted practices of the world."[33] This often-cited statement reflects an effort to reevaluate the moral foundations of social practice. In the phrase "accepted practices of the world" *(tenchi no kōdō),* there is a sense of universality—a universal norm that is to ground practice. The "evil practices" to be abandoned referred primarily to *meishin*—superstitious beliefs inconsistent with civilization and its universal norms.

While the Charter Oath only vaguely referred to "evil practices," Nishimura Shigeki, in an 1875 speech concerning ethics and governing, provided specific examples of the kind of actions so-called civilizing legislation targeted.

> Today, wise persons in the upper classes, detesting barbarism [*yaban*], have a deep craving for civilization [*bunmei*]. They establish excessively detailed regulations for the correction of customs and the proprieties, and they punish all manner of things such as baring the legs and urinating in public. Thinking such rude conduct close to barbarism, they especially fail to understand that the rude conduct of officials and nobles is still more barbaric than urinating in public.[34]

In this passage, Nishimura's intent was primarily to call attention to corruption among governmental leaders. Nevertheless, this passage illustrates the nature of some of the regulations enacted at this time. Three years earlier, in late 1872, new regulations went into effect in the Tokyo area, listing certain major and minor contraventions. Major contraventions included "unsightly exhibitions sponsoring snake charmers or mixed sumo wrestling matches between the sexes" and made it illegal "for anyone to operate a bathing house that permitted men and women to enter the water together." Those guilty of such violations were required to pay a fine ranging from 75 to 150 sen or, if unable to pay the fine, subjected to "ten to twenty blows with the rod."[35]

Mori Arinori (1847–1889), one of the founders of the *Meiroku zasshi* and minister of education from 1885 until his death, called for legislation to reform the institution of marriage. Linking the mistreatment of wives to barbarism, he wrote, "Among the customs common among barbarians, mistreatment of wives by their husbands is especially intolerable to witness."[36] Mori proposed new legislation to protect wives and concubines, asserting that the legal situation as it was "injures our customs and obstructs enlightenment."[37] Again, we find a close connection between customs, morals, and enlightenment.

Regulations such as these, by what they were designed to suppress, reflect a commitment to certain norms of civilization. They reflect also an appropriation of the "civilized values" of the West. The advocates of civilization and enlightenment were eager to claim a place for Japanese society within the space of civilization, a discourse in which it participated, but a status it had not yet attained. Civilization, according to this discourse, was the telos to which all societies aspired and progressed. The "stages of civilization" framework relied upon the authority of universal truth as its proponents sought to universalize it.

The Critique of Knowledge Acquisition and Legalism

By the late 1870s and early 1880s it had become clear, many intellectuals believed, that neither the acquisition of knowledge nor legalism alone was a sufficient means for reforming social practice. Critics of education centering on knowledge acquisition complained that the school curriculum, with little attention to moral education, was off course. And critics of legalism asserted that while it was effective as a means to control action, it could not sufficiently affect thought. Morality, on the other hand, had the capacity to affect not only external action, but the human interiority as well.

For Nishimura Shigeki, morality, not knowledge, had to take precedence in the education of Japan's populace. Nishimura explained the social failings of his day as resulting primarily from an overemphasis on the acquisition of knowledge at the expense of morality. He believed that during the 1870s the goals of civilization and enlightenment, which stressed a knowledge-based education, had undermined the importance of moral education. While he admitted civilization and enlightenment to be an admirable goal, he gave higher priority to the establishment of a wealthy nation and a strong army. Striving for civilization and enlightenment, he said, will have little meaning if we lose the independence of our country.[38]

"The Great Principles of Education" (Kyōgaku taishi, 1879), a document ostensibly reflecting the thoughts of the emperor but in fact drafted by the court official and Confucian scholar Motoda Eifu, called attention to the lack of emphasis on moral training in the Education Code of 1872.

> In recent days, people have been going to extremes. They take unto themselves a foreign civilization whose only values are fact-gathering and technique.... Although we set out to take in the best features of the West and bring in new things in order to achieve the high aims of the Meiji Restoration...this procedure had a serious defect: It reduced benevolence, justice, loyalty, and filial piety to a secondary position.[39]

Motoda feared that these moral principles might be forgotten if the "fact-gathering" that accompanied the indiscriminate emulation of the West continued, and he concluded that education was off its proper course. Although the 1880 revision of the Education Code placed moral training (shūshin) higher on the school curriculum, many complained that educators continued to devote most of their attention to the intellectual side of instruction.

Itō Hirobumi (1841–1909), a leading political figure of this time and later Japan's first prime minister, agreed with Nishimura and Motoda regarding the decline of morality. Depicting a state of moral decline similar to that of Nishimura, he wrote in 1879, "Deceit is praised and profit pursued without shame. Benevolence is forgotten and rivalries and conflicts prevail. Manners have collapsed and ethics have declined." Unlike Nishimura, however, he did not attribute weak morals to the content of the education system. Rather, he explained moral disarray by the unprecedented reform that had taken place since the Meiji Revolution. "The damage to our customs comes from the excessiveness of the change."[40] Various social problems attended this excessive change, leading Itō and others in government to rely heavily upon the law to preserve order.

But legalism too came under attack as a means for ordering society and suppressing uncivilized activities. Yamagata Aritomo (1838–1922), war minister and later prime minister, was troubled by the social unrest generated by the Movement for Freedom and Popular Rights and by the Takehashi Uprising of 1878. In his Precepts to Soldiers and Sailors (Gunjin chokuyu) of 1882, he urged members of the armed forces "neither to be led astray by current opinions nor meddle in politics, but with single heart fulfill your essential duty of loyalty."[41] He saw morality as a corrective to these social difficulties and criticized excessive dependence on legalism. In 1879, as army chief of staff, Yamagata commented on the obvious need for laws to preserve society, but lamented that many seemed to have forgotten that a society was also maintained "with morals and customs."[42] Nishimura Shigeki agreed with Yamagata's critique of legalism. He noted that some viewed legalism as a unique discipline because of its power to cure the great ills of society. Supporters of legalism argued that the law was necessary to pacify society. Nishimura countered that legalism lacked the spirit to pacify the people, that only morality had this spirit. "Law has the power to prevent people from falling into evil," he admitted, "but it has no power to make them do good." Consequently, the reformation of society, he believed, must start with morality, regardless of how comprehensive a country's laws may be.[43] Four years earlier, in 1882, Nishimura declared, "Law lacks the power to educate, it lacks the power to advance manners and customs.... [O]nly the power of morality can rectify the minds of the people, beautify manners and customs, elevate the conditions of society, and spread the glory of the nation in all directions.... Law cannot possibly serve as a substitute for morality."[44]

By the end of the 1870s, moral training had moved to the top of the education curriculum. Motivated in part by Motoda Eifu's "Great Principles of Education," "The General Plan for Elementary School Teaching Rules" of 1881 read, "The elementary school curriculum is to comprise basics in moral training, reading, writing, and arithmetic, as well as singing and calisthenics."[45] The Memorandum for Elementary School Teachers, issued the following month, also emphasized moral education. "To lead a person toward goodness is of greater importance than to make a person knowledgeable. For this reason, educators must emphasize moral education above all else in teaching their students." Instructors were directed to act as models of virtue and to "provide students with a thorough knowledge of the great path of ethics."[46] Here, knowledge acquisition had become secondary to moral training. For Yamagata, Nishimura, and others, morality was the best corrective to the social failings plaguing the nation.[47] Morality, by the late 1870s, had become central as a means for cultivating civilization and suppressing foolishness because of its capacity to control, guide, and restrain not only action but also thought. It was at this time that Inoue wrote his *New Theory of Ethics,* attempting to create a scientific basis for the refutation of "foolish practice" and the unification of the human interiority under a common morality of civilization. But not all, of course, were content to be subjected to civilizing, and many expressed their dissent simply by ignoring civilizing regulations, by choosing not to attend school, or by continuing to rely upon folk remedies when ill, for example. Yet it was through satire that dissenters launched a more subtle and subversive attack on the norms of civilization.

The Foolishness of Civilization

While Inoue's *New Theory of Ethics* was squarely situated within the space of civilization, texts (both written and visual) that sought to subvert notions of civilization marked the boundaries of this space. Critics of civilization, for example, found the above-mentioned effort to represent meat eating as a civilized practice an easy target for satire. As with so many other aspects of civilization, it was Fukuzawa Yukichi who led this encouragement of meat eating. In his 1870 article "A Theory of Meat Eating" (Nikushoku no setsu), Fukuzawa strove to dispel the commonly held view in early Meiji Japan that eating meat is repugnant and to popularize meat (as well as milk) as a vital source of nutrition. An accurate understanding of the human body and human nature, Fukuzawa argued, makes the merits of meat eating obvious. He pointed out that although few in the past had eaten meat, new methods have been developed for raising cattle and sheep, and these methods can and should quickly be adopted in Japan. He was critical of those who rejected this civilized practice and who held instead to anachronistic customs, such as Buddhist prohibitions against eating meat. "There are many who arbitrarily find the eating of meat to be repugnant. To eat meat, they say, is a loathsome practice and goes against thousands of years of custom. This view, however, is an empty theory of the uneducated and ignorant that discerns neither the principles of the human body nor the nature of humanity."[48] Without meat, Fukuzawa maintained, the body weakens and the mind loses its vitality. This is a loss, he argued, not only to the individual person, but to society as well. Superstitions, then, stood in the way of this nutritious and civilized practice that could promote the welfare of both the individual and the social body.

We see in artist Kawanabe Kyōsai's *The Civilizing of Fudō* a satirical reply to Fukuzawa and his views on meat eating. (See figure 2.) Fudō Myō-ō (Acala Vidyārāja, or the King of Immovable Wisdom associated with esoteric Buddhism), a wrathful defender of Buddhist law, is often represented with a sword in his right hand (to slice through the entanglements that bind the ignorant to delusion), a rope in his left (to bind the passions or those governed by them), and seated amidst purifying flames that burn away one's material desires. In Kawanabe's painting, however, Fudō tends a great pot of meat stew. He has used his rope to secure the pot to his sword, which he has affixed above the flames. Seitaka, his attendant at bottom right, prepares additional meat for the pot,

Figure 2. *Civilizing the King of Immovable Wisdom* (*Fudō Myō-ō kaika*), a satirical critique of civilization by Kawanabe Kyōsai. Reprinted with permission from the Kawanabe Kyōsai Memorial Museum, Saitama Prefecture, Japan.

while Kongara, the attendant at left, warms a bottle of sake in the flames. Here, as Japan enters the age of "civilization and enlightenment," even Fudō diligently reads through his copy of *Shinbun zasshi,* the Ministry of Education's weekly journal offering instructions on how to become more civilized.[49]

The humor in this image relies upon an inversion: Fudō attains "enlightenment" not by adherence to Buddhist teachings but by abandoning the principles and beliefs (as well as their implications for ethical practice) he has hitherto defended. Buddhism's moral injunctions against the eating of meat become obstacles to the new civilized morality. Thus even the most "foolish" may become truly "civilized." Or alternatively, even the most diligent defenders of Buddhist belief and practice may become a foolish enthusiast of civilization. Viewers of this image would have had a familiarity with Fudō and with the fact that the killing and/or eating of animals is a grave Buddhist offense, at least for the more seriously minded Buddhist practitioners. Kawanabe, then, sought to undermine the seriousness of this ethics of civilization with satire and humor.

But perhaps the most outspoken of civilization's critics were writers of *gesaku*, a literary genre understood as "lowbrow literature" by proponents of civilization but as "the literature of play" by those who wrote and read it.

Writers of *gesaku* were criticized for their refusal to "participate in the Enlightenment."[50] Proponents of civilization disdained writers of this genre of literature, a genre that still receives only marginal attention in present-day histories and critiques of Japanese literature. One scholar of Meiji literature asserts, "With rare exceptions, the later *gesaku* writers had nothing to say."[51] Yet their efforts to subvert civilization and to deflect the representation of foolishness by redeploying it in different directions warrant consideration.

Kanagaki Robun (Nozaki Bunzō, 1829–1894), a *gesaku* writer and journalist during the early Meiji period who worked closely with Kawanabe, questioned the merit of civilization, often by satirizing the works of this period's great "enlightenment thinkers." In 1868, for example, Fukuzawa Yukichi published a text titled *Illustrated Explanations of Scientific Principles (Kyūri zukai)* that provided simple explanations of various natural phenomena for use as a primary school science textbook. Four years later, Robun published his parody of this work. He gave it the homonymous title *Kyūri zukai,* but used ideographs that conveyed a meaning very different from Fukuzawa's work: "the uses of cucumbers."

Dismissing this work as "nonsense," as some literary scholars have done, perhaps misses or underestimates the seriousness of satire and its subversive potential.[52] While Fukuzawa in his work explains the properties of the atmosphere *(kūki),* Robun expounds on the characteristics of a country bumpkin, traveling from one restaurant to another, seeking to satisfy his insatiable appetite *(kūki).* Robun compares the "resounding acclaim" Fukuzawa's work received to the fart of a *kappa* (a kind of water sprite or fairy). "Like a *kappa*'s fart, though it momentarily resounds within the water, it soon floats to the surface as a bubble and disappears."[53] Here, Robun suggests that the high acclaim for Fukuzawa's work is unwarranted, exaggerated, and temporary. If not quite "profaning the sacred," Robun at least ridicules Fukuzawa's earnest devotion to civilization.[54] Municipal authorities in Tokyo responded by issuing regulations, directed at writers of *gesaku*, designed to mitigate obscenity and to promote works consistent with "civilized" conventions of decorum.[55]

Fukuzawa's 1870 article advocating meat eating provided Robun with another opportunity for parody. Robun's reply is his *Usha zatsudan aguranabe* (roughly: Sitting cross-legged before a pot of stew and chatting at a beef restaurant, 1871–1872). Here, Robun drew a mocking characterization of "the civilized man." This beef restaurant patron praises the Western (and therefore civilized) custom of eating beef.

He turns to his neighbor, who is also eating beef, and speaks: Excuse me, but beef is certainly a most delicious thing, isn't it?...I wonder why we in Japan haven't eaten such a clean thing before....We really should be grateful that even people like ourselves can now eat beef, thanks to the fact that Japan is steadily becoming a truly civilized country. Of course, there are still some unenlightened boors who cling to their barbaric superstitions [yaban no heishū] and say that eating meat defiles one to such an extent that one can no longer pray before Buddha and the gods. Those who hold to such a view don't understand the study of the true principles of things [kyūrigaku]....Savages [ebisu] like that should be made to read Fukuzawa's article on eating beef. In the West they're free of superstitions. There, it's the custom to do everything scientifically.[56]

Robun, by having his protagonist embrace the desire to "do everything scientifically," is calling into question this very desire. This text, then, is not simply an example of "the comic aspects of enlightenment," as some maintain.[57] This satirical account of eating beef (formerly discouraged in Buddhist thought as unclean, but here described as "such a clean thing") exemplifies a possible means of deflecting the universalization of civilized practice. The beefeater, even as he spoke of "unenlightened boors," "savages," and "barbaric superstitions," was himself made to appear foolish. In this way, Robun brings civilized conduct and foolishness together, collapsing the opposition upon which the advocates of civilization relied.

Later in this same work, Robun applied foolishness to himself. In a section about an old man who loves newspapers because of their capacity to enlighten those who read them, the old man says, "Newspapers, however, are not without errors. A report appeared in the *Yokohama Mainichi Newspaper* that Kanagaki Robun was fined for urinating in a public thoroughfare."[58]

Why did Robun include this account of himself in his own book? Clearly, Robun was not reproaching himself for his "uncivilized" behavior. His texts reveal not a complicit internalization of the foolishness representation, but rather an ironic appropriation and redeployment of foolishness. It is worth noting that the name "Kanagaki Robun" itself reflects this strategy. "Kanagaki" (仮名垣) can mean "written in the *kana* syllabary" and Robun (魯文) "foolish letters"; hence, his name itself ("foolish words written in *kana*") is ironic and self-deprecating.[59] Moreover, the "ro" of "robun," (also read "oroka," meaning foolish or stupid) parallels the "gu" of "gumin" (also read "oroka" and meaning foolish). In this sense, Robun literally took foolishness as his own signifier. In short, by *ostensibly* internalizing the values of civilization (i.e., by representing himself as foolish) Robun subverted the civilized/foolish opposition.[60] Robun's strategy was to invoke foolishness to signify a space of "eccentric wisdom." Something like this strategy can be found in the Taoist classic *Lao Tzu.* Here, the author of this text represents himself as foolish: "The multitudes all have a surplus... I alone seem to be lacking. Mine is the mind of a fool—ignorant and stupid!"[61] But this is the stupidity of one who sees beyond what the multitudes see. It is an eccentricity labeled as foolishness by those who misunderstand it.

These *gesaku* texts asserted, through satire, that there is something foolish about the relentless and enthusiastic pursuit of civilization and the norms it demanded, while in the adherence to "foolish" practice there is an unwillingness to be judged by the values of others. "It won't do," wrote Mantei Ōga (Hattori Kosaburō 1818–1890), another writer of *gesaku,* "for Westerners to judge the right and wrong of other countries' customs on the basis of the customs of their own countries."[62] Ōga's statement is insightful because it captures precisely the operation of the discourse on civilization. "Civilized" morality, although posited as universal (i.e., based on universal truths such as the fixed laws of nature), was in fact culturally specific. Underlying Ōga's statement is a conception of civilization as a "cultural convention."[63] For the proponents of civilization, relativistic views such as Ōga's above were "frivolous and contemptible."[64] Ōga's relativism had to be disavowed, as it was incompatible with a civilized practice rooted in a universal conception of civilization. Those like Kanagaki and Ōga—speaking from an enunciative position that civilization's advocates sought to neutralize or suppress—delineated the borders of civilization and its norms.

Conclusions: *Rinrigaku* and the Universal

Inoue Tetsujirō, in his *New Theory of Ethics,* attempted to objectify the good in accordance with the new modes of moral inquiry that came to be called *rinrigaku.* A detailed examination of Inoue's moral theory, together with a study of the underlying epistemology that enabled these new modes of moral inquiry, is taken up in the following chapter. The task of this chapter has been to situate *rinrigaku* within the moral discourse of the early Meiji period. *Rinrigaku* emerged out of the moral space of "civilization" and in opposition to "foolish" thought and practice. In providing philosophical justification for the state's civilizing project, *rinrigaku* supplemented pedagogical and legalistic efforts to disseminate and regulate civilized norms. As we will see in what follows, *rinrigaku* came to play an increasingly central role in the dissemination of state-sponsored moral views.

Yet how do we account for the contempt and hostility proponents of civilization had for the "foolish people"? How do we explain, for example, Inoue's hostility toward those he encountered at Mansei Bridge, or Fukuzawa's contemptuous remarks concerning the hateful nature of the people's "blind stupidity?" The ethics of civilization included everything from abandoning superstitions and adopting scientific ways of thinking to meat eating and the adoption of Western-style clothing. Although civilized practice itself was not universal—many in Japan saw themselves as merely "semi-civilized"—it was upheld as rooted in a universal and irrefutable rationale. In this sense, Inoue's ethical views were part of a discourse on civilization that understood certain conceptions of appropriate conduct to be universally binding. Yet these "universally true" norms of civilization came to be exposed as the provisional claims of a contingent and perspectival discourse, despite its proponents' insistence upon its universal status.

The space of this putatively universal discourse on civilization was constituted through the exclusion of its foolish other. In other words, civilization defined itself in opposition to what it was not (i.e., foolishness). From the initial positing of civilization as "universal," it was confronted by that which it had excluded, and thus the fictive nature of its universality (its supposed capacity for all-inclusiveness) was revealed.[65] As Judith Butler, in a discussion of the universal, has observed, "The all-encompassing trajectory of the term [in this case, "civilization"] is necessarily undone by the exclusion of particularity on which it rests."[66] The excluded particularity examined here was "foolishness." Through the parodic repetition of civilized practice (e.g., the eating of meat in Robun's writings), gesaku writers and artists opened up the discourse on civilization, making it possible to see something foolish in civilization itself. Here we have a possible explanation for civilizers' hostility toward the "foolish masses." This "other" had to be suppressed or eradicated not only to universally disseminate the norms of civilization (i.e., to create a common moral space within Japan), but also to verify or substantiate civilization's claims to universality.

At stake in this examination of civilization and foolishness is the potential of the "universal" to dominate and determine the moral subjectivity of the "particular," and the sometimes violent resistance that this engenders. This will remain a central theme in the following chapters, as I explore the various ethical theories developed by rinrigaku academics, the underlying epistemologies out of which these theories emerged, and the tensions that developed between rinrigaku and competing social ethics associated with civilization.

CHAPTER 2

The Epistemology of *Rinrigaku*

Because behind and supporting...the understandable prestige
of the natural science model, stands an attachment to a certain
picture of the agent. This picture is deeply attractive to moderns,
both flattering and inspiring. It shows us as capable of achieving a
kind of disengagement from our world by objectifying it.
—Charles Taylor, *Human Agency and Language*

Kyakkan (object): things we know of as existing outside the body,
such as mountains, rivers, streams, oceans, grass, trees. There is
not a single kind that is not an object. So the object is something in
opposition to the functions that take place within the mind, such
as pleasure and pain, that is, in opposition to the subject.
—*Kyōiku shinri ronri jutsugo shōkai* (Explanation of terms for
education, psychology and logic, 1885)

In the first two decades of the Meiji period, a number of
texts appeared that took up the question of ethics. Some of the most important of these works included Nishi Amane's "The Three Human Treasures";
Inoue Tetsujirō's *A New Theory of Ethics;* Katō Hiroyuki's *A Reconsideration
of Human Rights* and *The Relationship Between the Right of the Strongest and
the Moral Law;* and Nishimura Shigeki's *On Japanese Morality.* Except for the
last text, these writings approached ethics from a utilitarian or evolutionary
standpoint. In all of these works, their authors linked the "good" to state power
and social order. Contemporary scholars of Japanese philosophy—Kōsaka
Masaaki, G.K.Piovesana, Matsuzaki Minoru, H.G.Blocker and C.Starling, and
Robert Carter—have either ignored these works or dismissed them as eclectic,
superficial, and important only as intellectual background for the more mature
moral philosophy that appeared in the early twentieth century.[1] The authors
of such critiques, however, begin with their own conceptions of ethics and the

appropriate methodology for moral philosophical inquiry as they ask the question, "What is the good?" In this chapter, I am concerned not with some essentialized, ahistorical notion of the good, but with how the good was understood in early *rinrigaku* discourse, and further, with how such conceptions were produced. More specifically, I ask what were the conditions for moral truthfulness and how were they legitimized? We can begin to address the question of moral truthfulness and the conditions of its production in early Meiji Japan by examining the underlying epistemology out of which *rinrigaku* emerged.

The academic discipline of ethics *(rinrigaku)* emerged from within an epistemology, already authoritative by the early Meiji period, which contested Chu Hsi Confucianism and aligned itself with "Western knowledge" and "science." *Rinrigaku* scholars of the early 1880s claimed to speak from an objective and value-neutral position, a position from which to inquire into and apprehend "the good." Their methodologies and ethical theories, however, were invariably rooted in culturally and historically specific epistemological presuppositions, that is, in their own perspectival presuppositions about knowledge, knowing, and truth. Indeed, the possibility of "value-free objectivity" was itself one such presupposition. While the preceding chapter focused on the moral space of "civilization" that *rinrigaku* drew upon, this chapter examines the underlying epistemology that shaped and authorized *rinrigaku* and its claims concerning the good.

Epistemological Antecedents: *Ri* and *Jitsugaku*

The epistemology of *rinrigaku* was not new in the 1880s. Although the writings of Nishi Amane (1829–1897), a student of philosophy with a particular interest in the thought of Comte and J.S. Mill, provided a detailed statement of this epistemology's key features during the first decade of Meiji, it is possible to locate its antecedent traces in the thought of eighteenth- and perhaps even late seventeenth-century intellectuals. Indeed, a good deal of scholarship exists on the intellectual labor during the Tokugawa period (1600–1868) that enabled the revolution called the Meiji Ishin. A central feature of this revolution was the move away from Neo-Confucianism and other modes of thought toward new (often and problematically called "Western") ways of apprehending the world. One way to approach this transition is through the shifting meanings of terms central to both periods and epistemologies. *Ri* (principle), for example, a concept central to Confucian metaphysics, was reconfigured to signify "reason," "laws of nature," and even "science." A second example, *jitsugaku* (practical studies), underwent a similar transformation from an affiliation with Confucianism to an association with the "truthful knowledge" of the West. We can begin to approach the emergence of this epistemology through a brief genealogy of *ri* and *jitsugaku,* terms that were of central intellectual importance during both the Meiji and Tokugawa periods.

One of the most fundamental features of the epistemology that informed *rinrigaku* was the separation of fact and value. Although antecedent traces of such views of knowledge can be located in the eighteenth and even in the late seventeenth centuries, it was not until the mid-nineteenth century that this fact-value distinction was forcefully articulated.[2] The positing of fact as distinct from value—an epistemological position requiring the critique of much that Neo-Confucian thought presupposed—was perhaps most clearly put forward by Nishi Amane.[3]

In a number of writings from the 1870s, Nishi put forward a new set of pre-suppositions about knowledge in stark contrast to various views of knowledge and knowing collectively called Neo-Confucian. Nishi's articulation of this new epistemology was at the same time an attack on the Neo-Confucian (specifi-cally Chu Hsi) concept of *ri. Ri* (Chinese *li*), usually translated as "principle" in contemporary English language works on Chinese philosophy, was a central component of Neo-Confucian metaphysics. The historian of Chinese philoso-phy Fung Yu-lan describes Sung dynasty thinker Chu Hsi's conception of prin-ciple (*ri,* the essence of an object) in relation to material force (*ki;* Chinese *ch'i,* an object's physicality, the matter from which it is constituted).

> The case is like that involved in building a house. Though bricks, tiles, wood, stone, etc., are essential as building materials, there must also be an architectural plan or form in order that these materials may be used in construction. The materials are the "instruments" [*ki*] used for building the house, whereas its form or plan is the principle [*ri*] that provides the "source" from which the house is constructed. Moreover, after that house has been built, its principle, i.e., its plan or form, still inheres in it.[4]

Every object, whether material or ideal, contains within itself the principle that makes it what it is. Further, the various principles of all objects are identified in the source of all principle, an absolute that resolves difference called the Great Ultimate (Taikyoku). There is no distinction between moral and amoral prin-ciples. Indeed, there is a distinct moral aspect to the Chu Hsi conception of *ri.* Although an object's *ri* makes it what it is, *ri* is not merely descriptive—it is the principle of what the object *ought* to be. Not to be in accord with one's *ri* was a moral transgression. In this way, both good governance, for example, and the falling of the rain had a moral component.[5]

Nishi attacked this conception of *ri* as a confusion of two discrete types of principle. "Nowadays, when anyone even mentions the term principle *(dōri)* they make not the least distinction among the principle of loyalty to one's lord and filiality to one's parents, the principle of the falling of the rain, and the principle of the shining of the sun—all of these they call principle." Here Nishi suggested that to view the virtue of loyalty and the natural phenomenon of the rain as guided by the same principle was to confuse two different kinds of principles. "Because the vast majority of people think of these as one thing," Nishi argued, "a great mistake is made."[6]

This confusion of two distinct kinds of principle, according to Nishi, was responsible for the persistence of superstitions. "In Japan, many people believed that, because of the *kamikaze* [divine wind] of Ise or the influence of Nichiren's prayers, a typhoon arose to capsize the Mongol warships...or that rain fell on the drought by virtue of the *Ise* poems."[7] As discussed in the previous chapter, the eradication of superstition was an integral part of the civilizing project of the state in the early Meiji period. For Nishi, these superstitions obstructed the dissemination of truthful knowledge and consequently hindered moral discourse. "Until these people let go of their blind adherence to these superstitions, a discussion of truthful teachings will be impossible."[8] Nishi used the term "teachings" *(oshie)* to refer to "the Way of humanity" *(jindō)*, an explicitly moral term. This statement, then, shows that at least one of Nishi's objectives in his critique of the Confucian conception of *ri* was the clarification of morality. In *Hyakuichi shinron*, Nishi wrote that although the term *oshie* is often translated into Western languages as "morality" (he uses the katakana *moraru*) or as religion *(rerijiun)*, he said, "I use the term here solely to indicate the teachings of the Way of humanity."[9] It seems likely that Nishi understood the Western terms "morality" and "religion" in a Christian context. "Truthful teachings" as "the Way of humanity" then transcended the regional and cultural particularity of the morality and religion of the West and implied a moral teaching of universal scope. To apprehend the truth of this universal morality, it was first necessary to address the confusion generated by the Neo-Confucian assertion of unitary principle.

In contrast to this Neo-Confucian conception of a unitary *ri*, Nishi differentiated between human principle and material principle, or more precisely, between the *ri* of the mind *(shinri)* and the *ri* of the material world *(butsuri)*. "Though we may speak of this principle and that principle as the same, *ri* in fact has two paths and we must realize that the two are not even slightly related. To distinguish the two, I call one *shinri* and the other *butsuri*."[10] *Butsuri*, as natural principles *(shizen no ri)*, referred to "physical laws that apply to all creatures and that cannot be defied." As examples of natural laws or principles,

Nishi listed Newton's law of gravity, Kepelar's law of planetary motion, and so forth. None of these, Nishi pointed out, have any relationship to human affairs, though it is only through human discovery that these physical laws are revealed to us. *Shinri*, on the other hand, referred to principles governing the human realm. Here, Nishi's examples referred primarily to moral principles. These are principles arrived at through the use of reason and that "prevail only among humans." "Although they are based on nature," Nishi explained, "you can defy or alter them if you wish."[11]

For Nishi, these two types of principle were universal. Western scholars, he pointed out, used a variety of terms (because of their different languages) to refer to these principles, but as Nishi posited them as essential objects, all terms referred to the same thing. *Ri* in the West, Nishi argued, is expressed by the terms "reason" and "law of nature," the former corresponding to *shinri,* the latter to *butsuri.*[12] In other words, "reason" corresponded to the human realm, while "laws of nature" belonged to the material realm. Of course, this was not merely an explication of the usage of terms in Western languages. By linking the term *risei* to Western terms, Nishi undermined its alternative meanings in its Japanese context. He was concerned to divest this term of any prior meanings. Again, Confucianism was the object of his attack. "We must understand that the sense of *tenri* [principle of heaven] or *tendō* [Way of heaven] is not conveyed by the terms *risei* or *dōri*." In this way, Nishi endeavored to disqualify these alternative meanings and to fix these crucial terms to his new definitions. The establishment of a fixed conceptual vocabulary was essential for the legitimation of this new epistemological framework.

Reason was of particular importance in this framework because it served as the tool for apprehending both physical and moral principles. "The essence of intelligence" Nishi argued, "is to know the principle *(dōri)* of an object through the application of reason *(risei),* that is, to see the effect of a phenomenon and to know the cause, or to witness the cause and measure its effect."[13] By subjecting an object (a physical or mental phenomenon) to instrumental reason, its governing principle could be known. Nishi used the term *dōri* to signify an object's principle, and *risei* as the faculty for apprehending that principle, that is, as the human capacity for rational thought.[14] Reason, according to Nishi, functioned as "the basis for making distinctions between right and wrong."[15] And because this was a universal human faculty, it could be applied to apprehend universally true moral principles. Moreover, for Nishi, reason *(risei)* served as a restraint on desire so that one could pursue moral action. He described a condition in which "both intellect/reason and emotion are constantly at war with one another in one's innermost heart."[16]

In this epistemological framework, the physical world was objectified. The subject position of the knowing or observing human agent was detached from the material world and the laws that govern it. This calls to mind Charles Taylor's "picture of the agent" where disengagement from the world becomes possible through its objectification.[17] "Nature" for many Meiji thinkers was an object whose secrets could be revealed through empirical observation. This view of nature, of course, represents a radical departure from pre-Meiji conceptions and calls attention to the fluidity of "nature" in Japan. In fact, as Julia Adeney Thomas argues in her study of ideologies of nature in Japan from the early nineteenth to the early twentieth centuries, "the intellectual and political leadership of Japan repeatedly and consciously reconfigured the concept of nature."[18] As formulated by Nishi, nature operated in accordance with laws. These laws of the material world, Nishi maintained, "are not laws that are decided on the basis of the imagination of the human mind." Rather, "they are inherent in the object *(kyakkan ni zoku suru mono nari).*"[19] *Butsuri,* then, according to Nishi, referred to *a priori* physical principles. But moral principles were also objectified. Though they belonged to the human realm, they were treated as objects with an essence that could be revealed through instrumental reason. Unlike physical principles, however, moral principles were not arrived at through deduction (reasoning from the general to the particular) but through induction (reasoning from the particular to the general, from the part to the whole). In this sense, Nishi described them as *a posteriori* principles.[20]

Nishi's distinction between *shinri* and *butsuri* was also a separation of fact and value. By divesting the material or natural world of value, he denied it a subjectivity or consciousness of its own. As mentioned above, Nishi was critical of views that attributed some kind of agency to nature—that is, views of events in the material realm (such as the *kamikaze*) responding to events in the human realm (e.g., Nichiren's prayers). Nishi was thus attacking and refuting a conception of nature with agency capable of adjudicating human action.

For those whose thought was guided by such epistemological presuppositions, only those claims (ethical or physical) that were consistent with *ri* could legitimately be called truthful. It was in this sense that *rinrigaku* scholars sought to legitimize their ethical claims by asserting their "rationality" (*gōri;* here meaning not only consistency with reason but with natural laws as well). As prior modes of knowledge and knowing were rejected, "truthful knowledge" became the collection of claims that could be verified through this new form of epistemological adjudication. The authority of this epistemology lay in its connections with social utility and power. In the utilitarian atmosphere of the 1870s where "useless knowledge" was disdained and practical knowledge was seen as a means to attain wealth and power, "truthful knowledge" became a synonym for "practical studies" *(jitsugaku).*

The intellectual position taken by *rinrigaku* scholars in the 1880s was possible because of prior intellectual labor. The authority *rinrigaku* quickly acquired for itself was rooted in an already available epistemology—one that incorporated a reconfigured conception of *jitsugaku.* From the early part of the nineteenth century, "Western knowledge" gradually came to displace epistemologies associated with Confucianism as truthful knowledge. Indeed, by the end of the Tokugawa period, *jitsugaku*—a term once signifying Confucian learning—came to be understood and defined as the "truthful learning" of Western knowledge.[21]

In texts from the Tokugawa period, *jitsugaku* was generally used to refer to Confucian learning. By the early part of the nineteenth century, however, moral views associated with Buddhism and Confucianism were gradually losing legitimacy, while the authority of the practical sciences of the West steadily increased. In the 1830s, for example, critics of the Tokugawa *bakufu* government such as Watanabe Kazan and Takano Choei had criticized Confucianism as "empty learning." Kazan argued that Japan's problems resulted from a reliance on "grand and lofty abstractions borrowed from China."[22] In *On a Serious Matter (Shinki ron),* he wrote, "We have been influenced by the abstract scholarship of China and allowed the growth of this learning which, though noble in rhetoric, is empty in content." By contrast, the West, according to Kazan, had "dominated the world" by "acquiring knowledge of the entire world."[23] For Kazan, the overwhelming power of Western knowledge had been clearly demonstrated in Britain's defeat of China in their conflict over the opium trade. Kazan's colleague Takano Choei expressed a similar dissatisfaction with Confucian knowledge in one of his works comparing Chinese and Western medicine. The former he described as "a collection of unsubstantiated ideas" while the latter he viewed as "fact-based."[24]

In the 1850s, Sakuma Shōzan, who would become an advisor to the shogunate on matters of defense, repeated this criticism and called for the practical study of the technical knowledge of the West. The Confucian moral order had been called into question by the conviction that the power of the West stemmed from knowledge. Shōzan distanced himself from the "empty" Chinese learning and focused instead on the investigation of contemporary conditions. In 1858 he wrote that the learning of China and Japan "must be supplemented and made complete by inclusion of the learning of the entire world."[25] And while for Shōzan Western knowledge provided a much-needed supplement to shore up the increasingly delegitimized epistemology of the *bakufu* government, by early

Meiji "enlightenment" thinkers such as Fukuzawa Yukichi were calling for the complete displacement of Confucian knowledge with that of the West.

Fukuzawa criticized the "blind adherence to invalidated old ways."[26] In *An Encouragement of Learning (Gakumon no susume)*, Fukuzawa criticized conceptions of learning associated with Confucianists and scholars of Japanese learning.

> Learning does not mean useless accomplishments, such as knowing strange words, or reading old and difficult texts, or enjoying and writing poetry. These accomplishments...should not be slavishly worshipped as the usual run of scholars try to persuade us....[T]his kind of unpractical learning [*jitsu naki gakumon*] should be left to other days, and one's best efforts should be given to practical learning [*jitsugaku*] that is close to everyday needs....This is the practical learning that all men, without distinction of rank, should acquire.[27]

For Fukuzawa, *jitsugaku* included geography, natural philosophy (a "learning that seeks to know the workings of the ten thousand things in heaven and earth by observing their nature"), history, economics, and ethics (i.e., *shūshingaku*, a form of learning that "relates the natural principles [*tenzen no dōri*] by which one must discipline the body, interact with others, and make one's way through society").[28]

By the 1870s *jitsugaku* had come to refer to the West's form of empirical studies. "In the final analysis," wrote Tsuda Mamichi in the *Meiroku zasshi*,

> learning falls into two major categories. There are empty studies [*kyōgaku*] that are devoted to such lofty doctrines as nonexistence and Nirvana, the theory of the five elements, or intuitive knowledge and intuitive ability [i.e., associated with Buddhism, Sung Confucianism, and Yomeigaku, respectively]. And there are practical studies [*jitsugaku*] that solely explain factual principles through actual observation and verification, such as astronomy, physics, chemistry, medicine, political economy, and philosophy of the modern West.[29]

Here, in the early 1870s, roughly a decade before Inoue Tetsujirō would write his *New Theory of Ethics*, a methodology for ascertaining truthful knowledge emphasizing observation and verification is clearly asserted.

Contemporary studies of this transformation of *jitsugaku* describe it in terms of a shift from ethics to physics, from an epistemology infused with value

to one guided by fact. The scholar of Tokugawa intellectual history Maruyama
Masao asserted a discontinuity in conceptions of *jitsugaku* during the Tokugawa period and in early Meiji. While Fukuzawa Yukichi's writings on *jitsugaku*
are generally understood as an assertion for the need of "practical learning,"
Maruyama claimed that "Fukuzawa's truly revolutionary shift in *jitsugaku* did
not lie in the assertion of the need for a union of learning and everyday life, for
a practical usefulness of learning itself." Rather, the shift "appears as a revolution from ethics [*rinrigaku*] to physics [*butsurigaku*]."[30]

One problem with this argument, as historian Minamoto Ryōen has
pointed out, is that it indiscriminately categorizes all Tokugawa thought on
jitsugaku as "ethical." Minamoto argues that while the thought on *jitsugaku* of
some Tokugawa thinkers (such as Fujiwara Seika, Nakai Tōjū, and Itō Jinsai)
certainly had a moral component, ethics was not the central theme in other
thinkers' conceptions of *jitsugaku*.[31] Moreover, he asserts that in Fukuzawa's
conception of *jitsugaku* there are both ethical components and aspects reflecting the authority of the physical sciences.[32] In other words, Tokugawa conceptions of *jitsugaku* were not purely ethical, just as early Meiji conceptions of this
term were not purely a matter of physics.

Yet both Maruyama's and Minamoto's accounts of the transformation of
jitsugaku presuppose the possibility of a value-neutral position. Maruyama
claimed that by early Meiji "practical studies" referred to an epistemology
predominately guided by a fact-based form of inquiry in turn guided by the
physical sciences. As for Minamoto, his claim is essentially that in both the
Tokugawa and early Meiji periods, some conceptions of *jitsugaku* were concerned with ethics *(rinri)* and some were not. Both of these accounts fail to
recognize that all views of *jitsugaku*, including those guided by the physical
sciences in early Meiji, reflected some kind of value orientation.[33] The epistemology out of which the academic discipline of ethics emerged, one grounded
in the physical sciences and fact acquisition, was by no means value neutral.

This brief genealogy of *ri* and *jitsugaku* brings into view certain distinctive
features of a new epistemology that was taking shape. The material world of
butsuri became objectified in a way that allowed it to serve as a final foundation for knowledge. But for "nature" to be the final ground for value, nature
itself had to be valueless. Nishi contributed to the prior intellectual labor that
divested nature of value through its de-subjectification. In other words, nature
became an object devoid of moral content—it was no longer a subject capable
of moral adjudication. Nishi's separation of the human realm of *shinri* from
the material realm of *butsuri*, then, was also a separation of value from fact.
This gave rise to an empiricist methodology presupposing universal laws of

nature apprehended through the application of instrumental reason, observation, verification, and evidence. I call these presuppositions about knowledge an "epistemology of representation."[34] As I apply the term to late nineteenth century *rinrigaku,* I use "representation" to refer not centrally to representation per se (i.e., an image of the mind that represents the real object in the external world), but to the subject/object opposition it implies. Representation in this sense informed the methodological framework underlying *rinrigaku* texts of the 1880s.

Moreover, this was an epistemology authorized by its claims to practicality and power. The military and industrial power of the West was viewed as an outgrowth of its knowledge and skills. Such "truthful and practical knowledge" *(jitsugaku)* was in turn a product of this epistemology. When attention came to center on the power that stemmed from social and moral unity in the Social Darwinist environment of 1880s Japan, *rinrigaku* drew on this same epistemology to produce conceptions of the good with which to order and unify society. In the section that follows, I outline some of the major ethical theories associated with *rinrigaku* in order to further outline the epistemology in which they were rooted.

Early Meiji Theories of Ethics

Nishi Amane's Three Treasures
In the early years of the Meiji period, Nishi Amane approached morality with many of the same concerns as Inoue Tetsujirō and Katō Hiroyuki in the 1880s. In 1873, Nishi published "The Three Human Treasures" (Jinsei sambō) as a contribution to the journal *Meiroku zasshi.* Nishi's primary concern in this work was the ordering of society with the use of a social ethic authorized by a compelling moral foundation. The primary object of his critique was Confucian morality. Confucian virtues no longer had the power to quell social disruptions and to compel each person in society to accept his or her social position. His answer to this lack of a guiding morality was, as he called it, the "three human treasures" of health, wisdom, and wealth, the "fundamentals of morality."[35]

Drawing upon the utilitarianism of Mill, Nishi asserted that the idea of the greatest happiness for the greatest number was indeed the "chief objective of mankind." By honoring, maintaining, or seeking out the three treasures, the ultimate end of happiness could be attained. Without attention to these treasures, however, governing oneself, managing one's family, and ruling the nation would be impossible.

Further, Nishi described the three treasures as a "path for ordering the world" *(yo ni shosuru no michi)*.[36] In a passage that clearly reflects this abiding concern with social ordering, Nishi wrote,

> If men truly honor the three treasures without any reservations, however, what will prevent them from being regular members of society even though they may differ in social station? For example, it is a matter of course that old men who repair pipes, young men who gather trash paper, common women who sell beans, and children who gather manure follow vulgar professions and are not elevated in their ways.[37]

But Nishi argued that from the standpoint of social intercourse, monarchs and ministers and common people who gather trash and manure are all members of society. All are alike in possessing the three treasures, and these treasures are "equally precious without regard to men's differing social station."[38] "If we assess their utility and their merit, they must all be counted even though they may differ in size."[39] Likening social intercourse to links in a chain, Nishi asserted that each link is equally a part of the chain; each has its use and its role to play. "Just consider the injury to the chain . . . should one of its links . . . be defective." Should even a single individual neglect the three treasures, the whole of social intercourse would be negatively affected. To protect the chain of social intercourse, Nishi introduced a number of "rules" for social interaction dealing with honoring and helping to cultivate the three treasures in others. Translating an attack on the three treasures into legal terminology, Nishi argued that to infringe upon the health, wisdom, or wealth of another must be understood as assault, deception, or robbery.

Nishi's inquiry into the good reflects the use of a methodology consistent with the epistemology of representation. He based his arguments on "observable facts." Health he called a human treasure because of the observable fact that all have a desire for life. Similarly, wisdom was based on the observable fact that all desire to surpass others, and wealth on the desire to "acquire things for their use." Moreover, his views reflect the shift in emphasis from physical to mental power that was a part of the discourse on evolution and its doctrine of "survival of the fittest." Wisdom, for example, Nishi described as "surpassing others," not with bodily strength but with mental power, since man after all is "a rational being." Here, wisdom and its cultivation are discussed in terms of competition and warfare. Nishi noted, "Even in war there has recently been more emphasis on mental power than physical power."

Nishi's desire to put forward a morality that could compel certain types of practice is evident not only in his emphasis on observable facts, but also in the "indisputable retribution" that befalls one who takes the three treasures lightly. He pointed out that although one may disregard some of the old Confucian virtues without serious consequences, this was hardly true of the three treasures. Disease, ignorance, and poverty were the fate of those who did not cultivate health, wisdom, and wealth.[40]

This text shares with the moral texts of the 1880s a concern with ordering society around compelling moral standards grounded in an epistemology of representation. Yet Nishi preceded the effort to establish ethics as an academic discipline. Central in this endeavor was Inoue Tetsujirō.

Inoue Tetsujirō's *A New Theory of Ethics*

When the Tokyo Kaisei School (the successor to the *bakufu*'s Institute for Barbarian Learning, or Bansho Shirabedokoro) merged with the Tokyo Medical School in 1877 to become Tokyo University, one of the first concerns was the organization of the courses of the three departments.[41] The Department of Letters (Bungakubu), together with the Department of Law (Hōgakubu) and Department of Sciences (Rigakubu), was established at this time.[42] Together with general courses on Western philosophy, the history of Western philosophy, mental philosophy, and logic, the philosophy curriculum within the Department of Letters included a course titled Dōgigaku (literally, the study of the way of righteousness, morality, or humanity). This course was offered in the Department of Letters from 1877. Not until 1893 was a lecture course on *rinrigaku* set up, the same year in which an academic chair for ethics was established.[43] Yet efforts to establish ethics as an academic discipline were visible more than a decade earlier.

In 1881, just one year after graduating in philosophy from Tokyo University's Department of Letters, Inoue Tetsujirō lectured there on "the great foundation of ethics." Two years later this lecture was published as *A New Theory of Ethics (Rinri shinsetsu)*. This text represented the first sustained effort to establish the terms, concepts, and methodologies for the academic inquiry into the good in Japan.[44]

Inoue's central concern in this work was to uncover the "great foundation of ethics." Drawing upon utilitarian philosophy, Inoue asserted that the ethics of all philosophies and religions aim at the same thing: happiness in life. But these ethical theories and doctrines, Inoue argued, lacked a credible foundation—one that he set out to provide through an argument based on evolutionism. The "true form of the universe," Inoue maintained, is the ultimate source of moral knowledge. Evolution is a partial manifestation of the workings of the universe. Although from this one part we cannot know the whole, we can nevertheless intuit an ethical imperative from evolution: to improve oneself or perish. This moral imperative, then, which calls upon each individual to strive to realize his or her own ideal, is based upon evolution, an observable aspect of the universe, and ultimately on the true form of the universe itself (or as Inoue otherwise described it, *banyū seiritsu*, or universal existence). Hence, as Inoue stated in his preface, "the foundation of morality lies in the attainment of a level of perfection by following the law of evolution."[45]

As a methodological starting point, Inoue examined a wide variety of statements on morality, both philosophical and religious, and looked for commonalties. Following the utilitarian philosophy of Henry Sidgwick, Inoue divided ethical teachings into intuitionism and hedonism, and he argued that these categories could be applied to all of the ethical teachings throughout history.[46] "From ancient times, all ethical teachings fall within this categorization.... For both intuitionism and hedonism, obtaining happiness is life's purpose. Only the method in attaining this happiness differs."[47] Happiness in life, then, is the aim of all ethical teachings. Yet Inoue was dissatisfied with these teachings because none could provide an adequate explanation of why happiness must be our aim. This led him to his next task: to compare the foundations of these various ethical teachings.

In his examination of various ethical theories, Inoue observed that all attempted to ground their teachings in some higher order concept:

> There are those, like the Christians, who take divine will as the foundation of morality. Others, like Hobbes, assert it is the will of the ruler. For those like Cudworth, Clark, and Price, the foundation of morality is reason [*risei*]. For Shaftebury and Hutcheson, it is moral sense [*dōnen*]. For Mandeville, it is self-interest (personal gain). Then there are those who accept utility as the foundation of morality, those like Bain and Mill. However, this present work is based on evolutionism, and asserts that the foundation of morality lies in the attainment of a level of perfection by following the law of evolution.[48]

Not only does this list demonstrate Inoue's familiarity with various strands of Western moral philosophy, it also reflects moral philosophy's overriding concern with foundations for "the good"—the foundation providing irrefutable testimony to one's putatively universal (and universalizing) ethical claims. As mentioned above, this was Inoue's overriding concern as well, as the original title of his *New Theory of Ethics* (initially *The Great Foundation of Ethics*) makes clear. Although the names for these above-listed moral foundations differed, Inoue contended that all were attempts to express the same thing—the unknowable mystery of the universe. Apparently following Hegel, Comte, and

Lewes,[49] Inoue called this mystery "universal existence" *(banyū seiritsu)* or "the true form of the universe" *(utchū no hontai),* and he asserted that this was in fact the ultimate foundation upon which all ethical teachings are based. In this respect, because these ethical teachings attempted to apprehend universal existence, all of them contained some truth. Inoue was dissatisfied with these teachings, however, because none could provide an empirical account of any part of universal existence, their moral foundation. Consequently, because people are "unable to understand universal existence by means of human knowledge," they "fear it, make it into a god, respect it, and worship it." For Inoue, the moral pronouncements of religious and philosophical thinkers remained rooted in mystery and therefore could not properly be considered ethical knowledge. It was Inoue's task to uncover moral *knowledge* from this mystery whose true form in its entirety was ultimately unknowable. He argued that of all the mysteries of the universe, change was the only certainty.

The certainty of change allowed Inoue to extract a moral imperative from the uncertainty of the universe. "In all of creation, there is nothing that is at rest, nothing that does not change.... With the passing of a single minute, the universe is not entirely the same as before.... Everything is constantly changing." This change is the working of the universe, the law of evolution—it is the "tendency of the force of the true form of the universe." Change guided by the principle of evolution, then, was the only stable certainty.

> The tendency of evolutionary force...is the law of evolution [*kajun no kiritsu*]. It is reasonable that the condition of the universe is such that there was a cause that gave rise to the beginning of the world. To claim this is not so is the same as saying that for an effect there is no cause, and this runs counter to the laws of science [*kagaku no kiritsu*]. In the case of vegetation, a pinecone produces a pine tree; a melon seed produces a melon. A melon seed does not produce a pine tree, nor does a pinecone produce a melon. Consequently, today's conditions have been produced by an original seed. In other words, within the original nature of the universe was contained the seed which was to inevitably develop into these current conditions. So this seed follows the evolution of the universe.

The doctrine (or, in Inoue's understanding, the "scientific law") of cause and effect was an integral feature of evolution. Evolution, too, for Inoue, was not a theory but a law. The law of evolution, Inoue argued, is a form of knowledge that is ultimately based on the nature of the universe. Although it is impossible to *know* the true form of the universe, this does not mean we must fall back on faith or superstition. We are not completely cut off from knowledge about the universe's true form, because we can apprehend and verify a part of it as manifested in the law of evolution.

> Universal existence is, namely, the true form of the universe. People can only see one part of this image. Consequently, it is not possible to know the universe. If we were to take one wheel of a vehicle and show it to an ordinary person and ask him what it is, certainly he would be unable to answer. However, were we to show the entire vehicle, he would know. It is the same with the universe. By seeing only one part of the universe, certainly it is impossible to know what the universe is....People cannot know such things as their origin, their destiny, or how long they will live....Nevertheless, there is something that serves as a guide. This is none other than the tendency of evolutionary force.

This manifestation of universal existence (i.e., the law of evolution) provided Inoue with "ethical knowledge"—*knowledge,* according to Inoue, because it was ultimately derived from and based upon an observable and verifiable scientific law. As the theory of evolution involved not only the idea of change but of progress, Inoue concluded, "Day by day, month by month, all living things—not only people...evolve [*kajun shite*] and approach a level of purity and perfection." Hence, the ethical implication Inoue derived from evolution was the imperative to improve oneself, to strive to realize one's own ideal. But Inoue was motivated not merely to elaborate an abstract theory of ethics; *A New Theory of Ethics* reflects Inoue's close engagement with the social concerns of his day. His statements on moral progress and on attaining one's ideal show the importance he attributed to the moral cultivation of the individual.

Inoue directly commented on the ills of his present society. "Our society is overflowing with people who do not seek to attain this ideal, who neglect responsibilities and take their ease, who in the end have strayed down an evil path—everyone is like this. Because of this, our society today is enveloped by calamities of every kind."[50] *A New Theory of Ethics* was an effort to confront these calamities by offering a foundation upon which to reorder social behavior.

By establishing a foundation for morality, Inoue hoped to lend authority to and illustrate the urgency of his moral imperative. "Because the law of survival of the fittest is always at work, those things which cannot by themselves improve even a little, which cannot adapt to the tendency of evolution's force, must die out. So only those things that properly improve survive."[51] The law of evolution, then, allowed Inoue to assert an ethical imperative not simply to improve, but to improve or perish.

But what did it mean to improve oneself? Obviously, this could be interpreted in many ways. Inoue did not provide a listing of virtues to which one should adhere, nor did he establish a rule-based code of behavior. His statements about correct moral behavior are left rather vague. Nevertheless, Inoue's notion of the "sage" provides information on his view of correct ethical behavior.

> He who adapts to the tendency of evolution's force, avoids transgressions however slight, and lives a pure life, is called a sage. If one does not adapt to the trend of evolutionary force, then even a single word or a single act will certainly produce an unhappy result, and one will be unable to survive. "The tree that does not bear fruit is cut down and thrown into the fire" is not a worn-out proverb.... So the difference between one who attains purity and perfection and one who does not lies in a single word, in a single act. If one does not wear appropriate clothing in midwinter, one will certainly become ill. The reason for this is that this person did not adapt to the tendency of evolutionary force. To be indulgent and idle, to be licentious in the way of manners, this is the detestable feature of humanity. This too is the result of not adapting to the tendency of evolutionary force. If one does not study, and fails to improve, he will certainly lose out to others. This too is the result of not adapting to evolutionary force. In view of this, care for your body, observe common customs, and observe the high and the low [*sezoku to jōge shi*], polish your knowledge, and in this way you must endeavor to adapt to the tendency of the force of evolution.[52]

The above shows that Inoue's goal was not so much to establish a new set of moral rules to be obeyed as it was to provide an argument as to why one must improve. "Improvement" was a matter of production, of utility. Those who did not produce, that is, the socially useless, would fare like the "tree that does not bear fruit." The productive member of society, however, adapts to change brought on by evolution through studious and upright rather than indulgent behavior. He will observe "common customs" rather than abandon these for a new code. He will also observe "the high and the low (*jōge*)." This last point implies that one should know one's place in society. *Jōge*, meaning "high and low," "above and below," can also be interpreted as "ruler and subject" or as "the government and the people." All of this indicates that although the individual is directed to improve, such improvement must not disrupt society.

Inoue's *New Theory of Ethics* has generally been considered to be of little importance and has consequently received little attention. Studies of Inoue's thought tend to center on his later writings—his "Commentary on the Rescript on Education," his *Outline of National Morality,* and his contributions to the

1890s debates between education and religion, for example. Scholars who have written on *A New Theory of Ethics* criticize Inoue's eclecticism and point out weaknesses in argument. In other words, they provide a philosophical critique of what they take to be a strictly philosophical work.

Kōsaka Masaaki, for example, describes this work as an example of Inoue's "lack of Western scholarly philosophical spirit...manifested in his facile and rather hasty eclecticism and in the synthesizing tendencies manifest in his concepts." He asserts that "Inoue's demonstration [of an ethical foundation] does not go beyond a rather careless eclecticism." Toratarō Shimomura, in what appears to be a paraphrasing of Kōsaka, writes that Inoue's "synthesis [of Western and Eastern thought] did not go beyond a simple, hasty, easily constructed and superficial eclecticism." G. K. Piovesana, in his survey of Japanese philosophy, writes, "Inoue's eclecticism attempted a combination of Sidgwick's theory of happiness, Spencer's evolutionism, and Oriental ethics contained in the 'sage,' the ideal man in pursuit of happiness." In a more extended critique of Inoue's text, Matsuzaki Minoru questions the philosophical merit of *A New Theory of Ethics.* He contests Inoue's view that "universal existence" can be the foundation for ethics. "[Inoue] does not positively touch on the theoretical content of universal existence.... [C]onsequently, because universal existence is originally something we cannot comprehend...it cannot be a standard for morality." He goes on to argue that "the assertions in Inoue's work are not at all thorough" and that Inoue's concept of the ideal to which we all must aspire is subjective. Because no one can define a subjective ideal such as this, he reasons that "one cannot use this concept of the ideal to propose a standard of morality that is universal." He also argues that "one cannot necessarily say that the pursuit of the ideal is a moral good." Matsuzaki concludes with the verdict that Inoue's *New Theory of Ethics* is "nothing more than an eclectic collection of ethical views combined with evolutionism."[53]

My concern here has not been to refute these assertions of eclecticism and weak argumentation directed at Inoue's *New Theory of Ethics.* Rather, I have been concerned to show the importance of this work in another sense. It serves as a valuable resource for examining the production of a perspectival set of ethical claims as well as the epistemology in which they were rooted. The ethical claims of Inoue's *New Theory of Ethics* were presented as truthful because they were consistent with the features of the epistemology of representation. In this work Inoue asked, "What is truth? Is it not that which points to a coincidence between ourselves and external objects? If so, we must first understand the relationship between ourselves and external objects."[54] Here, Inoue clearly shows an acceptance of the subject-object dichotomy that was so central in this epistemology of representation.

Inoue understood the relationship between humanity and the external material world in terms of humanity's capacity to set ideals, to strive to attain them, and to adapt to the force of evolution so as to survive. As a partial manifestation of the universe's true form, evolution, Inoue repeatedly maintained, was the foundation for the good. In short, his conception of the good is legitimized by the natural law of evolution. His claims were thus in accord with *ri* in this one sense. (Again, to be *gōri*—"rational" in this term's modern translation, but literally meaning "in accord with *ri*"—was to be in accord both with the laws of nature and the human faculty of reason.) In regard to this latter sense of *ri* (i.e., reason), Inoue stated, "In this work, I do not inquire into the foundation of the good in order to advocate ethics. Rather, I dispassionately consider, *in terms of reason,* whether or not there really is a foundation for ethics."[55]

Koyasu Nobukuni, in an article on early Meiji ethics, cites this passage and calls attention to Inoue's emphasis on reason in *A New Theory of Ethics.* But Inoue's insistence that he had no ethical agenda to put forward must be interrogated. Koyasu states that Inoue was not concerned to assert some practical or social application of *rinri;* rather, his aim was simply to make use of reason as he engaged in the theoretical investigation of moral foundations.[56] But of course, the very attempt to "uncover" a moral foundation is political; it is to stake a claim to universal truth and the authority to universalize the ethical claims that the foundation supposedly substantiates. Moreover, Inoue's statements on "observing the high and the low," his far from dispassionate objections to those who "neglect their responsibilities" and follow an "evil path," and the "calamities of every kind" for which he believed them responsible are a clear indication of the ethical agenda that underlay his supposedly apolitical theorizing. Inoue's *New Theory of Ethics,* an initial effort to create and authorize *rinrigaku,* was soon followed by others texts with similar concerns.

Katō Hiroyuki's "Right of the Strongest"

Political and social philosopher Katō Hiroyuki, president of Tokyo University from 1881–1893, is perhaps best known as the author of *A Reconsideration of Human Rights (Jinken shinsetsu),* the most comprehensive and sustained attack on natural right doctrine of early Meiji. But Katō produced a number of important works on ethics as well. In 1888, he published *The Relationship between the Right of the Strongest and the Moral Law.* Five years later, writing on a similar theme, he published *Competition for the Right of the Strongest* (1893), followed by *The Progress of the Moral Law* (1894), *The Principle of the Evolution of the Moral Law* (1900), and *Nature and Ethics* (1912).[57]

The "moral law," Katō explained, is a standard for action that varies according to the conditions of each society. Just as there are differences between barbaric and civilized societies, and between developed and undeveloped societies, the needs of each differ as well. Barbaric societies have needs and interests that conform to their barbaric nature, while in civilized societies there are needs and interests that conform to civilization. "A standard for their actions is naturally established by the needs and interests that conform to each. In other words, this is called the moral law. Because of this, good and evil, right and wrong will necessarily differ in barbaric and civilized societies." As the needs of society change, so does the moral law.[58] But whose "needs and interests" determine the moral law?

In Katō's view, the strong determine moral standards. "Because the strong always suppress the weak...we must conclude it is a fact, one that no society can conceal, that the strong are the masters and the weak are nothing more than those who follow."[59] The moral law, then, as "a standard for action that emerges in accordance with the needs and interests of human society," is a reflection of the needs and interests of the strong of society alone. "As for the needs and interests of the weak, they are disregarded." This, according to Katō, is merely a reflection of the principle of survival of the fittest.[60]

Katō explained that in the struggle to survive, the stronger has the power and the moral right to conquer the weaker. Such power Katō called the "right of the strongest."[61] Katō noted that Western scholarship of the time viewed the idea of the right of the strongest in connection with barbaric societies. He argued, however, that governmental power exercised within constitutional monarchies and other cases of the "tranquil and refined power that is exercised in today's civilized societies" were demonstrations of the right of the strongest as well. Even the struggle to acquire the right of liberty is part of the struggle between the strong and weak of a society.

Drawing upon evolutionism, Katō argued that the shifting needs of the strongest cause the moral law not merely to change, but to progress. He viewed the evolutionary progress of society in terms of widening distinctions between ruler and ruled, high and low, rich and poor, and intelligent and stupid.[62] As part of this shift from social homogeneity to heterogeneity, a gradual evolutionary transition took place from the "vulgar and violent form of the right of the strongest of ancient times" to "the tranquil and refined right of the strongest" where superior intellect becomes the measure of strength.[63] Thus, in Katō's vision for Japan, a highly educated elite would lead society, while the lowly, stupid, and poor would allow themselves to be led.

Although Katō presented a view of a moral law that changes and progresses over time, he did in fact attempt to establish a universal good that transcended the shifting standards for action called the moral law. In *A Reconsideration of Human Rights,* Katō described this foundational good as

The Epistemology of *Rinrigaku*   41

the "favorable" or "beneficial operation of survival of the fittest." He explained this by way of example: "When the virtuous superior wins, defeating the ruthless inferior, the process may be called beneficial survival of the fittest; when a ruthless superior is victorious, overwhelming a virtuous inferior, the result may be called damaging survival of the fittest."[64] But who decides what is favorable or beneficial for society, and what constitutes virtue? It was not simply the strongest who decided this question. Katō stated, "The distinction between superior and inferior has to do with physical and mental strength, while the distinction between right and wrong, good and evil, indicates an opposition of moral sentiments."[65] Katō's point was that superiority and strength do not always indicate goodness. Katō's notion of goodness, that which benefits society, becomes clearer when we examine his statements on social order.

In a study of Katō's ethical thought, historian of the Meiji period Minamoto Ryōen argues that Katō's underlying concern in his moral thought during the 1890s and 1900s was to "ethically legitimize a theory of the state with power as its foundation." He states that Katō began to develop this theory in his 1893 work, *Competition for the Right of the Strongest (Kyōsha no kenri no kyōsō)*.[66] But Katō's concern with establishing the power of the state so as to suppress disruptive elements and order society was clearly visible even in the early 1880s. In *A Reconsideration of Human Rights*, Katō wrote of "radical elements who are covetous of power. They are stirring up the people in hopes of taking over society." Katō described them as uneducated, generally poor, ignorant of world affairs, morally degenerate, and "inclined to foment disorder in society."[67] His theory of the state was not as developed as it was to become, but his concerns with state power were certainly evident.

And while both Katō's views and the natural-right theory he opposed were based on a conception of natural law, Katō, like Nishi Amane, de-subjectified nature and thereby divested it of any moral adjudicating power. The moral law, according to Katō, was a function of evolution, or more specifically, the evolution of the right of the strongest. In turn, evolution was apprehended as a discovery of the natural sciences, reflecting precisely the kind of opposition between the material and human realms described by Nishi. This is clear from the outset of Katō's *Reconsideration of Human Rights*, where he discriminated between the physical sciences *(butsuri ni kakawaru gakka)* that study the "realities of nature" and, through experimentation, discovered evolutionary and other principles that "order all worldly phenomena," and the human sciences *(shinri ni kakawaru gakka)* in which "a few wise, clear-sighted thinkers" have begun to investigate "principles that govern human affairs, often with the assistance of the physical sciences."[68]

Nishimura Shigeki's Morality for Japan

In 1886, Nishimura Shigeki, a student of Confucianism and Western studies, a lecturer to the emperor, and a Ministry of Education official from 1873–1886, delivered an address at Tokyo University titled *On Japanese Morality (Nihon dōtoku ron)*. He explained in the preface to this work that the serious study of morality, his long-time concern, was necessary to provide Japan with moral direction. He believed that "through morality, the nation is established," and therefore hoped to "awaken the people's moral spirit" and thereby "solidify the foundation of the nation."

In *On Japanese Morality*, Nishimura began by distinguishing two types of moral teachings: those concerned with this world *(sekyō)* and those he called "otherworldly" *(segaikyō)*. The former included Confucianism and Western philosophy, the latter Buddhism, Shinto, Christianity, and other religions. "This-worldly teachings," he stated, "deal with the harmonization of society and the country; otherworldly teachings deal with this too to an extent, but they are concerned primarily with the return of the spirit after death." His first objection to otherworldly teachings, then, concerned their lack of social utility. These two teachings were further distinguished by those who follow them. "In the West, otherworldly teachings are associated with the middle and lower classes, while the mid- to upper classes are prone to follow this-worldly teachings."[69] The tendency among the lower classes to follow otherworldly teachings, according to Nishimura, was a condition not only of the West, but of Japan as well. Finally, and most fundamentally, Nishimura asserted that this-worldly teachings are based on *dōri* (an authoritative term because of its association with "reason," but in Nishimura's usage also conveying the idea of a "moral path" or "moral Way"), while otherworldly teachings are based on religious faith.[70] For these reasons, he concluded, "In establishing Japan's morality, we must abandon otherworldly teachings and make use of this-worldly teachings."[71]

But the teachings of this world (again, Confucianism and Western philosophy) had disadvantages as well. For example, Confucianism, he argued, should not be followed exclusively because in a number of ways, Western studies (such as physiology and psychology) surpassed Confucian doctrines in "the refinement of their investigation." Second, he believed Confucianism was inconsistent with the progressive atmosphere of the day. He was concerned that "unless a progressive spirit is cultivated, it will be impossible to extend the prestige of the nation." Third, he was critical of Confucianism because it sustained the disparity between the high and low of society. "Confucianism is advantageous for ascendants and disadvantageous for descendants. The ascendants seem to have rights but no obligations and the descendants seem to have obligations but no rights. Although such an arrangement is necessary in putting a country in order, the abuse seems to be a little too excessive." Here, he recognized the problem raised by advocates of popular rights, yet in his acceptance of this disparity between high and low and the unequal distribution of rights and obligations as inevitable in the process of social ordering, he comes closer to the views of Katō and Inoue. His fourth criticism concerned Confucianism's condescending attitude toward women, an attitude he believed to be "extremely incompatible with present and future conditions." Finally, he stated, "Confucianism regards antiquity as good and the present as wrong, and demands on every occasion that we imitate the peaceful reigns of Yao and Shun and the Three Dynasties.... Under the present conditions of Japan, of course, it is not possible to imitate Yao, Shun, and the Three Dynasties, and moreover, we should not try."[72]

Nishimura was equally critical of Western philosophy as a basis for morality. Though often theoretically sophisticated, Nishimura found the Western philosophical systems he had studied to be lacking in terms of their practical application to society. Further, because of the many competing schools within Western moral philosophy, there was no agreement regarding a single basis for morality.[73] Thus Nishimura's moral thought drew upon both Confucianism and Western philosophy, yet he remained critical of each.

Nishimura described his reliance on both Western philosophy and Confucianism to establish a moral foundation for Japan as an effort to conform to the "Middle Way." Most people in Japan, Nishimura observed, lean toward anything Western. They are obstinate and take things to a one-sided extreme. His response was to be equally obstinate in his defense of Confucianism so as to counterbalance the one with the other and thus to act in accordance with the Middle Way. He spoke of the Middle Way not as something confined to Confucian thought, but as a universal principle. "The Middle Way," Nishimura stated, "is a morality common to all the world." Referring to Aristotle's "Doctrine of the Mean," Nishimura pointed out that even the ancient Greeks asserted the virtue of following the Middle Way.[74]

Nishimura's unmistakable reliance on Confucian doctrine for his moral theory has led some scholars of his work to regard him as "conservative." Others, however, describe him as "progressive," rightly pointing out that he was critical of certain aspects of Confucianism and that he openly called for the adoption of Western philosophy in the formulation of a Japanese morality.[75] The problem with confining ourselves to these categories in assessing Nishimura's thought is that "conservative" here is understood as a return to the past, whereas "progressive" implies a willingness to adopt Western forms of knowledge. These are categories produced from within the modernization theory developed primarily in the United States of the 1960s and 1970s. The dubious theory that equates "progress" (with all its evaluative nuances) with the adoption and integration of Western knowledge and Western forms of social ordering must be approached critically. That Nishimura drew upon and reconfigured Confucianism in his moral thought is not an indication of conservatism. Moreover, though Nishimura drew upon Western philosophy and may himself have described this as progressive, we must interpret this from within the context of civilizational hierarchies and not as evidence of some ahistorical form of moral progress.

Nishimura's moral views overlapped in a number of important ways with *rinrigaku* scholars. In terms of their social aims, their opposition to Christianity and Buddhism, and the conceptual vocabulary they used, for example, there was a good deal of commonality. Yet Nishimura used the terms of the epistemology of representation in different ways from *rinrigaku* scholars. One example, as mentioned above, was his use of the term *dōri*, a word with a rich semantic history in Confucian and Buddhist thought but one that *rinrigaku* scholars sought to reconfigure as "reason." His views on cause and effect, a central authorizing principle for *rinrigaku* ethical claims, provide an additional example. While Nishimura accepted that "cause and effect is indeed a law established by heaven," he argued that not every cause results in an effect. "Though one may sow the seed of a plant, there are times when it will decay and not sprout." In cases where an effect was not tied to a cause, Nishimura asserted that a more precise term is "cause and response" *(in-ō)*.[76] Moreover, Nishimura claimed that good action does not always result in a good effect, just as evil action does not necessarily result in an evil effect. Nevertheless, he maintained that "doing good" is the only path or Way to happiness. And although this sometimes leaves one unhappy, this is a rare occurrence.[77] Finally, Nishimura's ethical views were not utilitarian and evolutionist. He was not as involved in the appropriation of these Western forms of ethical inquiry; rather, he made use of the authority of Western moral philosophy (particularly that of Aristotle) to legitimize his own reconfigured form of Confucianism. Yet he, like Katō and Inoue, was closely associated with the state, and his moral views were consistent with the needs of the state.

The Language of *Rinrigaku:* Fixing a Moral Vocabulary

The vocabulary through which this epistemology of representation was articulated also contributed to its production and legitimation. In other words, this epistemology did not simply come into being as an already formed and fixed object. Rather, it was produced (and continually reproduced) through the performative use of language even as this same language was used to articulate and legitimize it. Key terms of this epistemology appeared of course in the various writings by *rinrigaku* scholars, but they were also treated directly in dictionaries. Philosophical and other specialized dictionaries of the 1880s reflect an effort to codify key terms, to fix the meaning of the words and concepts that formed the epistemological foundation for *rinrigaku*'s normative orientation. Central in the codification of terms for *rinrigaku* discourse were Inoue Tetsujirō's *Dictionary of Philosophy* (*Tetsugaku jii*, first published in 1881, with expanded second and third editions appearing in 1884 and 1912), and the *Explanation of Terms for Education, Psychology and Logic* (*Kyōiku shinri ronri jutsugo shōkai*, 1885). These works were part of a struggle to establish a "standard" moral language with the authority to shape social practice. Included in these dictionaries were entries on ethics, knowledge, truth, subject, object, apperception, verification, reason, feeling, individual, nation, and so on. While these works were ostensibly designed to enable a clear discussion of philosophy, ethics, psychology, logic, and so forth, the selection of terms for definition in fact worked to delimit the objects, methods, and terms for "legitimate" ethical inquiry.

Inoue and Katō were central figures in this effort. Inoue, recalling his years as a student at Tokyo University, wrote,

> In discussing such things as philosophy, I found the terms to be insufficient. In my student days, because there was a need to fix these terms, I gathered together four or five friends and we met from time to time and decided on these words. The president [of Tokyo University] at that time was Prof. Katō Hiroyuki. Prof. Katō also agreed with us that this was necessary.

Inoue noted that Katō was for the most part responsible for deciding upon compounds to translate words associated with evolution. "Although I proposed the terms *junka* or *kajun,*" Inoue recalled, "we decided on Prof. Katō's *shinka.*" Katō's *shinka* connotes progress, while Inoue's *junka* and *kajun* both carry the more explicitly positive connotation of a "transformation into the pure." As stated above, Inoue described evolution as "an approach toward a level of purity and perfection."[78] "The terms *shizen tōta* [natural selection] and *seison kyōsō* [the competition for survival]," Inoue continued, "were also Prof. Katō's translations."[79] These various terms reflect both what was at stake (namely, Japan's very survival) and what lay ahead (a transformation into purity). A progressive, teleological conception of time is also evident here, such that Japan's present becomes a culmination of its past, and the future holds the promise of perfect or pure civilization. The good was to improve, to move toward purity and perfection (as understood within the *kaika* teleological framework), while evil was stagnation, for this meant Japan's eventual extinction.

In addition, both Katō and Inoue relied upon evolution as a moral foundation with which to ground their ethical claims. And although the "fact" of evolution itself was rarely disputed within or outside moral discourse, evolution as a "law of nature" was interpreted in different ways. As the foundation for their views of good action, both Katō and Inoue struggled not only to fix a term for "evolution," but to firmly establish its progressive and positive nuance. For example, as Katō emphasized in *A Reconsideration of Human Rights,* "It is incorrect to use 'survival of the fittest' as a pejorative term."[80] For Katō, "survival of the fittest" was simply an amoral principle. Yet while Inoue and Katō sought to legitimize evolution by casting it in the most positive light possible, others called attention to the destruction carried out in the name of evolution.

The Buddhist philosopher Inoue Enryō (1858–1919) questioned the unduly positive nuance of evolution. For Enryō, the evolutionist arguments of Inoue Tetsujirō and Katō Hiroyuki did not take account of the negative aspects of evolution. In contrast to Inoue Tetsujirō's terms *kajun* and *junzen,* referring to the level of "purity and perfection" to which evolution leads, Enryō used the term *tōta* (selection, or natural selection) to refer to evolution, a term carrying the connotation of leaving behind that which is useless or inferior. He asked, "Does the artificial selection of the North American aborigines in fact correspond to an advantage for society? Are the recent great advances made in European medicine, which through artificial selection extend the life of persons afflicted by disease, in fact a disadvantage for society?" Enryō's point was that artificial selection took negative as well as positive forms.[81] He called the systematic extermination of the North American Indians an example of the "savage law of selection" in a "savage society."[82] By contrast, he praised the "benevolent law of artificial selection" in "today's cultured civilization [*bunka kaimei*]" wherein doctors cure the sick and aid the suffering. In both savage and civilized societies, he admitted, both types of selection might contribute to the advancement or evolution *(shinka)* of society. But he maintained, "If we make use of the savage law of selection of older days in today's society which attributes importance to benevolence, we must know that this clearly is a disadvantage for evolution."[83]

Needless to say, *rinrigaku,* Inoue's neologized translation of ethics,[84] was another contested term in moral discourse. Inoue noted, "At first various proposals were made, such as *shūshingaku, dōtokugaku* and so on, but I translated this as *rinrigaku* because *rinri* is a word used in the Chinese classics. This translation eventually became fixed in the academic world."[85]

These two terms, *rinrigaku* and ethics, once equated by Inoue, came to mutually determine one another. *Rinrigaku,* according to Inoue, now signified all that "ethics" signified, while ethics necessarily broadened to include (and legitimize) the moral thought of "oriental philosophy." Moreover, *rinrigaku* continued to be epistemologically weighted even after Inoue equated it with the English term "ethics." In other words, *rinrigaku* was not (and could not have been) an empty container for ethics, a neutral term that signified the same field of meaning as the term "ethics." *Rinrigaku* continued to carry with it its Confucian traces. Even by the mid-1880s, several years after Inoue's translation had supposedly been "fixed," *rinri* for some signified a morality specific to China, calling to mind the "five relations" *(gorin)* of Confucianism.

In *Opinions on Textbooks for Moral Education (Shūshin kyōkasho no setsu,* 1890), Nishimura Shigeki discussed the meaning of the terms "ethics" and "morality."

> Five or six years ago, I asked a teacher about the meaning of the terms *shūshingaku* and *rinrigaku*. The first, he replied, is used in primary school courses; its English translation is "morals." The second, *rinrigaku*, should be used from the time of middle school and translates as "ethics." But this teacher's reply mistakes the usage of these terms. "Morals" is from Latin; "ethics" is from Greek. The meaning is basically the same and any difference is unimportant. Further, *rinri* is not the same as "ethics." *Rinri* is a fixed expression in China and is said to reflect the moral viewpoint of a Ming scholar who defined *rinri* as the only thing that distinguishes people from animals.[86]

Nishimura went on to explain that ethics in Western countries has a very wide range and does not deal specifically with *rinri*. The term *rinrigaku*, therefore, was an inappropriate translation for "ethics." The first character of *rinri (rin)*, Nishimura stated, refers to Confucianism's Five Constant Relationships *(gorin)*, while the second character *(ri)* refers to how those relationships should be characterized: father-child (close); emperor-official (integrity); husband-wife (difference); older-younger siblings (order); friends (trust). "*Rinri* is a morality *[dōtoku]* characteristic of China. Misunderstanding and argument have arisen due to inappropriate translations."[87] In short, Nishimura maintained that there is only one correct definition for *rinri*.

Another example of the struggle for terms and their meanings was the above-mentioned *Explanation of Terms for Education, Psychology and Logic*. In the preface, this work's compilers stated their reasons for putting together this dictionary. They represented their work of translation as an effort to facilitate communication.

> In the fields of psychology, education, and logic, there is a fixed terminology, and one must not arbitrarily amend it. Yet, in our country, from

ancient times, there have been none who have lectured on these fields. In recent times, these fields have been for the first time taken from the West and those engaged in the translation of works from these fields have each selected ideographs...and have thus created translations. For this reason, though the original language each translator translated from was identical, the translators have differed and so consequently the translated terms are not the same. For those who study these fields, it is as though they wander blindly through a thick fog.

This dictionary, then, according to its compilers, was designed to facilitate communication, to establish a "fixed vocabulary" *(ittei no jutsugo)* to assist those involved in the study of these "advanced fields" newly taken from the West. But establishing such a fixed vocabulary was certainly more than a matter of convenience. The terms selected (and omitted) for translation reflect a certain normative predisposition. Moreover, this dictionary was a project for the authorization of a vocabulary through which *rinrigaku*'s epistemology of representation might be produced and sustained. Sociologist Pierre Bourdieu speaks of the production of a "standard language" as a "struggle for symbolic power in which what was at stake was the formation and re-formation of mental structures. In short, it was not only a question of communicating but of gaining recognition for a new language of authority, with its new political vocabulary...and the representation of the social world which it conveys." And the dictionary, as Bourdieu points out, "is the exemplary result of this labour of codification and normalization."[88] The reformation of "mental structures" in the case of 1880s Japan was a matter of establishing and legitimizing an epistemology of representation. The following terms assert the subject-object opposition characteristic of the epistemology of representation.

> *Chikakuryoku* (perceptive faculty): The capacity to know in one's mind things in the external world through impressions of the senses, that is, the five sensory organs, is called the perceptive faculty.

> *Saigenryoku* (representative faculty): The mind does not merely perceive things of the external world through its perceptive faculty; it has the capacity to retain these things in the psyche and reproduce them on another day. This is called the representative faculty.

These definitions both worked to establish and legitimize the idea of an internal world of the mind set in opposition to an external world of nature. The observer of the external world is detached from that which is observed; in other words, there is a distinct opposition between subject (observer) and object (observed). This becomes all the more apparent in the following definitions.

> *Shukan* (subject): "Subject" is the general term for the many varied conditions that occur within the internal world, that is, within the mind. It is a term used in contrast to objective [*kyakkan teki*] knowledge, i.e., knowledge of the external world [*gaikai*]. If we classify our knowledge into different types, we will see that there is nothing other than objective and subjective knowledge. For example... the general term for the concepts of such things as rivers and stones is "object" [*kyakkan*], while the general term for the concepts of pleasure, pain, and so on is "subject" [*shukan*].

> *Kakukwan* [mod. Japanese *kyakkan*] (object): that which exists outside of our bodies... is called the "object." That is, things we know of as existing outside the body, such as mountains, rivers, streams, oceans, grass, trees— there is not a single kind that is not an object. So the object is something in opposition to the functions that take place within the mind, such as pleasure and pain, that is, in opposition to the subject. The terms "outside world" and "non-self" also have the same meaning.[89]

All four of these above terms are also listed in Inoue's 1881 dictionary of philosophy, and it is likely that he played a role in the compilation of the *Explanation of Terms for Education, Psychology and Logic* as well.[90] Further, the subject-object opposition, so clearly articulated in the writings of Nishi Amane in terms of *butsuri* and *shinri* and perhaps the most prominent feature of the epistemology of representation, is also readily apparent throughout Inoue's philosophy dictionary. Among the many examples of this are "physical science" and "mental science" *(butsuseigaku, shinrigaku)*, "object" and "mind" *(butsu, shin/ shin-i)*, and "materialism" and "idealism" *(yuibutsuron, yuishinron)*. In short, the terms show a pronounced opposition between the material realm *(butsuri)* and the human realm *(shinri)*.

Further, the epistemology of representation that is being produced and substantiated in the above definitions served as a basis for the good. The above definitions locate pleasure and pain within the mind, as attributes of the subject. In the definition below concerning good and evil, pleasure and pain play a central role.

> *Kyōaku* (evil): "Evil" is a principle that is in opposition to the good [*zenryō*]. The good is something that conforms to our minds, that is, something that

feels pleasurable emotionally. But "evil" is the opposite of this, namely, something that does not feel pleasurable emotionally.[91]

Good and evil here are understood in terms of pleasure and pain, thus this is clearly a utilitarian conception of the good.

One of the key concepts with which academics identified *rinrigaku* was "reason." Academics posited reason as an inherent and universal faculty of humanity and as the basis for moral decision making. In the early 1880s Inoue Tetsujirō attempted to establish equivalence between the terms *dōri, risei,* "reason," and the German term *Vernunft* in his 1881 *Dictionary of Philosophy.* In Inoue's 1883 *A New Theory of the Psyche (Shinri shinsetsu),* a translation of Alexander Bain's *Mental and Moral Science* (1868), *risei* is associated with utilitarian ethics.

> *Risei:* that which makes it possible to attain the aim of future happiness by clarifying the many varied thoughts that arise in the mind and by distinguishing between good and evil, right and wrong.[92]

This definition, slightly enlarged, became the entry for *risei* in the 1885 *Explanation of Terms for Education, Psychology and Logic* mentioned above.[93] Here, in addition to its role in moral adjudication, *risei* is described as a requisite for knowledge and as a defining feature of the person: "*risei:* that through which knowledge is obtained ... through the workings of the rational faculty *(dōrisei)* peculiar to humanity."[94] In fixing *risei* (as well as *dōri*) to the idea of a universal human faculty for moral adjudication, alternative uses of these terms were de-legitimized.

These "definitions" by no means indicate the "meaning" of these terms in 1880s Japan; each term was semantically unstable. Rather, these definitions were part of an attempt to legitimize, first, the precedence of a certain set of conceptual terms (while marginalizing other possible terms), and, second, a certain space of meaning to which each term must be confined (i.e., a space of meaning these terms ostensibly signified, but one that they in fact produced). And while the foregoing discussion of the language of *rinrigaku* depicts a relatively uncontested effort to fix the meaning of terms, there was in fact an intense discursive struggle to define terms, as we will see in the following chapter. Control over the language of moral discourse meant the power to control the methodology for moral inquiry, the epistemological foundation that grounded such inquiry, and, ultimately, the good itself. In short, by establishing and legitimizing a unitary moral vocabulary, *rinrigaku* scholars sought the power to control the conditions for moral truthfulness.

The Dissemination of *Rinrigaku*

Although the preceding academic ethical theories share commonalties and many draw upon some kind of utilitarian tradition, they by no means form a unitary view of ethics, and there were of course the many and varied ethical views upheld by those outside of academia. In short, no single view of the good had attained hegemony (and hence the "moral chaos" to which so many referred). Those thinkers situated within the space of *rinrigaku* discourse sought to create a new conception of the good, one consistent with the needs of the state as it ordered and civilized society. But the naturalization of some new conception of the good, that is, establishing hegemonic authority for a conception of the good so as to create a "common sense" view of moral action, was not simply a matter of its discursive production and legitimation. Such moral hegemony required also, perhaps primarily, a specified and regulated set of practices that performatively produced the good through their repetition. Two points of contact between discursive productions of the good and the good established through practice were the so-called "morality societies" and moral training textbooks. Nishimura Shigeki was deeply involved with both.

Nishimura Shigeki was probably the central figure in the call for the establishment of morality societies. These societies were to function as media for the transmission of a clearly delineated set of moral stipulations, primarily to the adult population, so as to cultivate and regulate moral practice. Nishimura listed five stipulations that had long been a part of Confucian doctrine: improving oneself, one's home or household, one's village or surroundings, one's country, and, finally, the people of other countries.[95]

Through these morality societies, Nishimura hoped to abolish "misguided doctrines and theories," here referring to "superstitious religious beliefs" and other such "nonsense of illiterate or ignorant people,"[96] and to encourage "good customs." This latter aim was related to "building the character of the people." Character building, for Nishimura, was of the utmost importance. It was upon the individual's character, and the individual's sense of morality, that the good of the nation ultimately depended.

> This is the final objective of the morality society, and is the one most necessary for Japan. No matter how comprehensive a country's political and legal system, how strong its armed forces, how wide its education, even if it has a number of excellent people, the country's reputation overseas depends on the character of all the people. For this reason, I call upon all the people in the country, all those who truly believe this country is important, to work hard to improve the people's character. As the Englishman Smiles says in

his discussion of character, if the people's character is excellent, the country's reputation will shine and it will be respected by other countries.[97]

Finally, through these morality societies Nishimura sought to "unify the hearts of the people." Emphasizing the importance of this last point, he stated, "When a country falls ill, it is for no other reason than that the spirit of the people is not in harmony."[98] Creating a harmonized and unified spirit of the people was to be undertaken through the cultivation of patriotism. Nishimura discussed the need for patriotism and the willingness to sacrifice one's personal benefits for the good of the social whole: "People love themselves first, their family second, and third, their country. Some philosophers or religious leaders tell us that we should restrain this feeling of patriotism. But today, so long as the world has not united into a single country and disputes continue to arise, if a country has no patriotism, it will not be possible to preserve it."[99] Drawing upon the American revolutionary war as an example, Nishimura observed that because of the unfair tea tax, "there was not one person in the whole country who drank tea." Nishimura felt that patriotism in his own country was declining because, with the opening of Japan to trade and foreign goods, people were consumed by the pursuit of benefits but had forgotten how to sacrifice. Closely connected to the spirit of patriotism was reverence for the imperial family. "The spirit of the people should be given direction by fostering their devotion to the sacred imperial family, for it is a destiny unparalleled in the world that the nation had been ruled for 2,500 years by a single family of emperors of unmixed lineage."[100] The appropriate moral practice that Nishimura's morality societies were designed to cultivate, then, centered on moral and national unity expressed through patriotism.

For those who took part in these societies (both members and teachers), conduct was strictly regulated. The morality society, organized to enhance the edification of its members and society as a whole, would be run by two kinds of people. The first Nishimura called the guide or leader, who would strive to edify the people; the second, simply called a member, would assist the spread of morality by direct and indirect means. The guide, Nishimura emphasized, must above all cultivate himself *(mi o osamuru),* otherwise he cannot hope to cultivate others. For this reason, Nishimura laid down the following six rules to which the guide of the society must adhere: Do not say what is not true, overdrink, fornicate, become angry, become greedy, or become arrogant. In addition, the guides were to be honest and sincere, fair, tolerant, strong, and kind. Thus, qualified guides, together with the assistance of members, were to strive to fulfill the society's objectives. By instilling a set of stipulations and moral convictions in its members, and by demanding adherence to a set of carefully regulated practices, these morality societies sought to produce the "morally upright" person.

Membership was initially small but quickly grew. In 1876, Nishimura established the first such morality society, the Tokyo Society for Moral Training (Tokyo Shūshingakusha). By 1880 it had 32 members; by 1884 membership grew to 328, and by 1902 there were 130 local chapters and roughly 10,000 members.[101] Yet even at its height, the morality societies reached only a small percentage of Japan's population. More important in terms of numbers was the moral training of schoolchildren. Primary school textbooks for moral training became a focus of heated debate. Many questioned whether they should be used at all, while others who accepted their usefulness argued over content.

Issues of school curriculum and methods of instruction were unquestionably of primary importance in 1880s moral discourse. While Inoue Tetsujirō and other *rinrigaku* scholars would become deeply involved in the production of moral training textbooks during the 1890s, Nishimura and others produced the moral textbooks of the early 1880s. As mentioned in the preceding chapter, the 1880 revision of the Education Ordinance gave greater weight to moral training *(shūshin)* within the school curriculum. One year earlier, Motoda Eifu published his "Great Principles of Education," asserting that moral education focused too much on texts translated from Western languages and that more attention to Confucian morals was needed.[102] To comply with Motoda's views, which were issued as an authoritative Imperial Rescript, the Ministry of Education took steps to revise current textbooks, appointing Nishimura Shigeki to the post of chief editor of its textbook compilation bureau. In this capacity, Nishimura issued his own textbook, *Moral Teachings for Primary School (Shōgaku shūshin-kun).*

This work reflected a shift from content centering on European and American ethics to content with a much higher degree of "Confucian" ethics. It emphasized eight key virtues, and beneath each followed a proverb of some sort from Europe, America, the Chinese classics, or Japan that was meant to elucidate that virtue. Therefore, this textbook upheld the position that Nishimura was to later advocate in *On Japanese Morality,* that of relying on both Confucianism and Western philosophy for Japan's morality. But as editor of Kōdansha's *Outline of Japanese Textbooks* Kaigo Tokiomi points out, "Because it drew proverbs first of all from the *Doctrine of the Mean,* the *Analects of Confucius,* and the *Mencius* we must view this work as a textbook based upon Motoda's "Great Principles of Education" which took Confucianism as the foundation for moral teaching."[103]

In the preface to this moral training textbook, Nishimura stated that teachers should make pupils recite and memorize the lessons in the textbook. Although it would be difficult for young students to understand the lessons

(written entirely in classical Japanese), they should first learn them by heart—
later in life their meaning would become clear.[104] The performativity of this
pedagogy is important. The daily repetition of these moral lessons was a practice through which students learned to regulate themselves. It focused less on
why this or that action was moral than on the repeated recitation of a phrase
that was to guide conduct throughout a student's life.

Rinrigaku and the Epistemology of Representation

In his study of Nishi Amane, Thomas Havens describes Neo-Confucianism as
a repressive ideology that had obstructed Japan's discovery of Western empiricism. According to Havens, Nishi's thought "contributed greatly to destroying
the Shushi theory of knowledge, which had delayed truly empirical scholarship in Japan, by conclusively emancipating society and moral philosophy from
their repressive links with the Sung cosmology.... *Ri* itself was now liberated
from its Confucian overtones to become something ethically neutral, like its
English counterpart, 'principle.'"[105] Havens' statement reflects the authority
of modernization theory prevalent at the time that he wrote. In other words,
it is with Nishi that, according to Havens, Japan finally extricated itself from
its irrational theories of knowledge and adopted Western forms of empirical,
value-neutral scholarship. But of course, even Nishi's conception of physical
principle, or *butsuri*, was never "ethically neutral." It was part of a regulatory
structure for arbitrating truthful knowledge that was deeply rooted in its own
normative orientation. The same may be said of the other moral theories examined in this chapter. Although the approach of each toward the question of the
good differed, each was guided by a shared set of epistemological resources,
each drew upon a common moral vocabulary to articulate its views, and each
was ultimately rooted in a historically contingent normative orientation. None
of these works was an ethically neutral, objective inquiry into the good. Each,
rather, was concerned to produce a moral foundation with which to reorder
thought and practice, reorder society, and enhance the power of the state.

From this sketch of the moral theories of Nishi, Inoue, Katō, and Nishimura,
it is possible to discern several features of the epistemological context out of
which *rinrigaku* emerged. Inherent in these writings on ethics were certain presuppositions about knowledge and truth. A first presupposition concerns the
objectification of the good, nature, and so on. "Nature" was posited as an object
to be known, presented to the consciousness of the subject or knower. A sub-
ject/object opposition was therefore also presupposed, that is, the objectification of the world required a kind of disengagement from the world—the object

(that which is known) as discrete from the intending consciousness of the subject (the knower). A second epistemological presupposition concerns truth as essential and revelatory. That which is objectified is endowed with an essence or "truth," an inherent, fixed feature of the object. By subjecting the object to rational scrutiny, that is, with the application of instrumental reason, the truth of the object (nature's laws, for example) can be revealed. This epistemology, objectifying nature so as to uncover its truths, was authoritative because of its connections to power. Katō, for example, made this clear with his citation of a passage, included in his *Reconsideration of Human Rights,* from German materialist thinker Ludwig Buchner, the author of *Power and Substance* (*Kraft und Stoff,* 1876): "As [man's] intelligence advances... he investigates the principles of nature and gradually gains the ability to regulate it. It is hardly an exaggeration to say that man today is progressing to the status of God."[106] The same epistemology that allowed for the discovery of nature's laws and the regulation of nature authorized *rinrigaku.*

These presuppositions about knowledge I have called an "epistemology of representation." The discourse on *rinrigaku,* located within the realm of academia, philosophy, and science, was informed by this epistemology. But to what extent did this epistemology of representation also inform the thought of others? As we will see in the following chapter, religious thinkers who participated in moral discourse made use of much the same conceptual vocabulary as that in the works of Katō and Inoue. This does not indicate one monolithic epistemology underlying all thought at this time, but it does suggest a dominant set of presuppositions concerning knowledge. Given that this set of epistemological presuppositions was closely intertwined with academic moral inquiry and, further, that it was appropriated by religious thinkers and others outside of academia, academics had a basis for claiming a space of legitimacy from which to arbitrate the good and the true. In other words, *rinrgaku,* in its academic setting, had attained a high degree of authority to decide which beliefs or truth-claims that informed various social ethics would attain the status of "truthful knowledge" and which would be relegated to the status of "falsehood" and "superstition."[107] But ultimately, *rinrigaku* would be unable to control the various reconfigurations of its concepts and terms once appropriated by others.

The emergence of *rinrigaku* and the epistemology of representation marks a fundamental break with Buddhist and Confucian conceptions of the good, the person, and nature prior to the Meiji period. In the many Buddhist and Confucian views of knowledge during the Tokugawa period, there is nowhere so marked an opposition between subject and object as is evident in the 1880s. The Buddhist doctrine of no-self *(muga),* for example, or the Confucian conception of the unity of all things in its doctrine of "principle" *(ri)* and the Great

Ultimate (Taikyoku) did not present the "person" as a disengaged observer set apart from "nature." Moreover, by the 1890s key aspects of the epistemology of representation came to be questioned, even abandoned—specifically the emphasis on reason over feeling and the subject-object distinction. This has important implications for how we might think about "the good." It compels us to take seriously the claims that the epistemology of a given time and place is not fixed and, further, that no view of the good can be put forward that does not to some extent reflect the epistemological context in which it was produced. If these claims are accepted, then formulating "acceptable" principles of conduct that are timeless and universally valid (moral theory by some definitions) becomes problematic.

CHAPTER 3

Rinrigaku and Religion

The Formation and Fluidity of Moral Subjectivity

> Religion establishes a standard for good and evil *by the commands*
> *of God,* whereas *rinrigaku* establishes a foundation for morality
> *with scientific principles.*
> —Inoue Enryō, *An Outline of Ethics,* 1887

As the new discipline of ethics began to emerge out of the
social disruption and moral disorientation of early Meiji, it contended with religion for the authority to speak for "the good." At stake in this contest between
ethics and religion was the human interiority. To what extent, if at all, should the
state play a role in shaping the individual's moral conscience? *Rinrigaku* scholars argued that if the state is barred from such a role, moral unity will never
be realized. For many religious apologists, on the other hand, the autonomy of
one's conscience was inviolable. This struggle over interiority was carried out in
the form of competing representations of religion. *Rinrigaku* academics sought
to expel religion from legitimate ethical inquiry and to establish ethics as an
academic discipline guided by reason and scientific principles. By representing religion as irrational and as socially harmful and thereby undermining its
ethical claims, *rinrigaku* asserted its own rationality and social utility. In this
way, *rinrigaku* strove to establish for itself a space of legitimacy from which to
critique alternative ethical views and the truth-claims upon which they were
based and, vested with the authority of "science," to become the dominant arbiter of the good and the true. Religious apologists, of course, contested these
representations of religion.[1] In hopes of enhancing the legitimacy of their own
positions, Buddhist and Christian apologists drew upon the same authoritative conceptual vocabulary woven throughout the language and methods of
academic ethical inquiry. Evolution, reason and rationality, the law of cause
and effect, social utility—these concepts, each rooted in and drawing authority

from the epistemology of representation discussed in the preceding chapter, dominated early Meiji moral discourse. Few hoping to advance an authoritative moral theory could ignore them. Yet, as religious thinkers reconfigured their respective moral views so as to be consistent with the prevailing rules for legitimacy in moral discourse, they indirectly contributed to the authority of *rinrigaku,* if only by drawing upon the same conceptual vocabulary that *rinrigaku* academics posited as the basis for legitimate moral discourse. Moreover, their engagement with *rinrigaku* and the broader epistemology of representation in which it was grounded transformed the religious moralities they struggled to defend. An examination of this encounter illustrates the (re)formation and fluid nature of moral subjectivity.[2]

Religion as Irrational

For scholars of *rinrigaku,* religion *(shūkyō)* was irrational and therefore inappropriate as a basis for morality. To call religion irrational was to claim that it was "inconsistent with *ri*" (the laws governing the external realm of nature, and reason governing the internal realm of the mind).[3] Thus, *rinrigaku* academics asserted that religion's truth-claims could not legitimately be called "knowledge" because they were inconsistent with the laws of nature *(butsuri)* and with the human faculty of reason *(shinri).*[4]

One of the clearest examples of the call to separate ethics from religion came from Inoue Enryō, one of Buddhism's most articulate and prolific proponents. As both a Buddhist apologist and academic moral philosopher (he defended Buddhism, as I will discuss below, but also attacked religion, in this case Christianity, as a basis for morality), Enryō provides an excellent example of the tension between science and religion. In *Outline of Ethics (Rinri tsūron,* 1887), Enryō called for an ethics entirely outside the realm of religion. While both religion and ethics, according to Enryō, concern the morality of the individual, "[religion] establishes a standard for good and evil *by the commands of God,* whereas [*rinrigaku*] establishes a foundation for morality *with scientific principles.*" Enryō favored science, rather than the Christian God, as a basis for morality. "Scholars of today," he urged, "must endeavor to establish *rinri* as an academic discipline based on the rules of science, making it one type of pure science."[5] He therefore applauded efforts of Western scholars to establish a foundation for morality without relying upon religion *(shūkyō),* but remained dissatisfied with the way they continued to employ to some extent the supposition of God *(tentei)* in their moral philosophy.

Enryō's aim in *Outline of Ethics* was to establish an academic discipline of ethics that would be in accord with a scientific methodology and to replace *dōtokugaku* with *rinrigaku,* that is, to replace Buddhism, Confucianism, Taoism, and Christianity with the science and philosophy of the West. His ethics reflect the authority that utilitarianism and evolutionism held in early Meiji. "The aim of life," Enryō stated, "is the complete happiness of self and other." The promotion of happiness, then, according to Enryō, must be the standard for the distinction between good and evil. He supported his arguments with references to the law of natural selection and the law of evolutionary competition, in much the same way as Inoue Tetsujirō and Katō Hiroyuki.[6]

In fact, many academics opposed the Christian doctrine of creation to the "scientific law" of evolution. Katō Hiroyuki, the thinker primarily responsible for the introduction of social Darwinism into Japan, referred to "the survival of the fittest [*yūshō reppai*]" as "a universal law that is eternal, unchanging, and constant."[7] By contrast, "the doctrine that a creator had...created all things in accord with certain objectives," he argued, "is not the result of experimentation." According to Katō, this doctrine was "directly at odds with the doctrine of causality [*ingashugi*]" and therefore "could never be espoused by anyone who is cognizant of the empirical laws governing all things in the universe."[8] For Katō, then, truth results from experimentation and is consistent with the laws of nature.

The early writings of Inoue Tetsujirō provide another example of this emphasis on the need for a morality based upon the "unchanging laws of nature." In his *New Theory of Ethics,* Inoue proposed a theory of ethics based upon evolutionism, arguing that the law of survival of the fittest means that only those who strive after their own moral and intellectual improvement survive.[9] He attacked Christianity's truth-claims as an unsubstantiated basis for morality, asserting that with the rise of evolutionary theory, "the dawn has broken for the first time" on the "mistakes" and "falsehoods" of Christianity. Christian beliefs were "false" because, as Inoue asserted, "they cannot be proven."

> I must laugh at religious apologists who often tell in detail of the conditions of the next life. Think for a minute. Why would God create people, then lead good people to heaven and cast evil people into hell? What purpose would God have for doing this? What benefit would He derive? The religious try to answer this by saying that the mind of God cannot be grasped by human knowledge. But saying that God bestows rewards and administers punishments upon the dead is an idea produced by the religious themselves. In terms of scholarship, this cannot be proven.[10]

Like Katō, Inoue's primary critique of Christian knowledge concerned the doctrine of creation, as this directly contradicted the laws of cause and effect, and evolution. "It is reasonable," Inoue asserted, "that the condition of the universe is such that there was a cause that gave rise to the beginning of the world. To claim this is not so is the same as saying that for an effect there is no cause, and this runs counter to the laws of science."[11] "Evolution theorists," Inoue stated, "explain the impossibility of things coming into being all at once as asserted in the Bible. With this, religionists...fear that, if the theory of evolution is accepted, religion will be torn apart because its ethics will be seen as lacking in authority."[12] Here, Inoue draws a clear connection between truth-claims supported by evidence and the authority a social ethic can be seen to possess. These texts uphold proof established through experimentation and scholarship, and an agreement with the laws of nature and the methods of science, as requisites for the verification of truth-claims.

In response to these attacks on the doctrine of creation, some Christian apologists, rather than contesting evolutionary theory, argued that evolution in no way undermined the basic tenets of Christian belief. J. A. Ewing, for example, a professor at Tokyo University, maintained that evolution was only a partial explanation of the world, and that behind evolution lay the design of God. We are wrong, he stated during a Methodist lecture series in 1883, to believe that we know how a thing was produced when we can merely explain how it has grown.[13] Yet Christian apologists had to fend off not only *rinrigaku* attacks but the criticisms of Buddhists as well.

A common strategy among Buddhist apologists seeking to defend Buddhism was to appropriate the conceptual vocabulary legitimized by *rinrigaku* and use it to deflect the *rinrigaku* critique of religion onto Christianity alone. Inoue Enryō, for example, equated the Buddhist doctrine of cause and effect, or karma *(ingasetsu),* with "the scientific principle of conservation of energy."[14] A similar example can be found in *A New Discourse on Buddhist Morality (Bukkyō dōtoku shinron,* 1888) by Buddhist historian Murakami Senshō (1851–1929). "For every cause there is an effect and every effect has a cause—this is a universal rule that includes all things.... [I]t is a natural law of heaven and earth with a direct connection to ethics."[15] Murakami aligned the Buddhist notion of karma with evolutionism and was thereby able to call Buddhism's theory of cause and effect (karma) "a true religion that is in agreement with the rules of philosophy and science." He attacked Christianity and its doctrine of creation, calling it "a false religion that is inconsistent with the rules of philosophy and science."[16] Murakami's argument, contrasting karma and creationism, relied for its effectiveness on linking karma to the law of cause and effect in evolution, hence Buddhism was in agreement with the rules of science.

Not all Buddhists, however, connected karma and scientific laws as closely as did Enryō and Murakami. Zen Buddhist Shaku Sōen (1859–1919), for example, abbot of Engaku-ji in Kamakura as well as a student in his younger days of Western learning under the direction of Fukuzawa Yukichi, struggled to retain the Buddhist connotations of this term during its reconfiguration as a scientific law.

In some ways, Sōen's statements concerning karma seem to identify this Buddhist doctrine with the scientific law of cause and effect. In a paper titled "The Law of Cause and Effect, As Taught by Buddha" delivered at the World's Parliament of Religions held in Chicago in 1893, Sōen spoke of *ingasetsu* as a "law of nature." Moreover, certain passages of his paper even resembled those in Katō Hiroyuki's *Reconsideration of Human Rights*. He stated, for example, "There is no cause which is not an effect." But Sōen's notion of cause and effect only outwardly resembled the cause and effect of Katō's evolutionary and scientific discourse. Cause and effect, as understood by Sōen, was clearly rooted in *samsara*, the Buddhist notion of cyclic rebirth. Our present circumstances, our abilities, shortcomings, and so on, Sōen maintained, all result from the actions of our previous existence. "We are here enjoying or suffering the effect of what we have done in our past lives.... [I]n future lives each one will also enjoy or suffer the result of his own actions done in this existence." Morality was thus a matter of *samsara* and karma (i.e., *ingasetsu*). "Would you ask me about Buddhist morality? I would reply that in Buddhism the source of moral authority is the causal law. Be kind, be just, be humane, be honest, if you desire to crown your future! Dishonesty, cruelty, inhumanity will condemn you to a miserable fall!"[17]

Shaku Sōen's description of cause and effect indicates that not all Buddhists were prepared to simply identify it with "scientific law" (and thereby allow the term's Buddhist connotations to be expelled). Katō, who in the early 1880s had appropriated the term *inga* to signify "cause and effect" in evolution, succeeded in de-legitimizing the Buddhist conception of cause and effect. Defending this term's Buddhist connotation, for some Buddhist thinkers, was to defend the root of Buddhist morality.

Yet for Murakami, Buddhism required the authority of science and philosophy. Buddhism agreed with the rules of philosophy because, as Murakami maintained, it was itself a form of philosophy. "Although I seek the principle and standard of morality in the world of philosophy, these cannot be sought in Western philosophy or Chinese philosophy, much less in Christianity. These are things that need to be sought in Indian philosophy, namely, Buddhism."[18] Murakami hoped to legitimize Buddhism by linking it to the authority of the term *tetsugaku* (a term first coined by Nishi Amane in the 1870s to refer to

Western philosophy). This had the further effect of distancing his own moral views from Christianity.

Murakami concluded his work on Buddhist morality with a list of moral standards for adhering to "a general morality for all humanity."[19] He presented a moral framework consistent with then-current utilitarian moral categories of altruistic and individualistic hedonism, asserting that moral standards should be directed at benefit to oneself and to others.[20] He listed six "austerities" or modes of conduct that were to serve as standards both for self-preservation and for fulfilling one's duties to others: charity *(fuse)*, adherence to the Buddhist injunctions *(jikai)*, forbearance or resignation *(ninjō)*, abstinence or diligence *(shōjin)*, meditation *(zenjō)*, and wisdom *(chie)*.[21] It is telling that Murakami equated this last austerity, *chie* (Sanskrit *prajña*), with the term *dōri* and explained *chie* as "the wisdom to choose to follow the good and avoid evil."[22] For *rinrigaku* academics, *dōri* usually referred to the human faculty of reason that allowed one to distinguish between right and wrong. Murakami's explanation of the term *chie* reflects the internalization of the authority and centrality of reason in the moral discourse of his time. Yet once a part of his moral system, *dōri* becomes something other than what is was. Murakami redirects the power of dominant moral discourse such that *dōri,* a term perhaps too important or authoritative for any moral theory at this time to overlook, is indeed addressed, but becomes a synonym for *prajña.*

The implementation of Murakami's morality described above was primarily a matter of keeping in mind "the four blessings": the monarch's protection, a mother and father's nurturing, a social livelihood, and the exhortation of the three treasures (of Buddhism, i.e., the Buddha, the sutras, and the priesthood). "If people keep these four blessings in mind and never forget them, then they will never exhaust their loyalty to the state, their filiality toward their parents, their affection toward society, and their respect for the three treasures. To keep these blessings in mind, is not this the essential point for the implementation of morality?"[23] In the end, the "essential point" in Murakami's new Buddhist morality, except for his fourth blessing concerning the three treasures, has little about it that is distinctly Buddhist.

Buddhist apologists also drew upon the authority of "scientific principles" to oppose those, like Nishimura Shigeki and Motoda Eifu, who would establish a morality for Japan based on the doctrines of Confucius and Mencius. Inoue Enryō argued that Confucianism had certain faults or shortcomings making it inappropriate as a foundation for ethics. "There are many shallow features of the morality of Confucius and Mencius that are not sufficiently considered in terms of reason *(dōri)*."[24] Enryō criticized Confucian ethics on a number of points: its moral principles were unclear, with hopelessly muddled theories of originary good and evil in human nature *(seizenakuron)* it presented no fixed standard for good and evil, it inappropriately mixed politics and morality, and finally, it called for the imitation of an ancient morality and was thus not "forward looking." These aspects of Confucian morality did not conform to the "rules of logic," and consequently its theories could not serve as a foundation for the ethics of contemporary Japan.[25] Murakami Senshō leveled similar criticisms against Confucianism: "The theories of Confucius and Mencius explain the principles and foundation of morality on the basis of conscience as a gift from heaven. Such gift-from-heaven theories *(tempuron)* are contrary to the principles of philosophy and oppose the rules of the theory of evolution."[26] Such being the case, Murakami argued, "Confucianism cannot be a basis for establishing a moral foundation through an appeal to the principles of philosophy, or for devising an ethics that conforms to social evolution." He argued further that because the teachings of Confucius and Mencius prioritize an idealized past over the present, they are "inconsistent with today's evolutionary society" and therefore cannot be a standard for morality.[27] Nishimura Shigeki, whose own moral views relied heavily on Confucian discourse, offered a similar critique of Confucianism to those listed above. Arguing against following the "Way of Confucianism" exclusively (as noted above), he stated, "Confucianism regards antiquity as good and the present as wrong, and demands on every occasion that we imitate the peaceful reigns of Yao and Shun and the Three Dynasties.... Under the present conditions of Japan, of course, it is not possible to imitate Yao, Shun, and the Three Dynasties, and moreover, we should not try."[28]

Enryō's, Murakami's, and Nishimura's critiques of Confucianism, specifically their claims that it was inconsistent with reason, logic, and the needs of the progressive "evolutionary society" of the present, reflect an unmistakable internalization of the same epistemology, terms, and concepts upheld by *rinrigaku* scholars. Their statements show that, for them, only a moral foundation consistent with reason and natural laws would be appropriate for a social ethic with which to order Japanese society.

Buddhist thinkers therefore contested the argument that all religions lacked any rational foundation. Inoue Enryō, for example, sought to demonstrate the "intellectual" character of Buddhism to the "people of the world" who, as he put it, "believe that religion does not go beyond supposition, and that the only thing based on reason *(dōri)* is philosophy."[29] In *A New Theory of Religion (Shūkyō shinron,* 1888), Enryō observed that people generally view religion as something emotional, but, he claimed, "there is among religions a type that is intellectual." He argued, "[O]f all the religions currently in the world today, only one—Buddhism—is an intellectual religion."[30] For Enryō, the legitimization of Buddhism required that it be rooted in the intellectual rather than the emotional. His attempts to refute the idea of Buddhism as irrational only further attest to the authority attached to the "rational."

Dōri was also central to the moral theory of Nishimura Shigeki, a proponent of "civilization and enlightenment" in the 1870s and a key participant in the discourse on morality in the 1880s. But while he upheld *dōri* over religious faith in his works on morality, his conception of *dōri* cannot simply be equated with "reason." Nishimura discussed the term *dōri* as "the path of *ri*" or "the moral Way." As mentioned above, Nishimura drew a distinction between "this-worldly" and "otherworldly" teachings. This-worldly teachings, such as Confucianism and Western philosophy, were based on *dōri* (the moral Way), while the otherworldly teachings of Buddhism and Christianity were based on faith.[31] A morality for Japan, he argued, must draw upon the former and abandon the latter. The "moral Way" Nishimura advocated was that of *sekyō* (philosophy and Confucianism). That his moral framework ties Confucianism to Western philosophy belies his doubt that Confucianism can stand alone without the support of the authority of Western philosophy.[32] As Nishimura's moral theory proposed a path in which philosophy and Confucianism are joined, he needed to employ a conceptual vocabulary that could incorporate both. The polysemy of the term *dōri* allowed him to draw on the legitimizing authority of "reason" of Western philosophy without excluding the moral Way of Confucianism.

For some Christians, *dōri*, at least in the sense described above, was considered a useless basis for compelling moral behavior. In his discussion of Confucian and other moral teachings, Christian apologist Kozaki Hiromichi (1856–1938) was highly critical of *dōri* as a basis for morality. "Even if moral teachings can direct people to the moral path *(michi)*, they cannot provide the strength to follow it. Even if they can clarify the moral principle *(ri)*, they lack the strength to change the person's spirit. The path and the principle *(dōri)* are useless things."[33] And while Kozaki the Christian attacked Confucian morality by focusing on *dōri*, Fujishima Ryō-on (1852–1918), a priest of the True Pure Land, or Shin, sect, refuted the Christian teachings of original sin, Adam and Eve, and other aspects of Christian doctrine, finding them to be "simply inconsistent with reason *(dōri ni kanawanu)*."[34] The title of his text was *Christianity's Lack of Reason (Yasokyō no mudōri)*. These examples reflect both the centrality and the polysemy of the term *dōri* in moral discourse.

The texts examined above, whether putting forward an academic or religious viewpoint, or both, indicate the authority attached to laws of nature, scientific methods, and the use of a certain conceptual vocabulary where *ri, risei,* and *dōri* were central. Discernible here is a conception of nature as an object to be examined, with fixed laws (such as evolution and cause and effect) that can be revealed or known. Academics sought to establish this view of nature and knowledge as the only legitimate basis for ethical inquiry, opposing the scientific methodology of *rinrigaku* to the "falsehoods" of religion. Religious apologists, by attempting to demonstrate the scientific or rational features of their religious moralities, strengthened the academic claim that only a social ethic rooted in scientific principles would be authoritative enough to compel its acceptance.

Religion as Socially Useless

Another critique leveled at religious moralities concerned their social effect. Were they capable of putting forward moral theories that could be practically implemented and that would benefit society? *Rinrigaku* scholars attacked Christianity and Buddhism because of the divisiveness they were seen to generate in society. For Inoue Tetsujirō, Christianity threatened to destroy the foundation of the nation. Here, we examine the debate over whether religion *(shūkyō)* had any practical benefit for society. Religious apologists struggled to demonstrate the social utility of their social ethics while *rinrigaku* academics represented religious moralities as "socially useless."

Could the moral tenets of Christianity or Buddhism be practically applied to contemporary social problems, or were they more concerned with "the next world?" As seen above, Nishimura Shigeki classified Buddhism and Christianity as "other-worldly teachings." He argued that such teachings could have little practical benefit for society, as they were generally more concerned with the "next world" than with this world. Nishimura argued that this-worldly teachings deal with the "harmonization of society and the country," while other-worldly teachings are "primarily concerned with the return of the spirit after death."[35] Buddhist apologist Inoue Enryō voiced a similar critique, despite his own affiliations with Buddhism. Although Enryō upheld Buddhism as "one type of pure philosophy," he nevertheless found it lacking as a basis for morality because of "its tendency to search for truths outside of this world."[36]

Nishimura was equally critical of Shinto. He believed that Shinto, through its association with the government in the early 1870s, temporarily helped to lessen the decline of the people's morality, but the experiment with Shinto and the Ministry of Rites (Jingikan) ultimately failed because Shinto "in the long run could not keep up with the development of human knowledge at that time." As for Buddhism, he said that it had long been a teaching of the lower classes and that it was extremely rare for the middle and upper classes to believe in it. "Therefore it cannot serve to unify public sentiment."[37]

Religions, said Nishimura, tend to be jealous of one another. Such was the case with Buddhism and Christianity: "Buddhism maligns Christianity;

Christianity maligns Buddhism." For Nishimura, the two were clearly set on destroying one another and there could be no peace between them. This clearly disqualified them as a basis from which to build a Japanese morality.[38] According to Nishimura, then, as the suitable morality for Japan should be one based on reason, it should draw upon elements from Confucianism or Western philosophy. Religions, such as Buddhism and Christianity (as well as Shinto, which he included in the category of religion), he deemed inappropriate because they are based on superstition and faith and are "the product of a primitive age."[39]

Motŏda Eifu, advisor and instructor to Emperor Meiji, shared many of Nishimura's views, including his opposition to religion as a basis for a national morality. He described Buddhism and Christianity as one-sided and factional. He also called Shinto one-sided, despite its emphasis on respect for the emperor. For Motoda, however, religion was not merely one-sided, but a dangerous disease as well: "While the errors of Buddhism and Christianity render them unworthy of belief, their concern with life and death, misery and happiness, and gain and loss strikes a kindred note in the human mind, people become superstitious, and the disease becomes rooted and immovable."[40] In his autobiography, Motoda recalls that the trend from 1873 onward was to follow Western education. The preference for Western books shaped even the emperor's education. Other lecturers to the emperor, Motoda observed, used books that were "for the most part only trivial translated things." Motoda, on the other hand, taught "the purity of the Confucian Way, the harm of Christianity, and the errors of Buddhism and vulgar studies." He also reminds us that history favors Confucianism. In times of Confucian dominance, society was well ordered and peaceful. But "during reigns in which Buddhism received Imperial patronage...powerful subjects brought disorder to the court's decrees, and disturbances followed one upon the heels of another."[41] Motoda, then, in even stronger terms than Nishimura, attacked religion as a superstition and as a disease that brought disorder to society.

Inoue Tetsujirō's critique of religion was directed primarily at Christianity rather than at Buddhism. For Inoue, Christianity was not merely impractical in relation to the resolution of society's problems, but destructive as well. In the Bible, for example, Inoue found only absurdities. He related a number of stories that involved incest, disorder, and killing. "In the first chapter Cain kills Abel, and this is the beginning of brothers killing each other." Inoue points out that although the mother of Jesus was not married to Joseph, she became pregnant. "How was it that this sacred child was born out of wedlock?" he asked. "If people believe in these stories, the damage to morality will be extremely great." Inoue concluded that Christian knowledge was a poor guide for ethical action. More than this, belief in Christianity was to be condemned because it led one away from "real virtue." Christianity, Inoue claimed, cultivated belief in "evil sayings and falsehoods, belief in ridiculous things; in the end it disrupts ethics." For proof of its disruptive effects, one need only look to the history of conflict and war in the West. The "wars of Jesus," he said, brought political turmoil, killing, and death to many. Although Inoue admitted that conflicts had occurred in Japan in connection with Buddhism, these, he believed, were less severe. "But now," he warned, "Christianity has come to the East, and hence, the blood will begin to flow."[42] Indeed, anti-Christian sentiment had already led to bloodshed. The Mikawa Uprising of 1871, in which Buddhists attacked and decapitated a state official because of his supposed Christian sympathies, is but one example.[43] In contrast to the socially destructive nature of religion, *rinrigaku* represented itself as capable of restoring order to society in a way that could strengthen, enrich, and unify the country.

The claim to "practicality," however, was not confined to academics' efforts to legitimize their ethical views; apologists of both Buddhism and Christianity employed this practical/impractical opposition as well, both in defense of their own views and as a means to attack competing social ethics. In his work on Buddhist morality, Murakami Senshō wrote on "practical learning," stating, "[I]n general, there are two types of learning, theoretical studies [*rirongaku*] and practical studies [*jitsuyō gaku*]." Included in this first group, according to Murakami, are physics and chemistry, astronomy, and geology. Practical studies included ethics, logic, education, and political science. "Even if a type of learning can be considered rational investigation in terms of scholarship, if it cannot be put into practice, one must say that such learning is a useless thing."[44] Here, Murakami has clearly adopted the classifications posited in academia that emphasized the close relationship between moral discourse and its practical implementation as a means to ordering society.

Murakami contested claims that Buddhism made no practical contribution to the betterment of society. Describing his motivations for writing his new theory of Buddhist morality, he stated that he himself was driven by his devotion to protect the country and to benefit the people *(gokoku rimin)*. Here, Murakami transformed the earlier compound *gohō* (protecting the dharma) into the "defense of the nation," which parallels Inoue Enryō's *gokoku airi*, stressing the need to protect the nation and to love reason. That disloyalty is shown toward the state and that many take a less than benevolent attitude toward society, he observed, was cause for lamentation. This reflected something lacking in the observance of ethics, and his moral treatise was designed as a corrective. "I pray that this morality of Buddhism will be put to practical use...that it will guide people and that it will widely benefit society. We must not idly allow this Buddhist morality to become a lifeless thing."[45] His efforts to sustain this Buddhist morality were supported by his critique of Christianity.

"Proponents [of Christianity]," wrote Murakami, "say that moral education requires the power of religion, and the reason they favor Christianity rather than Buddhism is that Christianity is of immense benefit to the development of society, whereas Buddhism has not distinguished itself in the cultural progress of the state." Murakami contested this view, depicting Christianity as an obstacle to knowledge. "Has not Christianity, with its control of the minds of the people, smashed the knowledge of the people for nearly one thousand years and temporarily suppressed the cultural progress of ancient times?"

> In terms of national essence [*kokutai*], morality and politics are closely related. For this reason, the key point that must be considered above all else in regard to maintaining *kokutai* is the moral spirit of the people. Is Christianity's monotheism damaging or beneficial to our *kokutai*? I believe it is harmful and that it is of no benefit. Does Buddhism's doctrine of cause and effect [i.e., karma] conform to Japan's *kokutai* or interfere with it? I believe it conforms to it and there is no interference.[46]

Murakami's concern in this passage was the benefit Buddhism can bring to Japan's national body or essence *(kokutai)*. His reconfiguration of karma as the scientific law of cause and effect meant that it was in complete accord with and of benefit to Japan's essence. And while Murakami attacked Christianity as an obstacle to knowledge and progress, Inoue Enryō made the same claim about Taoism.

Enryō characterized the school of Lao Tzu and Chuang Tzu as an inappropriate basis for ethics. Taoism, he argued, with its emphasis on "no-self" and "no-desire" obstructs the progress and improvement of society. It suppresses the people's progressive spirit. But "the greatest proof as to why this teaching must not be implemented in today's society," according to Enryō, is that "it has a tendency to hamper the development of intellectual ability by making people content with their foolishness [*gu*]."[47] Thus, even in this Buddhist attack on Taoism, we see the great importance attached to intellectual development and the acquisition of knowledge on the one hand, and the great contempt for foolishness on the other.

Like Buddhist apologists, Christians were equally concerned to assert the social utility of their own religious doctrines. Many Christian apologists hoped to show the socially beneficial nature of Christianity by equating it with "Western civilization." They argued that in order for Japan to acquire the superior knowledge and skills of the West, it was necessary not merely to imitate those skills, but to incorporate into Japanese society the morality upon which Western knowledge was built. In other words, Christianity was seen to be responsible for the superiority of the West, therefore Japan needed to adopt Christian morality. Western missionaries in Japan propagated this same message. In 1882 during a lecture tour, Joseph Cook, a reverend from Tremont Temple in Boston, asserted that Christianity was responsible for the prosperity the West enjoyed. To an audience of fifteen hundred people in Kyoto, he stated, "Japan cannot successfully compete with Western nations unless she equips herself as thoroughly as her rivals are equipped, not only in science, art, and industry, but in moral and religious training as well. The secret of the prosperity of the free nations of the Occident is Christianity."[48]

Niijima Jō (1843–1890), who in 1875 founded the Christian Dōshisha school in Kyoto, was also convinced that Christianity could enhance the welfare of society. Irwin Scheiner, in his study of Meiji Christianity, states that for Niijima, the individual "was the repository of Christian virtue." The cultivation of the individual with a Christian morality, according to Niijima, would "strengthen the independence of Japan and bring about the peace and happiness of our nation." Thus, the inculcation of Christian morality was the necessary first step toward the transformation and betterment of society.[49]

For Niijima, advancing toward perfection required that selfish desires be overcome. It required change at a fundamental level. Nothing less than a "new people" imbued with a "new spirit" informed by Christianity would bring about such a transformation.

> Because Christianity is the wellspring of culture, I believe it will wipe clean the spirit of humanity which is now tainted by sin and uncleanliness, and make for the "continued prosperity of a new people" in the East. The new people are those who embrace a new spirit. If a person lacks this new spirit, what benefit will the many kinds of Western skills be? Learning, people's rights, politics—all will become slaves to people's selfishness and desires, and at some point tend toward corruption. This is clear from the examples of history. . . . The reason the Chinese people do not advance is solely due to their lack of this new spirit. And in our country Japan, the reason we are not flourishing today is also because we lack this new spirit. There is but one religion that can create this new spirit—Christianity.[50]

Connecting the superior skills of the West with Christianity was not a new idea. Some years earlier, Nakamura Masanao also addressed the need for the religion of the West. In 1872 Nakamura argued that if Japan were to successfully incorporate Western skills and legal structures into its own society, it would have to adopt the West's religion as well or else be like "a mannequin with face and eyes, and hands and feet, but without a soul."[51] Tsuda Mamichi drew much the same conclusion. In the *Meiroku zasshi* he wrote, "There is no religion in the world today that promotes enlightenment as does Christianity."[52]

For these Christian apologists, only Christianity could serve as the spiritual and moral underpinning necessary for the successful acquisition and internalization of the material and legal structures and skills of the West. Not only was Christianity *not* socially useless or divisive in terms of the knowledge and skills, wealth and power, and order and stability it could bring, but it was the basis for the most useful and unifying social ethic of all.

The forgoing paragraphs describe the formation of moral subjectivity among various social-ethical positions at odds in some way with *rinrigaku*. For many religious apologists confronted by *rinrigaku*'s representations of religion as irrational and as socially useless or harmful, the appropriation, or perhaps the internalization of the language, concepts, and methods of *rinrigaku* and its epistemology, provided a means to reassert themselves with the authority already associated with this epistemology. In so doing, however, they transformed, subtly or at times dramatically, the ideological space of their own religious moralities and helped to reinforce and legitimize *rinrigaku*'s own ethical claims.

Yet it would be a simplification of a highly complex discursive exchange if we were to assume that these epistemological features remained unchanged even as religious apologists drew upon them for the defense of their moral views. As seen, the "scientific laws" of cause and effect and conservation of energy became, in the moral views put forward by Murakami Senshō and Inoue Enryō, synonyms for or variations of the Buddhist doctrine of karma. For those defending a Christian morality, the "law of evolution" became one part of "God's plan." But in this engagement between *rinrigaku* and religion, a term of particular contestation was the concept of *ri*. As argued in the preceding chapter, the terms *ri, risei,* and *dōri* cannot simply be treated as signifying some essential idea of "reason." Although some academics in the 1880s attempted to equate some or all three of these terms with "reason" or *Vernunft,* others used these terms in very different ways. This is all the more evident in the case of religious thinkers.

Religious apologists generally accepted the central role of *ri* in ethical inquiry, but in their own usage this term became something other than what Nishi Amane, Inoue Tetsujirō, and other academics insisted upon. Buddhist Inoue Enryō and Christian Uemura Masahisa (1857–1925), for example, questioned the dualistic notion of natural and human principle *(butsuri/shinri)* characteristic of *rinrigaku* scholarship, putting forward instead a transcendent notion of *ri*.

While Inoue Enryō was indeed concerned to defend Buddhism as consistent with *dōri,* he also critiqued methodology distinguishing between two kinds of *ri.* In his preface to *The Renewal of Buddhism (Bukkyō katsuron joron),* Enryō discussed the "essence of *ri" (ritai).* He argued that the essence of the *ri* of absolute reality is neither material nor spiritual, that absolute reality, in other words, is not simply one or the other.[53] This did not mean, according to Enryō, that the essence of *ri* is completely separate from materiality and spirituality; rather, "both the material and spiritual aspects are precisely the *ritai* of absolute reality. We simply call this 'only ri' *[yuiri]."* Here, Enryō wanted to avoid what he considered a one-sided view of *ri.* While Nishi Amane and *rinrigaku* scholars posited a distinct opposition between *butsuri* and *shinri* and, allowing no room for ambivalence, asserted that a view is either in accord with *ri* or is not, Enryō sought to retain a view of ultimate reality that was "neither *butsu* nor *shin"* and yet one where *butsu* and *shin* are the "*ritai* of ultimate reality." That is, he asserted a position of "only *ri*" transcending the opposition—in short, a "neither and both" *(soku-hi)* argument of identity-in-difference. His implication was that the scientific methodology that insisted on the opposition between materiality and spirituality could not help but be one-sided and failed to see the deeper ground. A similar assertion for a transcendent space of moral adjudication came from Christian circles.

In his 1884 work *One Truth (Shinri ippan),* Uemura Masahisa, a leading figure in the Presbyterian Church of Japan, accepted that reason allows us to distinguish between good and evil, but maintained that human reason is based on the eternal reason of God and that the distinction between good and evil itself is furnished by God. In short, he did not contest human reason, but attempted to ground it in something deeper—the "reason of God." "God, who created all things, who established the laws of heaven and earth, is the legislator of the supreme law."[54] Uemura's "reason of God," then, functioned like Enryō's "only *ri*" as a space of moral adjudication that transcended the laws of science.

Three years later, Kozaki Hiromichi put forward a view quite similar to Uemura's, attempting not to contest the authority of science, but to ground it in an "original cause." He began by asking, "How are we able to acquire knowledge of the phenomena of the external world?" Kozaki explained that in order for us to ascertain truthful knowledge of the external world, two things are necessary: human beings must be endowed with *risei* (the human faculty for rational thought), and the universe must be endowed with *dōri* (here, meaning a kind of consciousness). "If we lacked *risei,* and if in the external world there were no *dōri,* it would be in no way possible to have knowledge of the world."

But how did it come about that the external world possesses thought and being *(dōri)?* "If the universe consists of thought, then we reach the conclusion that there must be a cause." The cause, Kozaki maintained, is God. "The reason science is possible is because the existence of God serves as a foundation."[55] It is possible to attain truthful knowledge only because of the existence of God. Kozaki's opposition between humanity (as subject) and the external world (as object), the importance of *risei* and *dōri* in his argument, and his reasoning relying on the notion of cause and effect reflect an acceptance of the epistemology of representation. Yet he maintained that both humanity and the external world possess thought and being, or a kind of reason *(risei/dōri),* and drew upon the philosophy of Hegel to argue for an identity of *risei* and *dōri,* subject and object. This was of course a marginalized viewpoint in the 1880s, but one that came to hold greater authority in ensuing decades. The opposition between *risei* and *dōri* outlined by Kozaki then was quite different from that of Nishi Amane. Although Nishi did indeed distinguish between the internal human world and the external material world, assigning *risei* to the former and, in some of his uses of the term, *dōri* to the latter, only the human realm possessed consciousness; the mechanical material realm did not. But, as seen here, Kozaki argued for the existence of a kind of consciousness in both realms.

The ethical claims of *rinrigaku* scholars, rooted in an epistemology of representation and its attendant methodologies, relied upon a clear distinction between *butsuri* and *shinri,* that is, between the material and human realms. It required that they remain separate. To deny this opposition or to argue for a deeper reality that transcends it, as certain religious apologists did, was to subvert *rinrigaku's* epistemological foundation. The majority of religious moralities from this time internalized certain features of the epistemology that shaped *rinrigaku.* But an argument for some kind of ambivalence is also apparent in the writings of the religious thinkers examined above. This allowed them both to accept and even incorporate some of the truth-claims of the dominant epistemology (e.g., the laws of nature, the centrality of reason in moral inquiry and moral decision making) on the one hand, and to defend a transcendent space of truth as a foundation for ethical claims specific to their own religious views. In short, religion in 1880s Japan was constrained to admit the truthfulness of truth-claims emanating from the epistemology of representation, yet struggled to retain a transcendent space beyond it. *Rinrigaku's* truth-claims could be accepted, but they were not final; they did not emanate from the higher or deeper realm of "only *ri,*" "the reason of God," or the "original cause" of God. Religion, then, with its claims to a transcendent space from which to adjudicate good and evil, was an obstacle to the universalization of *rinrigaku's* ethical claims.

The Objectification of Religion

Religion's "uselessness," that is, the representation that it had a negative, or at least no substantially beneficial, social effect, was in fact highly useful for *rinrigaku* scholars who sought to legitimize claims to their own social utility. This, and the "irrational" nature of religion, provided *rinrigaku* scholars the justification for excluding religion from moral discourse. But it soon became apparent that religious belief and practice could not be eradicated from Japanese society. *Rinrigaku* academics were therefore left with the question: How can this irrational and useless other called *shūkyō* be brought back into the social order *rinrigaku* envisioned?

The answer was that religion had first to be transformed, to forgo its otherness, before it could be readmitted. As William Haver observed, "One is accepted into the community of the 'we' only insofar as one accepts one's essentially passive objectness... only insofar as one rejects one's difference, one's singular otherness. Which is no integration at all, of course."[56] Religion became an object of scientific and philosophical inquiry. As studies of religion as a social phenomenon produced theories of its evolutionary development, religion in its present form became part of a temporal progression toward a higher-order teaching guided by science. With evolution, then, the irrational and useless religion of nineteenth-century Japan was to be pushed into the past and displaced. This was perhaps the greatest blow dealt to religion in nineteenth-century Japan—to turn it into an object of inquiry so as to foretell its eventual death by transformation.

Inoue Tetsujirō, Nishi Amane, Nishimura Shigeki, and Fukuzawa Yukichi all drew on the positivism of Auguste Comte to situate *shūkyō* at a particular stage on a trajectory of evolutionary development. Comte posited three stages of social development: theological, metaphysical, and positivistic. In the final stage, knowledge based on facts takes the place of dogmatic assertions as the interpretation of phenomena begins to be conducted scientifically. Comte argued that contemporary religion would be replaced by a "religion of humanity" guided by positivist philosophers. In fact, about thirty years after the publication of these views, some of his followers in the London Positivist Society (established in 1867) attempted to realize Comte's vision when they opened a positivist temple in London in 1870.[57]

Inoue Tetsujirō's statements on religion reflect this Comtian framework. He envisioned the emergence of a higher-order religion *(kōdō shūkyō)*—a collection of what he called "ideal teachings" *(risōkyō)* or "ethical teachings" *(rinrikyō)*—that would take the place of contemporary religion. This higher-order religion would be one that is consistent with science and facts. His dual conception of religion as the "irrational and useless" religion of 1880s Japan and as a higher-order religion of the future allowed him to attack the former while recommending the latter. "What I most abhor is to newly import from a foreign country *a particular religion* like Christianity. But I do believe that a type of *higher order religion* is necessary."[58] Inoue's "higher order religion" was a kind of scientific morality that would take the place of Christianity, Buddhism, and other institutionalized religions.

Educator Sugiura Jūgō (1855–1924) similarly foresaw the eventual displacement of contemporary religion with *rigakushū*, a term he translated as "scientific morality." Sugiura's idea of scientific morality was part of an effort to establish, "as a substitute for religion, a morality that did not conflict with the rules of science or with the fruits of research as explained through science."[59] Christianity, therefore, the "irrational" and "socially useless" target of most *rinrigaku* attacks on *shūkyō*, the other that could not be eradicated, could be allotted a provisional place within the "rational" social order *rinrigaku* hoped to organize only with science's promise that it would eventually evolve away, that its "singular otherness" would be displaced by a new, higher-order religion. But even here the "irrefutable doctrine" of evolution could be turned upside down to authorize precisely what *rinrigaku* scholars sought to expel. Christian Kozaki Hiromichi, for example, drawing upon a very similar evolutionary teleology, divided religion into two types—natural religion *(shizen shūkyō),* for which he provided the examples of Buddhism and moral teachings such as Confucianism, and revelatory religion *(tenkei shūkyō,* i.e., Christianity)—arguing that the former was merely a preparatory step toward the latter.[60] Once again, the appropriation of the same conceptual vocabulary on which *rinrigaku* relied—evolution in this example—resulted in a reconfiguration of religion.

Public vs. Private Morality:
The Struggle for the Human Interiority

For *rinrigaku* scholars and religious apologists (here, primarily Christians) alike, one area of common concern and particular contention was the role of the state in shaping the moral and religious lives of its citizens. Most *rinrigaku* scholars saw such a role not merely as unavoidable but as indispensable for the production of moral unity. They directed their attack at the moral divisiveness they saw in Christianity. Christian apologists, for the most part, demanded a space of autonomy for the people free from any moral intervention by the state. At stake here was the human interiority. Should "conscience" be regulated by the state? Responses to this question shaped moral discourse throughout the Meiji period.

"Ethics are the foundation for ruling the country," proclaimed Nishimura Shigeki in an 1875 speech before the Meiji Six Society. Nishimura, strongly committed to the unity of ethics and political affairs, lamented the Ministry of Education's general disregard for the importance of moral education. In short, he supported a state-sponsored morality as a means to unify the "minds of the people."

Referring to the Confucian classic *The Great Learning*, Nishimura discussed "the logical sequence of disciplining the individual person *(shūshin)*, managing the household, ruling the country, and keeping peace in the world."[61] These, according to Nishimura, were all matters of the rational world *(dōri sekai)*. And while all animals, he argued, are endowed with an animal instinct, "the rational instinct *(dōri bun)* is found only in men and never in beasts." He equated this rational instinct with *tenri* (the Principle of Heaven) and asserted that the central feature of *tenri* is conscience. So when Nishimura asserted that "ethics and governing the country are both matters of the rational world," he was attempting to provide justification for linking one to the other. In other words, *shūshin* (usually read as ethics but literally as disciplining the body [*mi o osame*]) becomes a state matter.[62] But *shūshin* as "disciplining the body" is also a somewhat misleading translation. In fact, the crucial feature of *shūshin's* effectiveness was that it not only concerned the disciplining of the body (exteriority), but of the mind (interiority) as well.

Even more explicitly than Nishimura, Sakatani Shiroshi called on leaders to "establish mental restraints" and to identify a "controlling principle" to ensure proper moral behavior.[63] "There could be no uprightness but for controlling principles. What is the most important principle that should control all men in the world throughout their lives? There are two moral ways extending through history and spreading through the universe—the good and the evil."[64] The controlling principle to ensure upright conduct, he reasoned, must be the good. Sakatani explained the operation of this principle through a metaphor drawing on the authority of scientific, medical discourse: that of doctor and patient. The doctor (the controlling principle) was "the master of the patient's mind" while the "patient afflicted by a serious disease" represented the people of the nation whose behavior was in need of improvement. (Sakatani used the same term *shu* both in the sense of "master," i.e., the doctor, and "controlling principle.") "With proper training," Sakatani pointed out, "even a dull person" can learn proper behavior. Sakatani's "principle" (a moral principle, the "moral way of the good") was to exert control over one's conscience, over the human interiority, and had, according to Sakatani, the capacity to "unite the myriad minds of men."[65] In short, both Nishimura and Sakatani called for a prominent state role in shaping the human interiority so as to attain social unity. This was Inoue Tetsujirō's position as well.

For Inoue, the state had an important role to play in shaping the religious and moral lives of its people. This issue, so closely intertwined with the unity necessary for national survival, was far too important an area for the state ever to attempt to dissociate itself from it. Indeed, the state, as Inoue envisioned it, must take the lead in fostering unity through education (especially moral education) and in quelling disruptive and divisive elements that threatened unity. For Inoue, then, religious apologists' calls to limit state authority in the realm of morality could not be left unopposed. A widely circulated text in early Meiji Japan informed his arguments: J. S. Mill's *On Liberty*.

Inoue understood the central concern of Mill's text to be the call to limit the role of the state in the affairs of the individual. Mill stated on the first page of his "Introductory" to *On Liberty*, "The subject of this Essay is...Civil, or Social Liberty: the nature and limits of the power which can be legitimately exercised by society over the individual."[66] Inoue cited this particular passage as it appeared in Nakamura Masanao's translation of Mill's text. "How must we decide the *limit* between the power of the individual and the power of society [*nakama renchu*]? This is the actual problem. It is from this point we must begin." After critiquing Mill on a number of points, however, Inoue concluded, "It is extremely difficult to clearly fix a limit between those conditions which chiefly concern the individual and those which chiefly concern the government." For Inoue, the two tended to blend into one another. He therefore opposed attempts by religious apologists to clearly delineate a space for the thought and practice of the individual from which the state would be excluded. He framed his opposition within a broader anti-Mill discourse stressing the link between the government, morality, and religion.

Inoue was familiar with some of the contemporary arguments in England opposing Mill's *On Liberty*. In his own refutation of this work by Mill, Inoue referred to a critic of *On Liberty* named Stephen and wrote, "Like Mr. Stephen, I too refute *On Liberty*."[67] Inoue was almost certainly referring to James Fitzjames Stephen (1829–1894) and the work *Liberty, Equality, Fraternity*.[68] More important than the question of any direct influence of Stephen's ideas on Inoue, however, is the fact that such an anti-Mill discourse made up part of the discursive space of 1880s Japan. It is useful to examine Stephen's arguments, then, as they were part of the ideological landscape out of which Inoue's position emerged.

In his critique of Mill, Stephen maintained that the governing of a country could never be separated from religion and morality. "Mr. Mill's principle about Liberty," he wrote, "is mere rhetoric.... [T]he principle which warns off the State from a whole department of life on the ground that it is 'spiritual' while the State is 'temporal,' is a juggle of words.... [T]he government of a great nation can never be carried on satisfactorily without reference more or less direct and frequent to moral and religious considerations."[69] Arguing that laws must be based on principles and that laying down principles for legislation requires an appeal to morality, he asserted that "all government has and must of necessity have a moral basis, and that the connection between morals and religion is so intimate that this implies a religious basis as well."[70] Douglas Howland, in a study of the appropriation of Mill's thought in China and Japan, points out that for Stephen "government was precisely that body in an appropriate position to encourage socially desirable ends among its citizens. What was needed was not less interference by society into the affairs of individuals, but *more*—a point that resonated soundly with Japanese critics of Mill's position in the 1880s."[71] Clearly, Inoue readily agreed with Stephen on this point. Like Stephen, Inoue would not permit government to be barred from religious and moral concerns. Inoue's concern, however, was not to argue that Japan's laws were rooted in religion, but to enable and legitimize state control over the human interiority, and this brought him into conflict with some of the foremost Christian thinkers in Japan at this time.

Uemura Masahisa, for example, called upon Christians to defend the realm of conscience against state incursion. He stated, "[H]umanity is provided with a direct knowledge, a direct intuition of the truth of God, and one can therefore recognize righteousness." This "supreme fundamental law" of righteousness is revealed through one's conscience; it "commands one to do good." Further, "righteous morality," Uemura contended, "does not depend upon the laws established by society"; rather, "the distinction between good and evil is furnished by God."[72]

For Uemura, a person's conscience is that which indicates God's law of righteousness. If the state impinged on the moral and religious lives of the people, then it was intruding upon the Christian's relationship with God. Uemura called on the individual Christian to defend this realm of conscience against the state. "The Christian, in attaching importance to his duty toward God, must uphold his freedom of conscience, maintain the right to believe in his faith, and stand up in the world to make clear the distinctions between God and man. Christ attributed great importance to this right, and as a result, was crucified for defying the rulers of his time."[73]

Uemura's emphasis on duty to God rather than to the state and his desire to establish a space of individual moral autonomy from which the state would be excluded placed him in opposition to Inoue. For Inoue, Christianity was the enemy of social unity. Rather than bringing together the "minds of the people," Christianity only drove them apart. In "Disputing the Teachings of Jesus" (Yaso benwaku jo), he wrote, "The reason a nation is able to stand is that the minds of its people are not separated. If separated, how can a nation stand? Today in our country, many believe in Christianity.... They look down on those who do not share their beliefs. In this way, the minds of the people have become separated. The foundation of our country, therefore, is crumbling."[74] He concluded this essay with a warning: "From outside, it may look like Japan, but from the inside it appears as a different country. The minds of the people are not as one. In such a state, nothing will be able to save it." Buddhist Fujishima Ryō-on also viewed Christianity as divisive. "Today," he stated, "with the spread of this teaching [Christianity], it seems the minds of our country's people are becoming divided. People of spirit are boisterously saying that in every respect Christianity damages our customs and our national essence."[75] Both Inoue and Fujishima linked Christianity with the division of the minds of the people.

But separating the state from the private space of morality and religion, Christian apologists argued, need not obstruct social unity. They claimed that only Christianity had the power to unify and compel virtuous action. The editors of the Christian journal Cosmos (Rikugō zasshi), for example, emphasized the need for social order. "In general, the public peace of society is maintained through the establishment of social order... and balance. In establishing order and balance in society, there must be a single force that governs." That force, they asserted, "lies in the idea of religion."[76] One of the editors of this journal, Kozaki Hiromichi, a graduate of the Christian Dōshisha school and later its president, was convinced that Christianity alone had the authority to compel virtuous conduct. Religious authority was necessary, he argued, because knowledge of good and evil does not ensure virtuous action. "Is the reason why people do evil," Kozaki asked, "because they do not know that one mustn't do evil and that one must do good?... If the cause of people's evil deeds is a lack of knowledge, we would expect that it would be a matter of course that those who are cultivated would be guided by the good."[77] But clearly this was not always the case. What was needed, according to Kozaki, was some absolute authority— a transcendent sovereign of morality who rewards the good, punishes evil, and exerts control over right and wrong.[78] For these and other Christian thinkers, only the transcendent authority of Christianity would suffice to engender virtue and promote unity.

Both *rinrigaku* scholars and Christian apologists, then, were deeply concerned with issues of morality, religion, and interiority. But it would be inac-
curate to represent *rinrigaku* scholars alone as advocates of moral sameness
and Christian thinkers as champions of moral diversity. *Rinrigaku*, of course,
did seek the power to shape and dominate the interiority of the subjects of the
state. Yet while religious apologists contested these efforts by *rinrigaku* and the
state, they too called for a "controlling moral principle." They merely lacked
the power to impose one. Whether Kozaki's "transcendent sovereign of morality," Uemura's "supreme fundamental law," or *Rikugō zasshi*'s "single force that
governs," each hoped to configure their own moral perspective as universal
moral truth, and thereby to produce, in Niijima's words, a "new people" whose
thoughts and actions were guided by the "new spirit" of Christianity. In the
struggle for the human interiority, then, the key difference between *rinrigaku*
and religion was the power to establish moral hegemony.

This conflict between *rinrigaku* and religion continued and intensified in
the years that followed. Uchimura Kanzō's (1861–1930) sensationalized "failure to bow" incident of 1891 set off the protracted dispute called the "collision
between education and religion." Inoue Tetsujirō led the attack that questioned
whether Christianity, with its loyalty first to God, could ever be compatible
with the demand for loyalty to the emperor and the state.[79]

Conclusions: Moral Subjectivity as a Condition of Possibility

The texts on morality by religious apologists and *rinrigaku* scholars employed
a common conceptual vocabulary that enabled communication despite broad
differences of opinion. Certain terms and concepts (evolution, reason, rationality or being in accord with *ri*, cause and effect, social utility, social order and
unity, public and private, etc.), particularly those associated with the methods
of "scientific inquiry," were generally accepted as central to any discussion of
morality, though their specific meaning was always a matter of contestation. But
it was *rinrigaku* scholars who identified these terms as central to "legitimate"
ethical inquiry through the performative function of their putatively descriptive statements. That is, as discussed in the preceding chapter, even statements
that seemed merely to describe the discipline of ethics or to evaluate a given
moral theory had the effect of producing its objects, methods, and aims. This
shaped not only the moral inquiry of *rinrigaku*, but also that conducted from
the standpoint of Christianity and Buddhism.

Rinrigaku defined and legitimized itself by undermining the authority of
moral visions for society associated with religion, while the various religious

ethics at odds with *rinrigaku* internalized many features of the epistemology of representation in an effort to defend their views. Certainly, such internalization also involved a redirection of the power of discourse such that the terms and concepts that informed *rinrigaku*'s style of moral inquiry came to be transformed and redirected to new ends unforeseen by those, such as Inoue and Katō, who first insisted upon them. But the internalization of this epistemology also transformed the moral space of religion. This discursive exchange between *rinrigaku* scholars and defenders of religion reflects the way the production of "the good" and epistemological preconceptions were inextricably bound to one another. Moreover, despite the efforts made at this time to speak on behalf of some timeless moral universal truth, it attests to the fluidity of moral subjectivity and the contested and indeterminate nature of its production. Viewed in this way, moral subjectivity appears as a condition of possibility, always fluid and therefore always open to its own re-creation. Paraphrasing de Certeau, we might say that although our moral subjectivity is composed with the vocabularies of established languages, its trajectories trace out the ruses of other interests and desires that are neither determined nor captured by the systems in which they develop.[80]

The struggle to speak for the good in 1880s Japan continued on in the decades that followed. By the end of the 1880s, however, even as *rinrigaku* had established for itself a high degree of authority largely through its reliance on the epistemology of representation described in this and the preceding chapter, the discipline of ethics underwent a dramatic epistemological shift. The notion of "spirit" came to occupy a central position in its conceptions of the good. An examination of this emergent ethics of spirit is the focus of the following chapter.

CHAPTER 4

Resisting Civilizational Hierarchies

The Ethics of Spirit and the Spirit of the People

Without infinite spirit, our own spirit would cease to be. Without our own spirit, we could have no aim, and with no aim, there can be no morality.
—Nakashima Rikizō, *On the British Neo-Kantian School*, 1892

With the flash of a sword and the roar of a gun, Japan's army demonstrated the pure and unparalleled posture of Japan's national moral spirit in a dazzling display before all the nations of the world.... Japan's national moral spirit is nothing other than the universal virtue of the human heart, and such virtue of the heart indeed reflects the purity of Oriental morality.
—Inoue Tetsujirō, *The Philosophy of Japan's* Yōmei *School*, 1900

In the 1890s, moral philosophers in Japan began to reconfigure the discipline of ethics. The utilitarianism and evolutionary naturalism that dominated the moral discourse of early Meiji gave way to a moral philosophy of spirit. This shift was part of an effort to resist the civilizational hierarchies imposed by the West and internalized by many Japanese thinkers during the foregoing decades. But this required not merely the critique of assertions of Western superiority in the realms of knowledge and virtue, two key markers of "civilization" upheld since Fukuzawa Yukichi's *Outline of a Theory on Civilization.*[1] It required also the destabilization of the epistemology that grounded and enabled this discourse on civilization. Referred to in earlier chapters as an "epistemology of representation," this framework for knowledge linked truth with the observable, the measurable, and the rationally verifiable. "Spirit," the unobservable and intuitively apprehended, provided a means to contest "civilization" *(kaika)* and its underlying epistemology, and transformed the topography of moral thought in 1890s Japan.

Moral discourse, both within and outside academia, played a central role in contesting civilization and articulating a desire for moral particularity. Moreover, the shift in ethics from an epistemology of representation with its marked opposition between subject and object to one positing an identity between self and other, subject and object, was not merely a *reflection* of the civilization critique, but was integral in initiating and furthering this critique.

The critique of civilization took various forms. This chapter will focus on two moral philosophers: Nakashima Rikizō and Inoue Tetsujirō. Both resisted civilization, but in different ways and with varying effect—Nakashima through personalism, an ethics that took "spiritual principle" as its animating force, Inoue through efforts to articulate the moral spirit of the Japanese people. In short, in moral discourse of 1890s Japan, resistance to civilizational hierarchies took the form of a new ethics of spirit and an assertion of "the spirit of the people."

National Character and Personality

The idea that each nation possesses its own unique "national character" shaped late nineteenth- and early twentieth-century moral discourse in Japan. Although references to common "Japanese" traits can certainly be found well before the Meiji period,[2] the discourse on national character did not become a part of Japan's intellectual landscape until the late 1880s.[3] Unlike prior essentializing efforts to establish Japanese commonality and to differentiate Japan from China and the West, the discourse on national character, asserting that all the people of a nation possess a common set of characteristics shaped by historical and geographical conditions, was closely intertwined with the notion of the "people's spirit," a concept with roots in late eighteenth- and early nineteenth-century German Romanticism.

Drawing on already circulating "counter-enlightenment" arguments, J. G. Herder, a historian and leading figure in the articulation of German Romanticism, argued that each society must be understood as a *Volk* (folk, people) with its own *Geist* (spirit or genius). Each *Volk* possessed its own unique values, language, customs, and beliefs. These expressions of the *Volksgeist* (folk spirit), when embodied in the national form, constituted national character. "Every nation," Herder proclaimed, "is one people, having its own national form, as well as its own language: the climate, it is true, stamps on each its mark, or spreads over it a slight veil, but not sufficient to destroy the original national character."[4] Herder refuted the conception of civilization whereby each society followed a uniform path of development, with some higher, others lower on the hierarchy of civilization. No outward standard, according to Herder, not even "universal reason," could be applied to judge and rank a particular *Volk*. For Herder, even reason was historically and culturally contingent. Each *Volk*, therefore, had to be judged "from within."[5] In short, Herder contested the putatively universal discourse on civilization in late eighteenth- and early nineteenth-century Europe by arguing for the contingency of its terms, standards, and concepts.

As Japan in the late nineteenth century began to appropriate the discourse on national character, the various epistemological features associated with this discourse, in addition to Herder's cultural and moral pluralism that he associated with the concept of *Volksgeist*, entered Japan as well. First among these was a reconfigured view of nature. No longer the "mechanism" of early Meiji enlightenment thinkers, nature was conceived of as a living, organic entity possessing "spirit." The idea of absolute and eternal spirit emerged in conjunction with the idealism of Fichte, Schelling, and Hegel and was further developed during the latter part of the nineteenth century by the idealist philosopher of ethics Thomas Hill Green. The folk spirit (*kokumin seishin*, or *Volksgeist*) was understood as a manifestation of infinite spirit. Finite consciousness was not separate from eternal consciousness. Rather, the two formed a unity. Feeling and intuition, rather than conceptual thought, were upheld as the best means to apprehend this unity. Just as these views interacted in complex ways with idealism in early nineteenth-century Germany, so too did their variants interact with personalism in nineteenth-century Japan.

In the decades immediately prior to and following the turn of the twentieth century, the notion of national character was used both to reinforce and to subvert the moral and civilizational hierarchies associated with this conception of civilization. By the Taishō period (1912–1926), for example, the idea of national character was transformed into the basis from which to subvert such hierarchies. Following the logic of Herder's claims, proponents of Japan's unique spirit of this time argued for the value of each nation's national character and asserted that each nation contributed in its own way to world civilization. This represented the emergence of a new conception of civilization—one emphasizing cultural struggle *(Kulturkampf)*, or in Japanese *bunka tōsō*.[6] In the last decades of the nineteenth century, however, national character remained deeply intertwined with hierarchical civilization, or *kaika*.

The connection between national character and *kaika* can be seen quite clearly in *The Soul of the Far East* by Percival Lowell, member of the Asiatic Society of Japan and, in this capacity, author of a number of studies on Asia. In this 1888 work, Lowell argued that the peoples of the "Far Orient" occupy an inferior position in the progress of civilization because they lack a sense of self. They lack "personality." "Individuality, personality, and the sense of self," Lowell explained, "are only three different aspects of one and the same thing." In other words, "personality" implied a self-conscious awareness of one's own individuality, and this in the thought represented here by Lowell became a prerequisite for civilization.

An advanced society, according to Lowell, had a highly developed sense of personality, while primitive societies did not. "Individuality [i.e., personality] bears the same relation to the development of mind that the differentiation of species does to the evolution of organic life: that the degree of individualization of a people is the self-recorded measure of its place in the great march of mind." Lowell's main concern in this work was to show the "impersonality" (which he took to be "the soul of the Far East") of Asian peoples, and thereby to demonstrate their low degree of civilization. "If imagination be the impulse of which increase in individuality is the resulting motion...the Far Orientals ought to be a particularly unimaginative set of people. Such is precisely what they are. Their lack of imagination is a well-recognized fact." By providing the "fact" of a lack of imagination among Oriental peoples as evidence, Lowell concluded that they also lacked the impulse toward individuality or personality. As a result, the development of the Oriental mind remained at a primitive stage.[7]

Nakashima Rikizō, four years before taking up the chair of ethics at Tokyo Imperial University in 1893, wrote a review of Percival Lowell's book while studying abroad at Yale University.[8] Importantly, Nakashima refuted neither the idea of a hierarchy of civilizations nor the notion of national character. In his 1889 review, Nakashima criticized Lowell's work for failing to understand "the spirit of the people" of Japan, "the real animating ethical power which has made Japan what she is today." Throughout this article, Nakashima demonstrated his familiarity with the idea of national character. He took great offense when Lowell failed to see the difference between the "national traits" of China and Japan. "The difference is familiar to him who knows anything of these two peoples. The one [China] is extremely conservative, while the other [Japan] is progressive. The one is slow and the other impulsive. The one is grave and sober, but the other quick-witted and lively, etc."

But honor, according to Nakashima, was the defining trait of the Japanese people and the basis of ethical decision making for "every true Japanese." "It is hardly necessary to say that no one can discuss the characteristic traits of any nationality without fully entering into the spirit of that people." Unlike Herder in the late eighteenth-century German states and certain Japanese thinkers, such as Inoue Tetsujirō at the turn of the century, Nakashima accepted the association of *Volksgeist* and national character with universal standards of hierarchical civilization, rather than making them the basis from which to contest such hierarchies.

Indeed, Nakashima remained respectful of "civilization," but his respect had an edge to it. He acknowledged Japan's "great debt to the United States" for the "advancement in civilization" that resulted from Japan's introduction to the society of Western nations. But, with a note of sarcasm, he rebuked the West for the injustices of civilization. Referring to Japan's unequal treaties with Western countries that allowed for extraterritorial rights for foreigners in Japan and tariff limits on goods imported to Japan, Nakashima stated, "May the time soon come when Japan will stand among the community of civilized nations as their equal; and possess the full political powers which are due to her as a sovereign State, but which are now unjustly taken away from her by the *Christian* nations of the world." Nakashima's italicized emphasis on Christianity may of course be interpreted to imply hypocrisy.

But as a lack of personality was Lowell's main critique of Japan's national character, and as this impersonality, according to Lowell, indicated a low level of civilizational development, Nakashima took pains to show that the Japanese did indeed have a notion of personality. For Lowell, "impersonality" was the very "soul of the Far East." The lack of personality among the "Far Orientals" meant they had yet to attain a full consciousness of individuality. Nakashima, again citing Lowell: "In short, 'they are still in that childish state of development, before self-consciousness has spoiled the sweet simplicity of nature. An impersonal race seems never to have fully grown up.'"

Addressing this claim, Nakashima refuted neither the idea of national character nor hierarchical civilization. Instead, he argued that Lowell misunderstood Japan's national character and that if correctly assessed, Japan is not as "primitive" as Lowell claims. Nakashima readily admitted that personality in Japan was less developed than in America. "No candid mind," he observed, "can deny it." Nevertheless, he rejected Lowell's assertion that the Japanese lacked personality altogether. Honor, he pointed out, is not "an entirely *impersonal* matter!" Moreover, Confucian principles such as a sense of duty implied personality as well. Thus, "the Extreme Orient," he reasoned, "is not quite so impersonal as [Lowell] thinks." By direct implication under the logic of Lowell's argument, Nakashima maintained that Japan was not as uncivilized either.

National character and its reflection on civilizational hierarchies are here internalized. To demonstrate that each Japanese does indeed possess a self-conscious awareness of his or her own individuality (i.e., personality) is thus a means for asserting that while Japan may not yet be on par with Western civilization, it is by no means "primitive." This close association of "personality" with civilization and national character, I suggest, helps to explain the emergence of the philosophical discourse on personalism in Japan. At the center of this discourse was Nakashima Rikizō, recently returned from his studies abroad.

This exchange between Lowell and Nakashima is illustrative of key features of academic moral discourse in late nineteenth-century Japan as it began to contest civilizational hierarchies. Notions of "national character" and "the people's spirit" inform the arguments of each. Lowell's usage of "national character" (as a means to reinforce civilizational hierarchies) reflects the continuing dominance and authority of *kaika* discourse. And while Nakashima did not contest this, other thinkers of this time such as Inoue Tetsujirō did. For Inoue, national character shaped by "the people's spirit" became a basis from which to redefine and elevate Japan's national particularity. Thus the idea of "national character" had the potential both to sustain and to subvert *kaika*.

The philosophical concept of "personality" was another central feature of Lowell's and Nakashima's exchange. For Lowell, and for Nakashima too, personality was a requisite for civilization. Lowell's argument linking the Orient's lack of personality with immorality is derived from Hegel. When Hegel suggested that in Oriental societies no truly ethical existence is possible, he predicated the possibility of "ethical existence" on one having a self-conscious awareness of one's own individuality, that is, on "personality."[9] It therefore became imperative that Japan demonstrate that its people did indeed have personality. Nakashima himself initiated the movement called personalism, which centered on the moral cultivation of personality. Finally, also evident in this exchange is an emerging conception of "the Orient" *(tōyō),* a space of particularity constructed together with "the Occident" *(seiyō)* in late nineteenth-century Japan. As seen above, Lowell made use of "the Orient" to elevate "the Occident," and Nakashima, though unable to assert a parity between the two ("no candid mind can deny," he stated, that personality is less prominent in "the Japanese character"), sought to elevate Japan's character over that of China. Thus, Nakashima's statements, as much as Lowell's, reflect an Orientalist discourse. "National character," "spirit," "personality," and "the Orient"—these, then, were central terms of academic moral discourse as Japan approached the end of the nineteenth century.

The Ethics of Spirit: Nakashima Rikizō and Personalism

With the introduction of personalism to Japan, the dominant terms and concepts of moral discourse among academics shifted. Prior to this time, the dominant theories of the good were guided by utilitarianism and evolutionary naturalism. Now, however, the utilitarianism of 1880s Japan came under attack. While securing the greatest happiness for the greatest number was regarded in the 1870s and 1880s as "the chief objective of mankind" and happiness itself was "the obvious standard" for distinguishing good from evil,[10] utilitarianism lost sway by the end of the nineteenth century precisely because of its close association with the hierarchical discourse on civilization *(kaika)*.

The utilitarianism circulating in the early Meiji period was largely that of J. S. Mill. Mill's text *Utilitarianism,* introduced to Japan through the works of Nishi Amane and translated in 1880 by Shibutani Keizō, had an enormous impact on the moral thought of this time. In this work, Mill's calculus of the good was not simply a measure of the greatest happiness for the greatest number, nor a question of a quantitative measure of happiness alone; the good, according to Mill, was also a *qualitative* measure. Mill posited "higher" pleasures as evaluatively superior to the "lower" pleasures. Roughly, this meant the superiority of intellectual over physical pleasures. Only one who had experience of both sorts of pleasure was in a position to judge the desirability of each. This effectively secured for the "intellectual" and the educated the authority to judge matters related to "the good," and excluded the uneducated (i.e., the "foolish people" discussed in chapter 1).[11] Thus, Mill's style of utilitarian ethics mirrored and to some extent helped to produce the early Meiji convictions on Japan's inferior civilizational status.

Moreover, the "person" in this utilitarian conception of society, though certainly considered a part of society, was never described as synonymous with the social whole. The epistemology that shaped the ethical thought of early Meiji (the ethics of civilization) presupposed a subject-object dichotomy: the observing subject was detached and distinct from the objects perceived. "Nature" was itself an object, a mechanism with discernible and unchanging laws that could serve as a foundation for the good. This objectification of nature was reinforced by a materialist philosophy of perception.

In the early 1890s, however, *rinrigaku* scholars began to ground their ethical views in a very different epistemology, producing a new vocabulary with which to articulate it. The person, society, and nature, as well as the subject-object dichotomy, all underwent a dramatic reconfiguration. The "person" was no longer an isolated individual in a society of isolated individuals, each with his or her own desires and (oftentimes conflicting) conception of the good. Each person, according to the new view that was emerging, apprehended him or herself in the other. The person, then, was not merely "individual" but also social. The new philosophy that was being introduced was a form of idealism called "personalism" *(jinkakushugi).*

Nakashima Rikizō was the central figure in the introduction and dissemination of personalism in Japan. His students included such notable philosophers as Takayama Chogyū, Kuwaki Genyoku, Ōnishi Hajime, and Nishida Kitarō. He outlined this new philosophy and its ethical implications in an article titled

"Concerning the British Neo-Kantian school" (Eikoku shin kanto gakuha ni tsuite), serialized in 1892 and 1893.[12] The focus of this essay, and the inspiration in the development in Nakashima's moral views, was the philosophy of British idealist Thomas Hill Green.

Central to the epistemology of personalism was the idea of "spiritual principle." Nakashima, following Green, described nature as a system of relations. All phenomena, whether objects or events, are what they are by nature of their relation to something else. This relationality implied consciousness—one object can be related to another only through the productive activity of some consciousness.[13] But certainly the finite consciousness of a single individual cannot apprehend the totality of nature's relations. Therefore, "there must exist an eternal consciousness for which the eternal system of relations is an eternal object." This "eternal consciousness" Green called the "spiritual principle."[14] Nakashima and other personalist philosophers in Japan referred to this principle as *eikō naru seishin* (eternal spirit) and as *seishin shugi* (spiritual principle).[15] Finite human consciousness was, for Nakashima, a particular manifestation of infinite spirit, thus the subject-object opposition (between, e.g., self and other, individual and social whole) is overcome in the infinite consciousness of absolute spirit.

These presuppositions about nature and humanity formed the epistemological foundations for personalism's ethical claims. The "good" in personalist discourse was described as an ideal, as the realization of one's self or personality in its unity with absolute spirit. This concept of self-realization (*jinkaku jitsugen* or *jiga jitsugen*) held a central position in the ethical thought of Japan's idealist philosophers.[16]

Nakashima thus drew a close linkage between Green's "spiritual principle" and the possibility of moral action. "Without infinite spirit, our own spirit would cease to be, without our own spirit, we could have no aim, and with no aim, there can be no morality. These are the important points of Green's theory of logic."[17] "Infinite spirit," then, was more than just a feature of Nakashima's moral thought; it was in fact the very condition for the possibility of morality.

Following the publication of Nakashima's article introducing Green's thought, articles on Green's epistemology and ethics, as well as translations of his writings, began to appear. In 1895 Mizobuchi Shinma translated Book One of Green's *Prolegomena to Ethics*, "The Metaphysics of Knowledge," into Japanese, and in the same year Nishida Kitarō, who had graduated from Tokyo Imperial University the year before, published a concise summary of Green's *Prolegomena* in the journal *Kyōiku jiron*.[18] Green's *Prolegomena*, therefore, became an integral part of *rinrigaku* discourse in Japan at this time. Nakashima, using this work as a classroom text, passed along to his students the centrality of "infinite spirit" for moral philosophy.[19]

Like Nakashima, the moral thought of his students presupposed and emphasized absolute spirit and the unity of self and other it enabled. In an 1894 study of Green's epistemology, Nakajima Tokuzō, who had studied with Nakashima Rikizō at Tokyo University, explained that the "eternal spirit" *(eikō naru seishin)* and the consciousness of each individual *(shiki)* are identical— the former manifests itself through the latter, and there can be no distinction between the two.[20] Another student of Nakashima, Takayama Rinjirō (Chogyū) (1871–1902), also developed an ethics of self-realization in his main ethical work, *On the Moral Ideal (Dōtoku no risō o ronzu)*. In this text Takayama wrote, "Society cannot exist apart from the individual. The two form a relationship of part and whole, and the one cannot possibly be separated from the other."[21] He went on to say that society is not merely an "inorganic substance"; rather, it possesses its own personality, and this is none other than the totality of the individual personalities of that society. Society has its own ideal and its own means for development. "Society," Takayama stressed, "does not develop by extinguishing the personality of the individual, nor does the individual come into being through the negation of society's personality. This, in other words, is the Buddhist idea of identity-in-difference *(byōdō soku sabetsu)*. The subjective ideal of morality in fact lies here."[22] In addition, Nishida Kitarō's conception of the good in his well-known work on this subject, *An Inquiry into the Good (Zen no kenkyū)*, was also expressed in the vocabulary of personalism. "The good," wrote Nishida, "is the realization of personality *(jinkaku no jitsugen)*." He described this realization as "the unification of consciousness—and its ultimate form is achieved in the mutual forgetting of self and other and the merging of subject and object."[23]

For these personalist philosophers, Nakashima as well as his students, ethics was deeply imbued with a spiritual component. This view was quite at odds with the first two decades of moral thought in Meiji Japan. Rather than construing the subject (the consciousness of an individual) as detached from and opposed to an external world of "objects," personalism asserted an identity between the two. The consciousness of each individual participated in the eternal spirit or consciousness of nature.[24] Thus, the "spiritual principle" that informed the ethics of personalism, with its capacity to resolve the opposition between subject and object, individual and society, had the capacity to subvert the fundamental tenets of the epistemology of representation that grounded *kaika* discourse. As this notion of an absolute and infinite spirit gained authority, the legitimacy of the epistemology separating subject from object was called into question. This made possible a critique of the truth-claims that were grounded in this epistemology. In short, the ethics of personalism held the potential to subvert the West's claims to civilizational superiority. Yet in Nakashima's thought, this step was not taken.

In one sense, the epistemology of personalism transcended civilizational hierarchies. Each person, whether of the Occident or the Orient, equally participated in absolute spirit, and therefore each equally had the potential to cultivate his or her own personality. Next to this, superior knowledge and skills were secondary, and claims to superior virtue could be dismissed. Yet Nakashima's concern with cultivating the personality of the Japanese reflects his sense that most people in Japan lacked an awareness of their personality and the need for its cultivation. In this sense, he accepted Japan's civilizational inferiority.

Nakashima formulated his thought at a time when others were emphasizing Japan's national character or the character of the "Orient." Clearly he opposed Western representations of Japan, such as those made by Percival Lowell above, as "primitive," "unimaginative," and utterly devoid of personality. Yet rather than seek to reconfigure the meaning of and conditions for civilized society, Nakashima accepted the centrality of personality as a marker of civilization. Thus, Nakashima's primary concern with the ethics of personalism was to develop "personality" among members of Japanese society.

Basing his arguments on a theory of social development perhaps drawn from Spencer, Durkheim, or Tonnies, Nakashima observed that as societies develop they become more complex, such that a high degree of cooperation among the population becomes increasingly essential for a society's continued development. Without respect for one another's rights and individuality (i.e., personality), such cooperation is impossible. "Cooperation in our country," Nakashima admitted, "is not sufficiently established." The explanation for this was that "people in Japan have not yet sufficiently developed the concept of mutual respect for one another's personality."[25] As "all the other countries" strove to enhance social cooperation through attention to the individual's personality, Japan was being left behind. "I believe that from this point forward, industrial competition will become increasingly intense." Such competition took place not only among individuals, Nakashima insisted, but among nations. "Industrial competition is peaceful warfare."[26] But this was precisely the area where Japan was lacking. Through the cultivation of personality, social cooperation would be enhanced, leading to a more industrially competitive Japan.

The lack of social cooperation to which Nakashima referred was reflected, for example, in the large number of labor disputes that emerged out of the economic depression that followed the Sino-Japanese War of 1894–1895, by some accounts more than 160 between the years 1897 and 1905.[27] The government responded to these labor disputes and to other forms of socially disruptive activity with the enactment of the Public Peace Police Law (Chian keisatsu hō) in 1900. This law, which took the place of the Peace Regulations (Hoan jōrei, enacted in 1887 and repealed in 1898), enhanced police control over labor disputes and strikes.[28]

Nakashima attempted to convey the importance of social cooperation in his textbooks for moral training. In his *New Moral Training Textbook for the Teachers' Colleges (Shihan gakkō shūshin shin kyōkasho)*, Nakashima warned, "Without a spirit of cooperation we will be unable to make progress in our undertakings," and social disorder will be the result.[29] He stressed the need to cultivate self-respect *(jiko jinkaku no sonchō)*, without which one would be unable to respect others, and equality *(byōdō)* of self and other, arguing that all are equal inasmuch as all possess personality. Moreover, he discussed the value and importance of each individual's liberty, although he added that such liberty must remain within the confines of the order of society and its laws.[30]

Nakashima struggled to find some kind of contribution that Japan could make to the world, and stressed that not all of Japan's past need be abandoned. Indeed, Japan, like all countries, had certain "beautiful customs" that must be protected and preserved. Yet other customs had to be discarded. This included Japan's style of moral education. Nakashima wrote that while Japan's political, economic, and legal thought all underwent dramatic change since the Meiji Revolution, becoming "Western," only Japan's moral education remained "Oriental" (Nakashima called it *shina fū*, i.e., "Chinese"). "With this approach, I believe that satisfactory moral education is in no way possible."[31] While he admitted that this "Chinese style" was not without some positive aspects, he called for attention to the "further clarification of the concept of personality" so as to bring the current methods for moral education into accord with Japan's political, economic, and legal thought. In short, moral education needed to be in the "Western style." He warned, "[I]f we do not adopt such a policy and continue as things are, I believe we will be unable to attain the positive results we have hoped for in moral education."[32] Fending off anticipated attacks from critics of "Westernization," Nakashima assured his readers that his proposals for the reform of moral education did not demand that Japan's past be abandoned or that Japan had only "evil customs." Nevertheless, he supported a "Western method" for moral education, one that encouraged virtuous action by going beyond the simple inculcation of virtues and by clarifying the conception of personality.[33]

Nakashima's emphasis on personality in moral education reflects a continued adherence to previously established conditions for civilization. He was clearly looking outward, concerned more with elevating Japanese society to the same level of the West than with creating a particular "Oriental" or Japanese morality. Still internalized in Nakashima's thought, then, was the connection between civilization and personality, and the conviction that Japan was deficient in both.

Despite the wide acceptance of personalism within academic moral discourse, Nakashima's views met with harsh criticism by those opposed to an ethics that focused solely on "the Occident" and ignored "the Orient." Inoue Tetsujirō was one such critic. He attacked "those like Nakashima Rikizō" who "introduce Western ethics through translation and lecture on the universal aspects of ethics without any discussion of Oriental Ethics, and above all, the morality of the Japanese people." This, according to Inoue, was "truly an inappropriate approach."[34]

Inoue Tetsujirō: Creating the "Spirit of the People"

The moral thought of Inoue Tetsujirō was instrumental in producing alternatives to the civilizational hierarchies associated with the discourse on *kaika*. His critique of the universalizing force of Western ethics and his efforts to articulate the "moral spirit of the Japanese people" reflect a desire for national particularity. Although much of his work on the unique moral sensibilities of the Japanese (an expression of their spirit and national character) was undertaken from 1910 in his writings on national morality, his concern with a common morality for Japan began well before this. Inoue's appeal to a common Japanese moral spirit owed much to a document he would later call "the sacred book of Meiji": the Imperial Rescript on Education.

The Imperial Rescript on Education was put forward as a moral document. Issued in 1890 as the official pronouncement of the emperor though drafted largely by Inoue Kowashi, Motoda Eifu, and other court counselors, the Imperial Rescript prescribed a particular code of moral conduct, one designed to foster social order and obedience to the state. It called upon Japanese subjects to "always respect the Constitution and observe the laws." It sought to enlist all national subjects in the collective defense of the state should its survival or that of the current social order be threatened: "should emergency arise, offer yourselves courageously to the State; and thus guard and maintain the prosperity of Our Imperial Throne." It rooted these demands in an appeal to timeless tradition. The imperial line (the "Throne") is represented as "coeval with heaven and earth." Loyalty and obedience to the state here become the "Way" (a weighted term conveying a sense of a moral path) and "the teaching bequeathed by Our Imperial Ancestors, to be observed alike by Their Descendants and the subjects." Not merely traditional, this teaching was an enduring and universal truth, "infallible for all ages and true in all places."[35]

The Imperial Rescript, then, was not a text directed to the individual and his or her capacity for rational moral judgment; rather, it spoke to the *kokumin*, the state subjects of Japan. The Imperial Rescript, moreover, employed a performative strategy, proclaiming the virtues of the people so as to make them virtuous: "Our subjects ever united in loyalty and filial piety" was a conceit that sought to produce loyal and filial subjects by proclaiming such virtues to be already innate within them. The aim was to redress social discord and action that was subversive to the state by teaching national subjects that they and their ancestors have always embraced these virtues. By adhering to the Way of obedience to the state, each subject became, in effect, what he or she had putatively always been, and joined a supposedly timeless moral community of identity. "So shall you not only be Our good and faithful subjects, but render illustrious the best traditions of your forefathers." Here, then, presented as the authority of tradition, is a prescription for moral action, for faithfully fulfilling one's duties as a subject of the state. By emphasizing "our" virtues, "our" ancestors, and "our" traditions, the Imperial Rescript contributed to the emerging narrative of the folk with which Inoue Tetsujirō was also concerned. Indeed, though many offered interpretations of this document, it was Inoue who provided the official government commentary.

In his "Commentary," Inoue explained the meaning and intent of the Imperial Rescript line by line. One particularly troublesome claim in the Imperial Rescript was the assertion that the values it espoused were "infallible for all ages and true in all places." In short, it laid claim to both a temporal and a spatial universality. It reflected a desire for moral particularity (to proclaim the moral identity unique to Japan) even while asserting the universality of these values (a moral identity with all the world). The "universal" provided a legitimizing authority for the values in the Imperial Rescript that was too powerful to forgo. Inoue was left to sort out this contradiction.

He began by addressing the timeless quality of loyalty. Over time, Inoue conceded, with fluctuations in the level of a society's culture and customs, there will be differences in the way these teachings are carried out. Nevertheless, he maintained, "the spirit of this principle is invariably one and the same."[36] And if the kind of loyalty proclaimed in the Imperial Rescript was not always evident in the actions of his ancestors, it existed in their thoughts. "Our people, from ancient times, have held the virtue of loyalty deep in their hearts."[37] To establish the truth of the Imperial Rescript's teachings "in all places," Inoue explained that the teachings of loyalty and filial piety are necessary for the establishment of any society, whether it lies in the East or the West. These virtues are to be esteemed in any country, Inoue stated, and "they are not limited to our country alone."[38] Yet while asserting the universal scope of loyalty and filiality, Inoue at the same time sought to lay claim to these virtues as the "old customs" and "ancient ways" of Japan.

He suggested that in the decades following the Meiji Revolution, "knowledge education" had improved but moral education had declined. "Since the Meiji Ishin...the learning of Europe and America has greatly flourished in our country...[but] many in Japan have come to hate old customs and to abandon ancient ways...such that the moral principles of loyalty and filial piety have become out of fashion." "People do not understand," he continued, "that however much the learning of novelties may flourish the teaching of loyalty and filial piety cannot be changed in the least. Thus, as they are inclined toward the study of the various fields of novel learning, such people lose themselves upon an evil course."[39] The fields of "novel learning," so crucial for the advancement of "civilization" during the early years of Meiji, are here linked to an evil path and the cause for moral decline. By linking the learning of Euro-America with a decline of loyalty and filiality, Inoue was able to claim these virtues for the Orient or perhaps for Japan alone. Thus the effect of Inoue's argument was to assert that loyalty and filial piety are true in all times (provided this was limited to Japanese history) and true (but not practiced) in all places.

Although Inoue was appointed to write the "official" commentary on the Imperial Rescript, he was by no means the only one to offer an interpretation. The debate concerning this document provides an occasion to discuss the thought of another important moral philosopher of the Meiji period, Ōnishi Hajime (1864–1900). In his short lifetime, Ōnishi wrote widely on ethics, logic, aesthetics, and Christian theology, but his own moral standpoint might best be approached through his social criticism. Ōnishi took issue with Inoue's commentary and with the Imperial Rescript itself. The virtues of loyalty and filial piety, he contended, could not be true in all times and all places. How loyalty and filiality are defined and understood, what they demand of a person, and how they are put into practice—all will change over time, he argued. "The practical application depends on the particular situation, and even then the necessity of a certain kind of application exists only in the opinion of one private individual. Yet if the application of the Imperial Rescript is limited entirely to this kind of situation, then its intent is not fulfilled." In short, the Imperial Rescript and the virtues it espoused can be "true in all times and all places" only by admitting a plurality of truths. But this would not cultivate unity among those who practiced them. "When the trend of the times is different, even the elucidation of loyalty and filial piety is different." To continually reinterpret the meaning of the Imperial Rescript is to relativize its meaning. For Ōnishi, the

Imperial Rescript could never serve as a static universal, but only as testimony to the timelessness of contingency.

Ōnishi's critique is powerfully subversive because it points to the contradiction in Inoue's commentary and in the Imperial Rescript itself: the effort to establish cultural particularity while claiming to transcend that particularity so as to draw upon the authority of the universal. The Imperial Rescript, Ōnishi noted, is put forward as "true in all places," and yet it is a teaching "bequeathed by Our Imperial Ancestors." He asked, "If the very name 'Imperial Rescript' necessarily refers to the morality of a particular country and a particular brand of ethics, then do not these limits on its authority provoke useless discussion and nullify the Rescript's intent?"[40]

Ōnishi pushed his critique of the values of loyalty and filial piety further, dismissing the Imperial Rescript as a basis for morality. The Rescript and its two key virtues of loyalty and filial piety, he argued, were merely part of the state's demand for obedience—obedience to the command of one's ruler in the case of loyalty and of one's father in the case of filial piety. According to this interpretation of the Imperial Rescript, moral action is obedience to the authority's command. One is not permitted to ask why a particular action is to be carried out or why it is deemed moral, because to do so would run counter to the demand for obedience.[41] Indeed, Ōnishi reasoned, upon close inspection "there is no basis for the moral distinction between right and wrong beyond or outside of this authority." "The reason we are to obey a command is simply that it is the command of one possessing authority."[42] Incidentally, we will see (in the following chapter) that philosopher Nishida Kitarō made this same argument about two decades later, though his critique was directed at the "national morality" of Inoue Tetsujirō, Fukasaku Yasubumi, Yoshida Kumaji, and others.

But mere obedience, Ōnishi argued, could not provide a foundation for morality, and he methodically explained why this was so. If loyalty and filiality together form the moral foundation for Japan, then this morality will have two discrete foundations and present the possibility of contradictions between the two. "Can we be certain that there will never be a situation where, in the desire to be loyal, one must be unfilial, or that in striving to be filial one must be disloyal?"[43] On the other hand, if one argues that loyalty and filiality are a kind of unitary virtue joined together by a deeper moral principle both share, then it is this deeper principle that must be foundational and at the center of moral inquiry, not loyalty or filial piety. Moreover, he continued, if this deeper principle can be shown to inform other virtues as well, not just loyalty and filiality, then this realization will push loyalty and filial piety even further to the periphery of moral inquiry. He concluded that since "the Imperial Rescript does not point out the basis of morality, the various virtues proclaimed in it cannot be construed as an absolute in ethical theory."[44] And in contrast to his own efforts to present a carefully reasoned and logical argument, he viewed his critics as lazy-minded and abusive. He criticized those who upheld loyalty and filial piety as the centerpiece of Japanese morality for not thinking more deeply on the meaning of these terms, observing, "They prefer merely to spit out random and emotional statements of abuse at their critics."[45] In the end, Ōnishi boldly asserted that to proclaim loyalty and filiality as the basis of morality is "irresponsible talk."[46] But the Imperial Rescript's demand for obedience presented more than a philosophical problem; it also posed a threat to freedom.

Ōnishi foresaw the possibility of hegemonic state power curtailing freedom.

> If we say that loyalty and filial piety mean obedience to the command of one's ruler or father, and we take this as the foundation for morality, we cannot establish morality beyond where the command of one's ruler or father extends. This is the inevitable result of such a view. Thus, the command of one's ruler or father would actually have to extend to every sphere of social action in all of its infinite complexity.[47]

In other words, if proper moral action lies solely in obedience to a command, without that command to obey or disobey, there can be no morality. Thus, Ōnishi reasoned, if the state truly sought to disseminate a state morality of obedience based on loyalty and filial piety (and there was every indication that such a project was already, by the early 1890s, underway), and if the state succeeded in making the entire population "moral," then none could be both moral and free: only the subservient could be deemed moral, while those who determined their actions through free moral adjudication, even when such actions corresponded with the good of the state, could not be deemed moral. Making Japan moral, universalizing morality throughout Japan so that it informed all thought and action, required that the authoritative command extend to all parts and people of the country. The debate discussed in the previous chapter on where to set the limits of state authority, on the extent to which the state was to shape moral interiority, was still very much at issue.

Finally, Ōnishi critiqued the Imperial Rescript for advocating a parochial and self-interested nationalism. While Inoue in his commentary (and the text of the Imperial Rescript itself) called for self-sacrificing action for the good of the state, Ōnishi viewed such a demand as misplaced. Instead, he called for nationalism that recognized its responsibility to all humanity. "Our state exists to provide for the welfare of the lives of the world's peoples."[48] Thus, the value of the state lay within and beyond itself, in its capacity to promote and realize this ideal. He argued that only a cosmopolitan nationalism of this kind could be justified. "Nationalism that does not look beyond the state," he argued, "lacks a solid and justifiable foundation."[49] Of course, this kind of indiscriminate concern for others was precisely the shortcoming Inoue saw in Christianity. Universal concern for others was incommensurate with the special concern a subject of the state was to have for the state and other *kokumin*. Ōnishi's moral views, then, were clearly at odds with the Imperial Rescript on Education and the morality that was taking shape at the end of the nineteenth century. Moreover, his cosmopolitan view of nationalism was directly at odds with Inoue Tetsujirō's efforts to establish a Japanese moral spirit.

In the first years of the twentieth century, Inoue published several works (each pertaining to the ethical thought of Japan's past) that contributed to the production of the "moral spirit" of Japan and the destabilization of civilizational hierarchies. These works were *The Philosophy of Japan's Yōmei School* (*Nihon Yōmeigakuha no tetsugaku,* 1900), *The Philosophy of Japan's Ancient Studies School* (*Nihon Kogakuha no tetsugaku,* 1902), *The Philosophy of Japan's Shushi School* (*Nihon Shushigakuha no tetsugaku,* 1906), and *A Compendium of Japanese Ethics* (*Nihon rinri ihen,* published from 1901), a monumental ten-volume collection of Japanese Confucian texts on ethics from the seventeenth and eighteenth centuries. Through these writings, Inoue sought to offset the universalizing force of "Occidental" ethics with an ethics of "the Orient." Further, he emphasized the way Oriental ethics, once appropriated by Japan, progressed into an even higher form of moral thought. This he called "Japanese ethics," or *Nihon rinri.* These texts represent Inoue's effort to produce, systematize, and legitimize Japanese ethics.

Throughout these works, Inoue was extremely critical of utilitarianism. In the earliest of these texts, *The Philosophy of Japan's Yōmei School,* Inoue observed that from about the time of Japan's Meiji Revolution of 1868, "the world's scholars" had advocated utilitarianism and egoism. Inoue believed that such ethical views were gradually destroying Japan's moral spirit. The theories of utilitarianism and egoism, he stated, "sap the vitality of the state and insidiously eat away at the spirit of public morals."[50] And although Inoue admitted that utilitarianism may be an acceptable doctrine in regard to the state economy, he viewed it as unsuitable as the guiding morality of an individual. Rather than cultivating the "virtue of the human heart" *(shintoku),* utilitarianism merely guided one by their individual desires. "It defiles the virtue of the heart which we in our country have ever held as sacred."[51] "Though utilitarianism is a skillfully thought-out theory, it is lacking as a moral teaching. And as for egoism, it is truly nothing more than destructive and worthless sophistry."[52] Recall that Inoue was one of utilitarianism's greatest advocates in the early Meiji period and that it was he who, twenty years earlier in his *New Theory of Ethics* proclaimed that "happiness in life" is the aim of all philosophical and religious theories of ethics, past and present.[53] Clearly his ethical views had undergone a dramatic change. Inoue's new ethical position represented not only an attack on utilitarianism, the morality most closely associated with the discourse on "civilization," but also the defense of the moral spirit of Japan.

The appropriation of civilization, its morality, and its underlying episte-mology in the preceding decades, Inoue believed, had left Japan in moral chaos. Its "moral spirit" was in jeopardy. "Today, Buddhism has died out, Confucian-ism has become weak, and Bushidō no longer flourishes. The traditional moral principles of our country are in their final days.... By contrast, Western moral principles have gradually been imported, apparently with the power to sweep over our spiritual world."[54] Inoue was deeply concerned about the way ethics in Japan was increasingly determined by "the Occident." Nevertheless, he believed the Japanese people possessed a "spirit of morality" with the power to con-test the West. "Even if the traditional moral principles of our country should somehow decline, this would merely reflect a decline of these principles as a teaching or as a field of study. The unseen power of these principles, concealed within the spiritual realm of Japan *(waga seishin kai),* would remain, and this is something we must certainly never take lightly."[55] Japan's "spiritual realm" was the site from which *kaika* could be contested.

Inoue's ethical writings at the turn of the century focused on the "moral spirit of the Japanese people" *(kokumin teki dōtoku shin).* In the first of his three studies of Confucian philosophy, *The Philosophy of Japan's Yōmei School,* Inoue argued that the existence of such a spirit was beyond question. "If we require facts before our eyes as evidence of the manifestation of our national moral spirit, I say look at the actions of our army in China." Here, Inoue was referring to Japan's participation in the allied suppression of the Boxer War in China (1899–1900), which was ongoing as Inoue wrote the preface to this text. Inoue believed that Japan had successfully used this allied action to show the "pure" and "unparalleled" posture of Japan's national moral spirit. "With the flash of a sword and the roar of a gun, Japan's army demonstrated the pure and unparal-leled posture of the Japanese moral spirit in a dazzling display before all the nations of the world."

> What was it that particularly stood out among our forces? It was that they did not engage in a self-indulgent plundering, they did not give free reign to unnecessary violence, they maintained military discipline, and they were not in any way moved by their own self-interest. If this is not a manifesta-tion of our country's national moral spirit, then what was it?[56]

For Inoue, the discipline, courage, and selfless conduct of Japan's forces had to be explained in terms of moral spirit. Any view that ignored spirit in its assessment of the Japanese army's valor he deemed "a superficial view of an inexperienced and blind philistine."[57]

Fukuzawa Yukichi was perhaps one of the "philistines" that Inoue had in mind. Fukuzawa, according to Inoue, rejected Chinese civilization and rejoiced in the importation of Western civilization, pointing out that Japan's victory in its war with China (1894–1895) was possible because of the useful tools of civilization. Confucianists demonstrated their "stupidity" most clearly, according to Fukuzawa, in their disregard for the trends of the times. Their views were in direct contradiction to the newly emerging civilization. Critical of this position, Inoue stated that Japan did indeed draw upon modern weaponry and other "tools of civilization" in its war with China, but China equally made use of such tools. That Japan was victorious despite this was an indication that civilization's tools and weapons were not the decisive factor. Japan's victory, Inoue insisted, was the result of spirit. "Civilization's tools are necessary, but most important of all is the spirit to make use of them."[58] Inoue's and Fukuzawa's debate over civilization, spirit, and the Sino-Japanese War reflects a growing ambivalence toward the concept of civilization itself.

An image carried in Fukuzawa's current-events newspaper, *Jiji shimpō*, during the first year of Japan's war with China captured this ambivalence. (See figure 3.) This image shows Japan (represented by a Japanese soldier in Western-style military uniform), China (as a decrepit and dying literati, marked by the Qing-style queue, an opium pipe, and fingernails that have grown long through lack of manual labor), and Korea (in the Japanese soldier's arms, a child not yet having reached the adulthood of civilization and therefore in need of Japan's protection). In the smoke from the gun (symbolic of the power and violence of Western technology and civilization) appear the characters for *bunmei*, or civilization, the term used from the 1870s in Japan to refer to the end point toward which Japan strove. Thus, the image represents the victory of Japanese civilization over Chinese barbarism. Indeed, Fukuzawa himself described this war as a *bunya no sensō*—a battle between civilization and barbarism. The image declares Japan's arrival among the civilized countries of the world while it legitimizes Japan's advance into Korea and its subsequent influence on Korea's civilizing "Kabo" reforms.

Yet the image can be, and in all likelihood was, read in more than one way. Alternatively, it represents disillusionment with civilization and the violence it projects. The characters in the smoke may also be read *wénmíng*, the Chinese reading that conveys not the hierarchical civilization of the West, but China's

Figure 3. Civilization, violence, and power during the Sino-Japanese War. The characters in the smoke read *bunmei* (civilization). This image was carried in Fukuzawa Yukichi's *Current Events News (Jiji shimpō)*. Untitled image, August 8, 1894.

wavering or perhaps now defunct conception of its own superiority and centrality in the world.[59] In this reading, the power and violence of civilization bring death to those, like China, unable to progress with the times. A decade after the Sino-Japanese War, art critic and scholar Okakura Kakuzō captured this perspective with eloquent irony: "[The average Westerner] was wont to regard Japan as barbarous while she indulged in the gentle arts of peace; he calls her civilized since she began to commit wholesale slaughter on the Manchurian battlefields." Even Fukuzawa himself as early as 1885 wove together his assurance of civilization's benefits with a justification for the use of violence against Japan's neighbors.[60] For Inoue, the technological advances associated with civilization were without question powerful and necessary for Japan. But his struggle to explain Japan's victory over China by way of spirit rather than civilization reflects a recognition of spirit's greater potential to mobilize Japan's population in times of war. Moreover, as long as civilization remained the key evaluative framework for comparing societies, Japan could take pride in its superiority over China but would remain civilizationally inferior to Europe and America. Inoue found an alternative to civilization in the idea of Japanese spirit.

    In an effort to clarify the meaning of "Japan's national moral spirit," Inoue proclaimed, "It is nothing other than the universal virtue of the human heart (*shintoku no fuhen naru mono*), and such virtue of the heart indeed reflects the purity of Oriental morality."[61] In this one important statement, Inoue drew upon the authority of the universal to authorize his conception of *shintoku* (a virtue common to all humanity), he claimed this virtue for the Orient alone (although universal, it had not yet been realized in the "rational" Occident), and he equated this virtue with Japan's national moral spirit and thus positioned Japan to speak for the Orient. Inoue himself, through his statements on *shintoku* and his efforts to systematize Japanese ethical thought, sought to speak for Japan. In other words, Inoue's works reflect a desire to demonstrate the moral particularity of Japan, an attempt to locate Japan within the broader space of particularity called the Orient *(tōyō)*, and finally, his struggle to oppose the "Orient" to the "Occident" so as to undermine the latter's claims to civilizational superiority.[62]

For Inoue, establishing moral particularity for Japan required the systematic organization of its past moral thought. His *Compendium of Japanese Ethics* brought together a great variety of moral texts from Japan's Tokugawa period (1600–1868), while his three studies of Confucianism in Japan (Yōmei, Shushi, and Ancient Studies) provided interpretive analysis and commentary. As the moral principles of the Occident "swept over" Japan, Inoue feared that Japan's moral spirit would be unable to withstand the universalizing power of the West. He therefore called for the study of the development of Japan's moral spirit. "If we wish to know the fate of the national moral spirit [*kokumin teki dōtoku shin*] in our country, it is necessary to comprehend the spirit of the moral teachings that have come to forge and educate the minds of the Japanese people." Through the study of Japan's moral past, Inoue hoped to resist the "illegitimate and heretical doctrines" (e.g., utilitarianism and egoism) with which the world endeavored to "wipe out Japan's national moral spirit down to its very roots," to "cure the current ills of society," to cultivate Japan's moral spirit, and in the end, to make clear to all the nation's of the world the true meaning of *shintoku,* the virtue of the human heart.[63]

Inoue's first major effort in this direction was his study of the philosophy of Yōmei Confucianism as it had developed in Japan. In this work, Inoue discussed the major Yōmei thinkers in Japan, such as Nakae Tōju, Kumazawa Banzan, Satō Issai, Yoshida Shōin, and others. He argued that Yōmeigaku would be beneficial in the cultivation of *shintoku* among Japan's younger generation. Inoue viewed Yōmei as a kind of "method of the heart," one that is peculiar to the Orient. No such method, according to Inoue, existed in the Occident, "certainly none like that of Japan." "In the ethics of the Occident, the cultivation of *shintoku* is not the main concern. Rather, most central is intellectual pursuit. In other words, through intellectual pursuit, they decide upon moral principles, and then afterwards attempt to implement them."[64] *Shintoku,* Inoue's "universal" virtue of the human heart, was the central concept in his effort to differentiate Oriental and Occidental moralities. For its cultivation, Inoue advocated Yōmeigaku.

But Yōmei was closely associated with anti-establishment movements in Japan's recent past. In the wake of the Tempō Famine of 1836, for example, Ōshio Heihachirō, deeply motivated by the Yōmei doctrine of the unity of knowledge and action, believed that knowledge of society's injustices demanded action against those responsible. He led a small group of followers in armed rebellion against the Tokugawa *bakufu* in 1837. In 1858 Yoshida Shōin, a student of Yōmei Confucianism, was executed for initiating a plot to assassinate high-ranking *bakufu* officials. Saigō Takamori, influenced by both the Zen and Yōmei traditions, was a central figure in the Satsuma Rebellion against the Meiji state in 1877. Later in the nineteenth century, Yōmeigaku played a role in the Movement for Freedom and Popular Rights. Nakae Chōmin, proponent of French liberal thought and natural right theory, was also a follower of Yōmeigaku, as was his disciple, Kōtoku Shūsui. Kōtoku was convicted of conspiring to assassinate the emperor and executed in the High Treason Incident of 1911. Finally, Okunomiya Kenshi, executed along with Kōtoku in the High Treason Incident and a participant in the popular rights movement in the 1880s, was also believed to be a follower of Yōmeigaku. Obviously, not all of these events are to be explained as inevitable outgrowths of Yōmei Confucianism. They do, however, explain Inoue's trepidations with regard to this school.

In his study of Yōmeigaku, Inoue compared it with Shushigaku and noted that of the two, the Yōmei School was clearly the more dangerous. "Although the Shushigaku faction is not without vices, among the various factions of Confucianism, it is the safest."[65] Later, in 1911, following the High Treason Incident, the *Tokyo Asahi shinbun* carried an article in which Inoue linked Yōmeigaku with anarchism and socialism. In the wake of the High Treason Incident, Inoue and others held a conference at Kokugakuin University to confer on social instabilities. Inoue, one of the discussants at this conference, elaborated upon "the dangers of Yōmeigaku, French revolutionary thought, and Socialism." Because the father (Okunomiya Zōsai) of condemned anarchist Okunomiya Kenshi was a well-known Yōmei scholar as well as a participant in the popular rights movement of the 1880s like his son, Inoue equated the dangers of Yōmeigaku with the liberal thought of Rousseau (whose *Social Contract* had been translated into Japanese by Nakae Chōmin, the teacher of another convicted anarchist, Kōtoku Shūsui).[66] With this long history of opposition to the Tokugawa regime and the Meiji state, why did Inoue draw upon this form of Confucianism?

First, Inoue felt he could separate out the dangerous elements from Yōmeigaku and focus only on the less violent, quietly reflective side of this school. He distinguished two types of Yōmeigaku: one contemplative, the other prone to action. While he condoned the former, he associated the latter form with "politicians, economists, and social reformers" who, though they may not have advocated utilitarianism, were "utilitarians all the same."[67] Linking this latter type of Yōmeigaku (which included some of the more violent social reformers such as Ōshio Heihachirō, Nakae Chōmin, Kōtoku Shūsui, and Okunomiya Kenshi) to utilitarianism, the form of Western thought that Inoue most despised, was one of the ways in which he attempted to de-legitimize it.

Inoue also drew upon the Yōmei School because it was, in his view, a teaching exclusively concerned with ethical matters. Inoue described Confucianism in general as a form of ethics. Although he admitted that it branched out to include other concerns, he stated, "[E]thics [rinrigaku] is the true spirit of Chinese philosophy in its entirety, from ancient times to the present."[68] But Inoue went even further with Yōmeigaku. That is, ethics was more than just its driving spirit. Yōmeigaku for Inoue was "ethics and nothing else."[69] Inoue presented a view of "intuitive knowledge" (ryōchi), a central conception in Yōmei thought, as intuitively apprehended moral knowledge, thus he closely aligned this concept with his own concept of universal virtue (shintoku).

A writer under the pseudonym "Tengaisei" took issue with Inoue for his depiction of Yōmeigaku and "intuitive knowledge." Inoue, writing in the bimonthly journal Yōmeigaku, claimed that Yōmei's disciples eventually began to investigate things outside of ethics, but since this took them outside the scope of what Yōmeigaku, as a form of ethical study, could rightly address, they were at times at a loss for answers. Responding to this claim, Inoue's anonymous critic stated, "Professor Inoue understands intuitive knowledge simply as the virtue [toku] of each individual's heart [kokoro]... but intuitive knowledge is not such a limited thing.... [O]f course, clarifying the virtue of the human heart is a matter of intuitive knowledge, but this is true of grass, trees, roof tiles and stones as well—there is nothing that is not based upon the operation of intuitive knowledge."[70] The point here is not for us to discern the "correct" interpretation of "intuitive knowledge," but rather that Inoue saw in Yōmeigaku, particularly in its doctrine of intuitive knowledge, a compelling teaching for the cultivation and clarification of the virtue of the human heart.

Finally, and perhaps most importantly, Inoue drew upon Yōmeigaku because it was best suited to disrupt and subvert the civilizational hierarchies of kaika and the epistemology of representation. This epistemology was one that objectified nature, upholding a dichotomy or dualism between the human realm and the realm of nature. Nature's laws were apprehended through experience and by observing the external world. This was the epistemology that Inoue sought to undermine. But many of these epistemological features he attributed to Shushigaku as well. This is clear from the way Inoue distinguished Shushi-gaku from Yōmeigaku.

In contrast to the government-sponsored educational style of Shushi-gaku, Inoue explained, Yōmei is directed toward the commoners of society and guided by private scholars. In addition, Shushigaku calls for extensive learn-ing, and from this derives rules for moral action, while Yōmei views moral action itself as a kind of learning. Further, Shushigaku interprets the world through a principle-matter *(ri-ki)* dualism, while Yōmeigaku asserts that *ri* and *ki* are inseparable, hence it upholds a *ri-ki* monism. In Shushi thought, Inoue continued, the mind or heart *(kokoro)* is divided up into *ri* and *ki*. But for Yōmeigaku, "the human heart is precisely *ri* and nothing else. If one can attain clarity of *kokoro*," Inoue emphasized, "*ri* becomes clear on its own. For this reason, it is not necessary for Yōmeigaku to widely investigate things of the external world so as to clarify *ri*. The important point lies simply in the clari-fication of the human heart." Moreover, for Shushigaku, *ri* is clarified through experience, reflecting a "tendency toward empiricism," while Yōmeigaku, by contrast, is disposed toward idealism *(yuishinron,* literally "the theory of only *kokoro*")* because truthful knowledge lies within the heart. Finally, Shushigaku calls upon one first to "know" and then to "act," whereas Yōmeigaku does not discuss which precedes the other, knowledge or action, but asserts an identity of knowledge and action. "Thus Shushigaku esteems the study of principles [*gakuri*], while Yōmeigaku values action."[71]

Inoue's comparison of Yōmeigaku and Shushigaku indicates the former's greater potential as a means to subvert *kaika* and its epistemology. Shushigaku as described here in many ways resembles the epistemology of representa-tion that Inoue contested. Both rely upon observation and "a tendency toward empiricism" to acquire knowledge of the external world (thus both possessed a kind of subject-object dichotomy). Both prioritize *gakuri* (the study of scientific principles, perhaps also interpreted as "academic reason" as the term *gakuri* was commonly opposed to "emotion," or *kanjō*) as a means to knowledge. Inoue's representation of "the ethics of the West" (which prioritizes intellectual pur-suits that reveal fixed moral principles, which *thereafter* provide the basis for moral action)[72] sounds remarkably similar to the Shushigaku described above (in which one first "knows" and then "acts"). Thus, the monistic and idealistic Yōmeigaku differed from both Shushigaku and the epistemology of representa-tion in that it looked inward to the heart for moral truth, rather than out toward the principles of some external world.

Moreover, Inoue was critical not only of the Shushi School; the Ancient Studies School of Confucianism (Kogaku) also had deficiencies. In his study of this school, Inoue frequently aligned Kogaku thinkers with utilitarianism.

Ogyū Sorai (1666–1728), for example, was "attached to utilitarianism." In addition, Inoue criticized Sorai for failing to adapt his "Chinese-style" thought to Japan. "The Ancient Studies of Sorai most of all had a Chinese style," Inoue complained, "so much so that one may well ask where the Japanese features were." And while Inoue praised Yamaga Sokō (1622–1685) as the most "Japanified" of Kogaku thinkers because notions of *kokutai*, Shinto, and reverence for the emperor figured prominently in his works, he too tended toward utilitarianism. Given Inoue's overwhelmingly negative assessment of utilitarianism, the Kogaku School did not provide the most suitable teachings for the cultivation of *shintoku*.[73]

Despite the shortcomings Inoue saw in Shushigaku and Kogaku, however, he by no means advocated the study of Yōmeigaku to the exclusion of these other two schools; these teachings had also contributed to the historical development of Japan's moral spirit. The Shushi School, for example, once introduced to Japan from China, was transformed and "improved." Inoue emphasized that the dualism of Chinese Shushigaku could not possibly be the end point for philosophy; oppositions had to be transcended to attain a new synthesis. Japanese followers of this school gradually came to reject such dualisms, positing instead a unity of principle and matter (*ri* and *ki*) reflecting a monistic view of the universe. "There can be no doubt," Inoue proclaimed, "that this was a sign of philosophical progress."[74] Inoue also depicted the Shushi School as "completely contrary to utilitarianism." He saw in its emphasis on self-cultivation a parallel with personalism's completion of the personality *(jinkaku kansei)*. "As for the morality of the Shushi School, although it differs in form, in spirit it is running on nearly an identical track with the current so-called theory of self-realization. Shushigaku and the statements of Green and Muirhead of the British Neo-Kantian School are often as two sides of the same coin." Here, Inoue suggested that the Shushi School of Confucianism was in no way inferior to the ethics of personalism popularized by Nakashima. In addition, Inoue's account of the evolution and "progress" of the school once it entered Japan reveals his concern with situating Japanese ethics at the top of a developmental hierarchy within the space of "the Orient."

Thus, while the quiet and contemplative form of Yōmeigaku held a privileged position over Shushigaku and Kogaku in Inoue's thought, Inoue never advocated the single-minded pursuit of Yōmei studies at the expense of other forms of Confucianism. His primary concern in his studies of Japan's past ethical thought was the cultivation of "the virtue of the human heart" *(shintoku)*, and for this Yōmeigaku was the most suitable. Cultivating the heart was also his concern in his textbooks for moral training.[75] Yet inasmuch as Shushigaku and Kogaku contributed to the production of Japan's moral spirit as well, Inoue, in his *Compendium of Japanese Ethics* project, gathered texts from all three Confucian schools in an effort to systematize Japanese ethics.

But Inoue was not alone in this effort. A similar effort was underway in various intellectual journals. The publishers of the journal *Shushigaku*, for example, stated their aims in the following way.

> We hear that Western scholars are currently establishing a field called "Oriental Philosophy" and investigating Oriental learning. If we do not immediately begin the study of the Oriental disciplines ourselves, Westerners will absorb them, carrying them off for their own benefit and leaving us, their originators, as mere bystanders. To avoid this disturbing prospect, we have begun publication of this journal and plan to gradually bring together here the morality, philosophy, poetry, literature, history, law, economics and other Oriental learning based upon the Shushi spirit of the investigation of things and the extension of knowledge.[76]

Like Inoue, the editors of this journal clearly saw themselves as the caretakers of "Oriental thought." Other journals, such as *Yōmeigaku,* conducted this same kind of systemization and collection of Tokugawa texts. Through the collection of past Confucian texts, Inoue and others sought to create the field of Oriental thought so as to check the universalizing force of "Western scholarship." Unlike proponents of one specific school of thought (such as the editors of *Shushigaku* or *Yōmeigaku*), Inoue's ultimate goal was not the absolute legitimation of Yōmeigaku alone, or even "Oriental thought," but rather the synthesis of the moralities of both "Orient" and "Occident."

Indeed, Inoue never called for the complete rejection of Western moral theory. As shown, he was deeply opposed to utilitarianism, but believed that Western moral theory had other viable alternatives. He did, however, emphasize the complexity and diversity of Western moral views, which raised the question, "Which to rely upon?" "The more we study these theories," Inoue pointed out, "the more puzzled we are likely to become." In *A Compendium of Japanese Ethics,* he asserted that since Japan must choose among the various Western moral theories, it should choose something that is both "correct" and "appropriate" for Japan. And for Inoue, the moral views of Kant and Hegel were best, but it would be necessary to harmonize and unify these views with Japan's own traditional moral principles.[77]

Inoue argued that the moral philosophy of Kant and Hegel had a great deal in common at a fundamental level with the morality of Japan. So much so, Inoue affirmed, that nothing could be removed from Japanese ethics that should not also be removed from Hegelian or Kantian ethics, and any positive quality adopted from the latter must also be adopted from the former, because the same fundamental qualities existed in both systems, Japanese and Occidental. Thus, Inoue aimed to place Japanese ethics on an equal footing with that of Hegel and Kant. Whereas Nakashima accepted the idea that certain aspects of Japan's national character had to be abandoned or overcome, and that Japan revealed its moral inferiority in its lack of cooperation and underdeveloped sense of personality, Inoue rejected such a position. The ethics of the Occident and the Orient were equally important and valuable.

For the study of ethics, Inoue argued, we require both "inquiry into scientific principles," the methodology that characterized the scholarship of the Occident, and the "cultivation of the virtue of the human heart" as in Japan. Neither, Inoue insisted, must be abandoned; the two needed to be brought together and unified.[78] Such a merging was natural, Inoue argued, because "Western civilization was initially imported from the Orient. Then, that civilization gradually spread outward, eventually extending to America . . . and finally came in contact with our country."

But bringing together the ethics of the Occident and the Orient meant "an abrupt collision," an interaction Inoue compared to the crossing of positively and negatively charged electric poles. The resulting conflict, however, simply indicated the "origination of a future morality." When the moralities of the Orient and Occident are brought together, taking the good points of each, Inoue maintained, "we will certainly realize a great morality unprecedented in past and present."[79]

Yet, Inoue pointed out, the world was already well familiar with the works of Europe's moral philosophers. The history of Japan's ethical thought, however, was virtually unknown in the world. "It would be deplorable," Inoue stated, "to keep secret something that holds the world's aspirations concerning moral education."[80] It was with the aim, then, to "fulfill the aspirations of moral education in the world" that Inoue systematized documents concerning ethics from Japan's past.

Self-as-Other: The Ethics of Spirit and the Broader Intellectual Context

Despite substantial differences in terms of their methodological approach to ethics, philosophers of personalism like Nakashima Rikizō and those like Inoue Tetsujirō concerned with Japanese particularity shared an opposition to the ethics of "civilization." More than this, however, their own presuppositions about knowledge, the person, and nature reflect an opposition to the epistemology that informed and enabled notions of hierarchical civilization. In other words, in contrast to the epistemology of representation that underlay ethical discourse during the first decades of Meiji, the ethical thought of both Nakashima and Inoue was rooted in a "hylomorphic" epistemology wherein dualisms such as the opposition between subject and object, self and other, are collapsed.[81] This is clear in Nakashima's view of absolute spirit and individual consciousness. It is also evident in Inoue's emphasis on the Yōmei concept of the identity of knowledge and action *(chikō goitsu)*.[82] The breadth of this epistemology, the extent to which it shaped not only moral discourse but the wider intellectual landscape of this period as well, can be gauged by its presence in the thought of those outside the field of academic ethics.

The thought of Buddhist historian Murakami Senshō followed the above-described epistemological shift from subject-object dichotomy to unity. Murakami, who in his 1888 publication *A New Discourse on Buddhist Morality* emphasized "karma" as the essence of Buddhist morality, focused in the mid-1890s on the idea of "no-self." His earlier view was an attempt to legitimize Buddhist morality by linking the Buddhist doctrine of cause and effect (*ingasetsu*, or karma) to the "scientific" law of cause and effect (also *ingasetsu*) that authorized *rinrigaku*'s evolutionist theories of this time. His later emphasis on no-self, however, reflects the redeployment of an old Buddhist concept marginalized in his earlier work, one that insists the opposition between self and other is false.

In "The Buddhist Theory of Anātman" (Bukkyō muga ron, 1896) Murakami asserted, "Buddhism arrives at truth through the idea of no-self."[83] As in his earlier work, Murakami maintained his interest in moral issues. He asked, "On what basis are we to establish a standard for good and evil, demarcate a boundary between delusion and wisdom, and distinguish illusion from enlightenment? Only through the two paths of *yūga* [self] and *muga* [no-self]." But the former alternative *(yūga)* represented "delusion" and "evil," while *muga*, on the other hand, Murakami described as "enlightenment" *(satori)*: "it is wisdom, it is good." In the end, Murakami asserted, "one must conclude that Buddhism from head to tail is a teaching of the doctrine of no-self, a teaching that attains the truth through the idea of no-self."[84] Thus, in this 1896 text, a doctrine denying the opposition between self and other is the essence of Buddhism and the only viable path for adjudicating moral action.

It is significant that this work on no-self emerged when it did. In this text, the doctrine of no-self is of central importance for Murakami's position on morality. The distinction between good and evil is established on the basis of no-self. In Murakami's earlier text, *A New Discourse on Buddhist Morality,* however, *muga* was hardly a central concern for Murakami, if, indeed, it was a concern at all. The term *muga* is listed nowhere in the twelve section headings of the introduction to this work. Nor does the term appear in any of this work's six chapter headings, thirty-four section headings, or twenty-eight item listings. Rather, Murakami understood *ingasetsu* (cause and effect, or the doctrine of karma) to be the starting point for discussions of moral foundations. Thus, the change in his view reflects the broader shift to a hylomorphic epistemology.

A similar monistic emphasis can be seen in the Confucian doctrine emphasizing a unity between human beings and nature *(tenjin goitsu)*. This doctrine received little emphasis in the 1880s among scholars of morality. But as the notion of subject-as-object gained ground through the works of scholars of personalism, the idea of *tenjin goitsu* could be legitimately reactivated within a new context. Uchida Kanehira, in an article titled "The Person and the Great Ultimate" (Hito to taikyoku), posited heaven *(ten)* as the foundation for morality, but made it clear that his notion of heaven was quite different from that of "religionists." Uchida associated "heaven" with the Confucian notion of the "Great Ultimate"—"a comprehensive name for the ten thousand principles." He argued for the doctrine of heaven-human unity. "Heaven is endowed with humanity, and humanity is nothing other than heaven.... [T]his is called *tenjin goitsu*."[85] Here again is the presupposition of subject-object unity.

Oyanagi Shiketaka, another Confucian scholar, compared T. H. Green's ethics of self-realization to the ethics of Confucianism and found a great many similarities. He argued that the "original nature" of the self in the theory of self-realization and its assertion that the "divine spirit" manifested itself within the finite body of the person bore a remarkable resemblance to the Shushi view of the absolute, according to which "our spirit is precisely the effect of the Great Ultimate [*taikyoku*]." Thus, both personalism and Confucianism in Oyanagi's account linked the individual and the natural world. But he noted that the school of self-realization continued to speak of the "relationship" between the natural world and humanity, conceiving of the former as object *(kyaku)* and the latter as subject *(shu)*. For Oyanagi, this still reflected a degree of dualism despite self-realization theory's view that the two were as one. Nevertheless, Oyanagi drew upon the authority of Green's personalism to authorize his Confucian view of ethics and to contest evolutionary views of morality. Because the good, Oyanagi argued, is a matter of cultivating one's innate spirit, the idea that moral progress is simply the result of "changes in environmental conditions, as the evolutionists claim" must be false. He concluded by calling for the development of a "new Confucianism" to ensure the continued prosperity of the nation and to serve as an ethical theory belonging solely to the Orient.[86]

Like Inoue, the publishers of the journal *Yōmeigaku* were responding to "the moral decline of recent years." The object of their reform efforts was "the spiritual realm of Japan," or more specifically, "the spirit of the people" (*kokumin no seishin,* or *fūki*). Since the basis of society is the heart *(kokoro)* of the individual, they argued, the best means must be sought for its cultivation, and there was no better school of thought for this purpose than Yōmeigaku. Their arguments show a reliance on the authoritative concepts of the day. The cultivation of the heart, for example, they sometimes linked to the realization of personality. In addition, statements concerning the unity of the individual and the social whole (e.g., "The spirit [*seishin*] of one person is the same as the spirit of ten million people") resemble those made by personalist philosophers of this time. The publishers of this journal linked the "fortitude of one person's spirit" with the morale of the entire nation, and in this way joined the propagation of Yōmeigaku with the promotion of the nation's welfare.[87]

Finally, the late Meiji philosophy of Nishida Kitarō also reflects this shift. In a discussion of spirit, Nishida stated, "We usually distinguish mental phenomena and material phenomena in terms of internal and external, thinking of the former as internal and the latter as external. But this kind of thinking emerges through the arbitrary assumption that sprit is within the body. When seen from the perspective of direct experience, all things share an identity as phenomena of consciousness and there is no distinction between internal and external."[88] Nishida too, then, collapses the opposition between the internal and the external, subject and object.

These various viewpoints described above all insisted upon some kind of unity between self and other. Certainly this view was not unheard of during the first decades of the Meiji period, but it was by no means dominant. By the early to mid-1890s, however, this hylomorphic epistemology informed *rinrigaku* scholarship and the thinking of intellectuals outside of academia as well. "Spirit" was the pivotal component that allowed for such an epistemology, and thus it was spirit that transformed moral discourse toward the end of the nineteenth century.

Conclusions: Relocating the Universal

Spirit reshaped the intellectual and moral landscape of Japan in the final decade of the nineteenth century. Spirit, centering on the metaphysical, the intuitive, and the human interiority, provided a powerful formula with which to contest both the inferior status assigned to Japan within the hierarchical framework of "civilization" *(kaika),* as well as the epistemology that enabled this framework. Moreover, it played a central role in the thought of moral philosophers Nakashima Rikizō and Inoue Tetsujirō. While Nakashima's ethics of personalism relied upon the notion of "absolute and infinite spirit," Inoue's pivotal concept of *shintoku,* the virtue of the human heart, was equated with the moral spirit of the Japanese people. Further, both Nakashima and Inoue developed their ethical thought from within the essentializing discourse on national character, but they engaged with it in different ways. Nakashima's appropriation of national character discourse and the notion of "infinite spirit" that informed his ethics, though not without the potential to subvert civilizational hierarchies, nevertheless functioned to reinforce them. Inoue, on the other hand, made use of national character and spirit in such a way as to subvert assertions of Western civilizational and moral superiority.

Nakashima's goal was the cultivation of "personality," that is, the self-conscious awareness of one's own individuality. This required that the individual be able to set his or her own ends and pursue them within a society that ensured equality, liberty, and respect for oneself and others. Nakashima, however, accepted personality as a measure of civilized society; Japan's underdeveloped sense of personality, therefore, implied civilizational inferiority. Inoue's aim was to create an essentialized moral spirit of Japan through the study and appropriation of Japan's moral past, in particular various schools of Confucian thought. While each school, Inoue believed, had contributed in some way to the development of Japan's moral spirit, the Yōmei School best suited his notion of *shintoku* and provided the best means for subverting the epistemology of representation that enabled *kaika* discourse.

Destabilizing or circumventing the universalizing force and authority of *kaika* discourse for both these thinkers involved the relocation of "the universal." In place of objective universal laws of nature as the ultimate foundation for the good, Nakashima asserted the universality of spirit. Absolute spirit, the ultimate moral ground and the ideal toward which good action aspired, manifested itself through the finite consciousness of each individual. Inoue and others, who viewed this "absolute spirit" as a synonym for the Christian God, believed Nakashima's personalism had completely disregarded the ethics of Japan. For Inoue, the virtue of the human heart was a universal value, one that had been cultivated in the Orient, and above all in Japan, but had yet to take hold in the Occident. Even the assertion of moral particularity (of the Orient, of Japan), then, required the legitimizing authority of the universal.

Moreover, there was a shift in the ways these universal foundations were manifested. In the case of the ethics of civilization, the universal manifested itself in uniform, constant ways (through the trappings of civilization, the fruits of universal knowledge such as canons, ships, etc., and through a "civilized" social order) and thus permitted a hierarchical framework of civilization in which all societies, if they survived, would follow the same path of development as the civilized societies of the West. In the case of spirit, however, this universal manifested itself in particular ways. Each society, in accordance with its own historical, geographical, linguistic, and cultural conditions, developed its own unique national character, a reflection of the spirit of its people, òr *Volksgeist*. The "national spirit" in Inoue's estimation displaced the universalizing claims of occidental civilization and even the eternal and infinite spirit of personalism, which to him resembled Christianity's God. In short, there was a shift from a universal manifested in universal ways to a universal spirit manifested through the particular national form.

Efforts by non-Western societies to contest the Occident and assert "national spirit" are central concerns in many works of postcolonial theory. Partha Chatterjee, for example, argues that anti-colonial nationalism "divide[s] the world of social institutions and practices into two domains—the material and the spiritual. The material is the domain of the 'outside,' of the economy and of statecraft, of science and technology, a domain where the West had proved its superiority and the East had succumbed." He describes the spiritual as "an 'inner' domain bearing the 'essential' marks of cultural identity. The greater one's success in imitating Western skills in the material domain, therefore, the greater the need to preserve the distinctness of one's spiritual culture."[89] Ostensibly, this is a realm, according to the non-Western societies that posit them, beyond the grasp of the West. While Chatterjee's analysis centers on anti-colonial nationalism, it is nevertheless useful in interpreting late nineteenth-century Japan. Inoue did indeed turn to what he called Japan's "spiritual realm" in an effort to establish Japan's authentic moral particularity. Of course, it was hardly beyond the grasp of the West; indeed, Japan constituted this "spiritual realm" (the folk spirit) through an appropriation of Euro-American intellectual currents.[90] Nevertheless, Chatterjee's framework should be taken neither as inevitable nor as universal, nor again, of course, as a theoretical endorsement to pursue one's desire for an authentic spiritual realm uncontaminated by the "outside." The genealogy of the late Meiji conception of "spirit" *(seishin)* suggests that spirit, in its varied forms, was by no means part of an "uncontaminated inner realm"; rather, it shows a close connection to early nineteenth-century German Romanticism and to mid-to-late nineteenth-century British idealism. Meiji intellectuals, moreover, were not unaware of this genealogy and the "spiritual" potential in European thought. The "West" was neither simply material or spiritual. It did not present itself as a uniform object. Thus, we find Okakura Kakuzō, who helped to produce "Japanese art" in much the same way that Inoue and others produced "Japanese ethics," asking,

> Where is the essence of the West [Ōbei] in the countries of Europe and America? All these countries have different systems; what is right in one

country is wrong in the rest; religion, customs, morals—there is no common agreement on any of these. Europe is discussed in a general way, and this sounds splendid; the question remains, where in reality does what is called "Europe" exist![91]

Okakura and others such as journalist Kuga Katsunan put forward this critique of an essentialized Occident in order to argue for diversity and for the particularity of each nation. Yet while they represented an undifferentiated and unitary "West" as a problematic category, the essentialized view of "the Occident" was too powerful and too useful to be abandoned. It allowed for the positing of "the Orient," a space of particularity within which Japan could assert moral superiority. This contradictory need for a West that was at once essential and fragmented reflects Japan's desire to be a part of a larger oriental civilization and at the same time to differentiate itself from other oriental societies.

In the foregoing chapters of this volume I have examined the role of "the universal" in the production, legitimation, and dissemination of various normative orientations associated with *rinrigaku*. In the present chapter, for the most part, the focus has been on Japan's engagement with the moral philosophy of the Occident as it sought to destabilize or circumvent the universalizing force of civilization, or *kaika*. But subverting the putatively universal underpinnings of *kaika*, in the thought of both Nakashima and Inoue, ended in the relocation of the universal. Even Inoue, as he sought to establish the moral particularity of Japan, was unable to forgo the legitimizing authority of the universal. Finally, while "the ethics of spirit" examined here (both Nakashima's ethics of "absolute spirit" and Inoue's "virtue of the human heart") relied upon a hylomorphic epistemology deeply opposed to dualisms, emerging at this time was the paradigmatic dualism of Orient and Occident. This suggests, perhaps, the impossibility of thinking or positing universality without simultaneously thinking or creating particularity.

In the chapter that follows, my focus turns away from Japan's engagement with the Occident and returns to the domestic social conditions intertwined with moral discourse in Japan. As personalism became increasingly marginalized, efforts to establish moral particularity intensified. The struggle to create an essentialized "Japanese" morality through the exclusion of alternative moral possibilities came together at the close of the Meiji period in an authoritative discourse called "national morality."

CHAPTER 5

Approaching the Moral Ideal

National Morality, the State, and
"Dangerous Thought"

There are those, like the treasonous group that was punished this
year, who embrace dangerous thought...the kind of unhealthy
thought that opposes or destroys national morality.... [But] as
long as we use national morality to regulate Japanese society, the
continued existence of the Japanese people is assured.
—Inoue Tetsujirō, *An Outline of National Morality*

People say that anarchism is a poison that comes from the mouths
of traitors and that it is an extremely evil and dangerous doctrine. I
do not know what they mean by traitors and rebels.... The society
that the great doctrine and spirit of anarcho-communism points to
is a society...which, by striving for the happiness and advantage
of everyone, will encourage the progress and improvement of
humankind.
—Sakamoto Seima, *A Word on Joining the Group*

The Taoist classic *Tao te ching* observes, "[W]hen the state is
in confusion, it is then that there are faithful subjects."[1] Such a statement might
well be describing turn-of-the-century moral discourse in Japan. At this time,
while the "dangerous thought" of anarchism, socialism, and individualism
threatened to undermine the foundation of the state, various state apparatuses
sought through a number of strategies to produce "good and faithful subjects." In
other words, "dangerous thought" and the "faithful subject" emerged together,
the one providing the negative condition against which the other was conceptualized and defined. National morality *(kokumin dōtoku)*, a state-sponsored
articulation of a "unique Japanese morality," was a central feature in efforts to
cultivate faithful subjects while suppressing dangerous thought.

National morality emerged as the dominant form of moral inquiry among *rinrigaku* academics in early twentieth-century Japan. During the decade that followed the 1912 publication of *An Outline of National Morality (Kokumin dōtoku gairon)* by Inoue Tetsujirō, a pivotal figure in this discourse, more than fifty scholarly works on national morality were published.[2] In his *Outline of National Morality,* Inoue discussed loyalty to the state, filiality to one's parents, the notion of the state as a "family," and other concepts that had been associated with national morality discourse from the turn of the century or before. And while "loyalty," "filiality," and the "family-state" were certainly key terms in national morality texts, contemporary accounts of national morality focus on these terms as its "defining elements" and, as a result, miss much that is important. National morality discourse was not merely a collection of statements on loyalty, filiality, and so on. When placed in its philosophical and sociopolitical contexts, national morality can be seen as an effort to configure the good as the pursuit of a moral ideal. Approaching this ideal involved the universalization of a state-centered normative orientation and the suppression of dangerous thought.

National morality functioned as an apparatus of the state working together with a network of bureaucratic institutions to produce a moral community of subjects perfectly loyal to the state. But equally central to national morality discourse was its strong opposition to a diverse set of intellectual positions— including socialism, anarchism, individualism, and literary naturalism—which it collectively represented as "dangerous thought." Not only national morality scholars, but also bureaucrats, legal scholars, politicians, and others warned that such dangerous thought jeopardized the existence of the state. National morality, then, can be seen as one aspect of a broader discourse to sustain and increase the authority of the state, to create homogeneous subjects all equally patriotic and equally loyal to the state on the one hand, and to suppress the disorder and divisiveness of dangerous thought on the other.

The various state apparatuses that endeavored to bring about loyalty, order, and unity produced and attempted to universalize a broad state-centered normative space—one asserting that the survival of the state was paramount and that the needs of the state therefore had to take precedence over individual needs. National morality scholars, arguing that the continued existence of the state was a requisite for the moral development of the individual, played a central role in the production, legitimation, and dissemination of this space. In other words, national morality did more than seek to universalize its own abstract and explicitly moral claims; it contributed to the universalization of this broad normative space and its prioritization of the state.

Scholars of national morality articulated this state-centered space in moral terms. That is, just as the legal structure of the state legislated this normative space, the police and military enforced it sometimes violently, educators disseminated it pedagogically, and various government ministries appropriated the figure of the emperor to represent this space symbolically, national morality scholars articulated this space in moral-philosophical terms. Through the conception of the "good" that it developed, national morality produced a moral-philosophical justification for the state's insistence on loyalty and its suppression of dangerous thought. In this way, national morality discourse legitimized the state's use of open, physical violence for establishing order and cultivating action that served the state; indeed, national morality, in its suppression of the alterity of the other through discursive strategies, was itself violent.[3]

Inoue Tetsujirō in his *Outline of National Morality* and the majority of scholars of this subject that came after him posited the good as the "approach" toward an ideal. Though coded in the philosophical jargon of personalism discussed in the preceding chapter, this ideal signified complete moral homogeneity—a community of subjects perfectly loyal to the state. That which facilitated the approach toward this aim constituted "the good," while whatever inhibited or obstructed this aim was "evil." In national morality discourse, then, an individual's actions were truly good only when they corresponded to the good of the state. Conversely, the "dangerous thought" of anarchism, socialism, individualism, and literary naturalism represented obstacles on the path toward the ideal and thus could legitimately be suppressed as social evils. National morality appropriated still powerful conceptions of loyalty and filiality from Japan's pre-revolutionary past and fused them with new conceptions of the person and the state developed within philosophical idealism to produce an argument legitimizing the state's efforts to cultivate the loyal subject and suppress or annihilate obstacles in the path of this goal. This particular formulation of national morality, appearing for the first time in Inoue's *Outline of National Morality,* represented a subtle but important reconfiguration of the discourse. This chapter addresses the following questions: How was such a reconfiguration of national morality possible and why did it take place when it did? What exactly was dangerous about "dangerous thought" and how did it come to occupy such a central position in Inoue's conception of the good? Finally, what strategies did national morality deploy for the suppression of dangerous thought and how were these resisted?

The passage from the *Tao te ching* cited above refers to a space of non-differentiation—the "One" or the "Tao"—that had been lost or rejected. Once outside of this space, distinctions emerge: good and evil, order and disorder, faithful and unfaithful subjects. National morality also posited such a space, but unlike this lost antiquity of Taoism, it lay in the ever-receding future, approachable but never finally attainable. Recognizing the unattainability of its ideal, national morality nevertheless sought to "approach" the ideal through the universalization of the state-centered normative space it helped to produce and through the annihilation of its other, "dangerous thought." National morality and its other, however, were inextricably bound to one another, each taking on meaning in opposition to the other. The "loyalty" of the loyal subject took on its significance precisely in opposition to dangerous thought, or, conversely, dangerous thought was "dangerous" only inasmuch as it encouraged defiance of (i.e., disloyalty to) the state and the moral position it sponsored. National morality could never bring about the complete annihilation of dangerous thought without changing or perhaps annihilating itself in the process. In this sense, the tension between national morality and dangerous thought was marked by a desire to annihilate on the one hand and a need to sustain on the other. In short, national morality was constrained to stop short of the complete annihilation of dangerous thought—to check, to control, but not finally to erase it. The discourse on national morality in Japan, then, reveals a close connection between the pursuit of the moral ideal and violence. It was the state's pursuit of this ideal that sustained the very social reality it sought to transcend, one of moral disarray, dissension, and violence.

Interpreting National Morality

In 1911 the Ministry of Education, as part of the state's efforts to create loyal subjects, appointed Inoue Tetsujirō to give a series of lectures on national morality. Lecturing in the summer of that year, Inoue criticized the unquestioned adherence many in Japan showed to the ethical theories of the West, arguing that an investigation and cultivation of the unique moral sensibilities of the Japanese people was of paramount importance in the effort to forge national unity and protect the state. He described national morality as "an expression of the [Japanese] folk spirit" *(minzoku teki seishin)* and urged his fellow academics to devote more attention to the study not only of Japan's national morality, but of the development of its folk spirit as well. Here, Inoue's statements on morality as an outward manifestation of the folk's inner spirit reflect the "national character" discourse prevalent at this time and suggest a blurring of the terms *kokumin* and *minzoku.*[4]

Kokumin dōtoku was a morality of the Japanese *kokumin,* the people living together under the authority of the same state. National morality's architects chose this term to describe their project rather than *minzoku,* a term that came to be used more frequently by late Meiji and signaled a kind of cultural grouping, a people sharing "common customs, values, language, and race." As a morality of the *kokumin,* then, national morality was clearly a state-sponsored morality demanding order and obedience from its subjects. Its concern was to suppress "dangerous thought" and to cultivate dutiful action within Japan. But national morality was nevertheless legitimized as a morality of the folk *(min-zoku);* the values of loyalty and filiality, for example, were not represented (in textbooks on moral training, in the Imperial Rescript on Education) as recent constructs imposed by the state to regulate society but as timeless tradition handed down by Japan's ancestors and articulated by Japan's emperor. More-over, national morality discourse presented "Japan's values" as distinct from those of other societies, both "Occidental" and "Oriental." National morality scholars, therefore, contributed to the production of narratives of identity in order to legitimize the moral demands of the state. In this sense, the discourse on national morality concerned both *kokumin* and *minzoku;* it was a morality for both "state-subjects" and "the folk."

In his discussion of Japan's morality, Inoue placed particular emphasis on patriotism, ancestor worship, and the virtues of loyalty and filial piety. Loyalty to the emperor (the father figure of the "family-state") was to be expressed in the same way one expressed filiality toward one's parents, hence the recurrent call for loyalty-as-filiality *(chūkō ippon)* in national morality texts by Inoue and others. In this way the metaphor of the state as a "family" was used to evoke patriotic thought and practice. Further, Inoue invoked the Imperial Rescript on Education of 1890, discussed in the previous chapter, as a foundational text for national morality, calling this education rescript "the sacred book of Meiji" and "the essence of Japan's national morality." "Within it," stated Inoue, "are listed all of those things considered to be the important points of national morality."[5] In short, Inoue reiterated many of the same points of national morality that were part of the discourse up to that time.

Contemporary works on national morality commonly list patriotism, loy-alty and filiality, ancestor worship, and the "family-state" as its defining ele-ments. To be sure, these were all central terms in national morality discourse, but the meaning of these terms was contested. Nevertheless, contemporary studies of national morality depict it as an essential object with fixed character-istics. This enables their methodologically problematic search for the "origin" of national morality. That is, if national morality has an essence that remains unchanged over time, then according to these studies, it must have an origin, and until this origin is located and explained, the national morality movement will not be fully understood.

In their concern to locate the "original statement" of national morality, con-temporary accounts have focused on a variety of texts and thinkers. Although a number of writings on *kokumin dōtoku* appeared in the years between the

1890 Imperial Rescript and 1911, Inoue's 1912 *Outline of National Morality* is often viewed as the formative statement on national morality. Indeed, this work offered a more comprehensive and detailed analysis of the subject than any prior text. Moreover, it initiated an upsurge in scholarly writings on the subject of national morality, no doubt in part due to its close affiliation with the Ministry of Education and its official state authorization. Such considerations may explain philosopher Funayama Shinichi's claim in his 1956 work on Japan's idealist philosophers that it was Inoue who established national morality, that he was the "originator" of this discourse.[6] But of course, Inoue was not the first to emphasize the family system, ancestor worship, and loyalty to the state. Moreover, the term *kokumin dōtoku* had been a part of moral discourse at least since the late 1880s. With these points in mind, others have sought to pinpoint the origin of national morality in the late nineteenth century.

Fukasaku Yasubumi, moral philosopher (from 1912) and chair of the ethics department (from 1926 until 1935) at Tokyo Imperial University, traced the beginnings of national morality to Nishimura Shigeki. In his *Essence of National Morality* (*Kokumin dōtoku yōgi*, 1916), Fukasaku stated that the term *kokumin dōtoku* first appeared in Nishimura's 1886 work *On Japanese Morality* (*Nihon dōtoku ron*). Similarly, moral philosopher Yoshida Kumaji concluded, "Nishimura must truly be viewed as the founder of academic national morality in our country."[7] Kōsaka Masaaki, in a similar pursuit of national morality's origins, emphasized that the various elements of national morality thought— loyalty and filiality, the family-state, the "unbroken" imperial line, and so forth—can be found in the writings of legal scholar Hozumi Yatsuka from the early 1890s. But there are fundamental problems with these views and their methodological approaches.

Implied in such a methodology is a sense that a subject cannot be fully explained until its origins and causes are known. This, however, is to presuppose national morality as a coherent whole, as an essential object with a fixed set of features such as the above-mentioned "elements" of loyalty, patriotism, family-state, and so on, that remain unchanged over time. As a result, these contemporary studies of national morality are often blind to important shifts in the meanings the term *kokumin dōtoku* conveyed and to changes in the intellectual context within which *kokumin dōtoku* was constituted.

Although both Nishimura and Hozumi must be considered participants in the discourse on national morality (provided this is understood broadly as part of the state's efforts to cultivate loyalty in its subjects), their views emerged out of different intellectual and social contexts. Nishimura's argument for a "Japanese morality" rested on a framework differentiating this-worldly teachings (including Confucianism and Western philosophy) from otherworldly teachings such as Buddhism, Shinto, and Christianity. He asserted that the morality suitable for Japan was one based not on religion but on the secular teachings of Confucianism supplemented by Western philosophy. In this sense, the object of his critique was not anarchism or individualism (as was the case with the national morality of the 1910s), but rather the "otherworldly teachings" of Buddhism and Christianity. As for Hozumi, his conceptions of loyalty, filiality, and patriotism were justified through an argument concerning "the great principle of ancestor worship" in a way quite different from the philosophical foundation created for national morality in the 1910s.[8] Thus, *kokumin dōtoku* was by no means a semantically transparent term signifying the same object and carrying the same meaning regardless of the context within which it appeared. The statements on national morality by Nishimura and Hozumi must be situated in their own contexts, and the same is true for Inoue's lectures in 1911.

Inoue's 1911 discussion of national morality, published the following year as *An Outline of National Morality,* did more than simply reiterate the elements of loyalty, filiality, and so on, that had in some form been a part of moral discourse from the 1890s. It initiated a subtle but important reconfiguration of the discourse on national morality. Inoue attempted to reground national morality and its demand for loyal subjects through the construction of a new foundation for its claims, one drawing on the metaphysics of personalism. In short, Inoue's *Outline of National Morality* represented neither a smooth continuation of national morality discourse nor this discourse's "original statement." Rather, it marked a shift in the discourse.

The search for the original statement of national morality in contemporary accounts is possible only because of their treatment of this shifting discourse as an essentialized object with certain "definitive characteristics." And this formalizing method can be maintained only by ignoring important shifts in the intellectual context out of which statements on national morality emerged. Inoue Tetsujirō's 1911 lecture series on national morality is an example of such a statement where attention to its philosophical and sociopolitical context is particularly important. It is at this time that national morality begins to co-opt the philosophy of personalism to legitimize the suppression of "dangerous thought."

The Philosophical Context: National Morality and Personalism

Particularly lacking in contemporary studies of national morality is any treatment of its connections with personalism, described above as a form of philosophical idealism centering on the moral cultivation of the personality of an

individual. In the few works that address both, national morality and personalism are treated as two separate forms of moral inquiry.[9] But the conception
of the good that Inoue Tetsujirō put forward in 1911, as well as those developed in the majority of moral-philosophical writings that followed, was closely
intertwined with personalism. National morality's prescriptive statements—its
demand that the people *(kokumin)* be loyal and filial, for example—rested on a
framework constructed with key conceptual resources appropriated from personalism. In other words, conceptions of person, the good, and the state developed within personalism enabled and informed national morality.

The implications of this are important. When national morality is examined in the context of personalism, a new interpretation becomes possible. We
come to see national morality not simply as a collection of statements about
loyalty and patriotism, but as a kind of "idealism" (in the sense that it conceptualized the good in terms of an ideal to be pursued). The pursuit of this moral
ideal proved dangerous for moral orientations at odds with national morality
because to approach the ideal was at the same time to suppress or eradicate
obstacles in the path of the ideal. Such obstacles included anarchism, socialism,
individualism, and literary naturalism, referred to by national morality scholars
as "dangerous thought." But before beginning a discussion of national morality,
dangerous thought, and the broader sociopolitical context, I turn to national
morality's appropriation and subsequent reconfiguration of personalism.

For philosophers of personalism in 1890s Japan, the "person" was not
merely individual, but social as well. Drawing upon an epistemology that
brought together subject and object, self and other, personalism reconfigured
utilitarian conceptions of the person as an isolated, socially atomistic individual, putting forward instead the view that the person was both individual
and social. To the extent that a person could both actualize their own unique
potentialities and cultivate a self-awareness of their sociality, he or she realizes
"the good." The good of the self, in this view, is the good of the other. The state,
in personalist thought, was the space within which such "self-realization" took
place. The primary function of the state was to facilitate the individual's social
actualization by creating the conditions necessary for this to take place. That is,
it functioned as the means to bring about the end of self-realization. If the state
stifled this process, it was not fulfilling its purpose.

Personalism therefore allowed for resistance to the state under certain conditions. British idealist philosopher T. H. Green, whose own writings in translation became an integral part of personalist discourse in Japan from the early
1890s, asked, "Must not the individual judge for himself whether a law is for the
common good? And if he decides that it is not, is he not entitled to resist it?"
To this Green answered "'yes,' without qualification."[10] Yet such resistance was

in fact qualified. Green argued that resistance should be conducted through legal channels wherever possible. While admitting that problems arise when legal recourse has little or no effect, he maintained that so long as the laws fulfill the ideal of the state, their evasion is unjustified. "There can be no right to disobey the law of the state," he argued, "except in the interest of the state."[11] In other words, disobedience to the state could be justified only as an attempt to bring the state and its laws more into keeping with its ideal.[12] This provided the individual with a role to play in deciding the good of the whole—if the state was moving away from its ideal (as the individual understood it to be), the individual was justified in opposing the state and its laws.

Here, the ambivalence of personalism is apparent. It had the potential to be taken in two completely different directions. It emphasized the self-actualization of the individual on the one hand, but called on the individual to preserve the space of self-actualization (the state) by submitting to its laws on the other.[13] With the theory of self-as-other occupying such a central position in its epistemology, personalist philosophers asserted an identity of individual and social whole. This paved the way for the equation (utilized by national morality proponents): the good of the individual equals the good of the social whole; therefore, the individual must act for the good of the social whole, that is, the state. But this identity in personalism was meant as a basis from which to refute extremes on both sides, both extreme forms of individualism as well as views that prioritized the social whole over the individual. Yoshida Seiichi, for example, a moral philosopher at Tokyo Imperial University and proponent of personalism, made this quite clear by expressing opposition to both "extreme individualism" and what he called "extreme universalism." Yoshida used the term "universalism" to refer to individualism's opposite extreme, that is, to "a situation in which only the group has power."[14] In fact, Yoshida argued that personalism is able to avoid both extremes precisely because of the way it identifies subject and object. Such an identity implied for Yoshida that neither subject (the individual) nor object (the group, the social whole) is prioritized.

Yet with the appropriation of the vocabulary of personalism by proponents of national morality, personality (jinkaku), actualization (jitsugen, kanzen), and the ideal (risō), as well as the epistemology equating subject and object or individual and social whole (each central features of personalism), came to be deployed in an effort to legitimize a new conception of the good—one that prioritized the state over the individual.

National morality described the good as the self-realization of the person or personality (jinkaku), that is, it posited the good in terms of an ideal to be attained. In his Outline of National Morality, Inoue Tetsujirō discussed personality and the ideal in much the same terms as personalism: "Attempting to complete *(kansei suru)* one's personality *(jiko no jinkaku)* is, namely, a method for realizing the ideal as a human being. And this method is morality *(dōtoku)*."[15] The "method" Inoue refers to here is not a methodology for moral inquiry, but rather the path of virtue, cultivating one's personality so as to approach the human ideal. Inoue pointed out that we can take "complete personality" as our objective precisely because personality is incomplete or imperfect.[16] In other words, so long as personality is incomplete, it is possible to "approach" the ideal of "complete personality."

Moreover, one approached the moral ideal only as a subject living within a state. "It is impossible," wrote Inoue, "for anyone to exist outside of the state."[17] One of Inoue's contemporaries, the national morality scholar Fuka-saku Yasubumi, amended Inoue's assertion to account for the "uncivilized." "Of course...most barbarians," he observed, "live their lives without constructing a state...but those who cannot be called *kokumin* [in this context, people belonging to a state, i.e., subjects of the state] are very few."[18]

In national morality discourse, as in personalism, the state functioned as the space of self-realization. Inoue pointed out, "It is within the state that one grows, is active, and develops. Thus, if separated from the state, it is impossible to attain one's aims as a human being." The state here, a space of growth, action, and development, is necessary for actualization of the self. The less "complete" or "perfect" the state is, the more problematic the cultivation of "personality" will be.[19] Thus, a well-organized, safe, and peaceful state is essential for the individual's self-realization. Fukasaku made this clear as well when he asserted that the state contributes to the individual's efforts to realize his moral possibilities. Such possibilities are best realized where the highest degree of safety can be maintained. And it is the state that best maintains order and peace and protects the lives of the people.[20]

But in national morality thought, the ideal of "complete personality" referred not merely to the self-realization of the individual, but to the realization or perfection of the state as well. This was because the state also possessed personality, one that national morality scholars identified with individual personality by drawing upon the subject-as-object philosophy of personalism. In short, "the completion of one's personality is the completion of the state, just as the completion of the state is the completion of the individual's personality." In this statement by Fukasaku, cultivating individual or state personality was merely "viewing the same fact from different perspectives." This enabled the assertion that "good" action on the part of an individual must contribute to the completion or perfection of the state. That is, as Fukasaku put it, "the individual's actions are truly good when they are at the same time for the good of the state."[21] The individual will be unable to complete his or her personality unless this is the case. This, then, served as a basis for the subject's loyal and dutiful action on behalf of the state. To make sacrifices for the good of the state, according to this national morality view, was precisely to perfect one's own personality.

National morality's reconfiguration of personalism was most apparent in its privileging of state good over the good of the individual (despite their ostensible identification). Whereas personalism posited the state as merely a means to the end of individual self-realization, national morality prioritized the completion of the state. "The aim of the state," Fukasaku maintained, "is to plan for the safety of the state itself and of the people, and thereby to bring about the completion of both. To achieve this aim, the state must above all plan for its continued existence and development." To this end, Fukasaku stated, "the people must all practice a fixed morality. The term *kokumin dōtoku* refers to the morality that the people, as a people, must practice."[22] Here, Fukasaku called for moral homogeneity as a prerequisite for the survival of the state. The moral inclinations of the individual, wherever they diverged with the needs of the state, would be suppressed, while social practice in general would be regulated by national morality. Indeed, as the epigraph at the beginning of this chapter indicates, Inoue advocated the use of national morality to "regulate society." The object of regulation was clearly the *kokumin,* the "people belonging to the state," according to Fukasaku's definition of this term.

Fukasaku pointed out that because of egoism, the individual will at times ignore the needs of others or engage in activities that oppose the state. "But, the power and the life of the state lies in suppressing the egoistic spirit *(shuga shin)* of the individual so as to resist this kind of anti-state activity and, in adapting the individual to the state, to finally bring forth self-sacrificing action in which the individual extinguishes his egoistic self and brings to life his eternal higher self on behalf of the state." Fukasaku called this "state personalism" *(kokka teki jinkaku shugi).* "I believe," he proclaimed, "that from this point forward, our national morality must be cultivated and ordered in terms of this state per-sonalism."[23] "Complete personality," then, meant perfected state personality, a morally homogeneous totality of all individual personalities. With this discussion of complete personality in mind, we may now turn to Inoue Tetsujirō's definition of "the good."

The moral ideal of complete personality served as the basis for Inoue's conception of the good. In his *Outline of National Morality* he stated, "Once this great aim [of complete personality] is decided upon, the good and the evil of human society can for the first time be settled. That which is in accord with this objective is the good, that which is not in accord with this objective is evil."[24] Here, in theoretical terms, Inoue has defined "the good" according to his national morality perspective. His definition asserts that whatever is conducive to bringing about the ideal of complete personality is the good. Obstacles in the path of the ideal can legitimately be suppressed as "evil." By equating the good of the person with the good of the state, and then carefully specifying what constituted the good of the state (e.g., loyalty, obedience), national morality discourse delimited the good of the individual. The good, then, was no longer the form of self-realization compatible with individual ends as put forward by personalism; the good now constituted conduct that served the state.

The ideal of complete personality therefore must be understood as a moral space in which there is perfect moral action, where every thought and every action of each subject served the state. In Inoue's definition, the good is not this ideal itself, but "the approach" toward this ideal end. To approach the ideal, then, was to universalize a contingent and perspectival discourse, that is, to attempt to establish a moral space determined by the terms of the national morality discourse on the ideal, and this involved the sometimes violent suppression of otherness. Yet the ideal, according to Inoue, would remain forever out of reach, meaning that personality would never be fully complete or perfected. The approach, then, had no end point. In this scenario, the state continually seeks to approach the ideal of the subject's perfect loyalty, but never attains it. As "approach" entails not only the universalization of the state's own normative views but also the suppression of moral alterity, the social reality of moral dissension, suppression, and violence is sustained. When Inoue's definition of the good is understood as allegory, we see that his ethical claims were not merely the objective conclusions of value-neutral philosophizing. They corresponded to the normative orientation of the state—one seeking to cultivate loyal subjects ready to serve the state on the one hand and to suppress dangerous thought on the other. In other words, Inoue's definition of good and evil referred to loyalty to the state and dangerous thought respectively.

The Sociopolitical Context:
National Morality and "Dangerous Thought"

In the summer of 1910, while Inoue Tetsujirō lectured on national morality to the East Asia Society, a study group that he had established, police were completing their arrests of several hundred supposed anarchist activists suspected of involvement in a plot to assassinate the emperor. In December of that same year, when the trial associated with this case began, Inoue, at the request of the Ministry of Education, was again lecturing on national morality, this time to instructors in charge of moral training at Japan's Teachers' Colleges. At the conclusion of the trial, twenty-four were sentenced to death. Twelve later had their sentences commuted to life imprisonment, while the other twelve were executed in January 1911. This came to be known as the High Treason Incident.[25]

That Inoue's lectures on national morality so closely coincided with the arrests, trial, and execution of these anarchist activists is suggestive of the close connections between national morality discourse and the state's efforts to suppress anarchism. Indeed, about six months after the executions had been carried out, Inoue alluded to the High Treason Incident in his *Outline of National Morality*. Published in 1912, this book began as a lecture held in June 1911 at Tokyo Imperial University. This lecture, like his previous one in December 1910, was at the specific request of Minister of Education Komatsubara Eitarō. There, to an audience of educators in the field of moral training, Inoue spoke of the enemies of national morality: "Within Western civilization lies very harmful thought. There is even a great poison. These poisonous elements, not surprisingly, were imported into Japan along with beneficial elements. As a result, there are those, like the treasonous group that was punished this year, who embrace dangerous thought."[26]

Here, Inoue referred to those involved in the High Treason Incident. He assured his audience that the threat of this dangerous thought to national morality had not ended with the execution of those twelve anarchists. While they had been punished, there still remained "those among a portion of society who embrace unhealthy thought, even though they go unpunished. It cannot be denied," he asserted, "that there are some who embrace the kind of unhealthy thought that opposes or destroys national morality." As the above indicates, there was a close connection between the discourse on national morality and the social disruptions it sought to control. Inoue advocated "the use of national morality to regulate Japanese society" so as to ensure "the healthy existence of the Japanese people."[27] As a threat to the health of Japanese society, dangerous thought had to be suppressed.

Inoue was not alone in his condemnation of this dangerous thought, which referred generally not only to anarchism (a mode of thought seeking to dismantle the state so as to bring about a society free from authority), but also to socialism (which called for the overthrow of the "immoral" capitalist system together with the class divisions and poverty it engendered) and individualism (which undermined the state's demand for national unity). Many thinkers, both within and outside national morality discourse, stressed the dangers of such thought. Like Inoue, the educator and materialist philosopher Katō Hiroyuki feared socialism and communism. In 1912, just after the conclusion of the High Treason Incident, he called them "extremely dangerous things" because, he believed, they were inconsistent with the good of society and the state.[28] Two years earlier, the "elder statesmen" and former prime minister Yamagata Aritomo collaborated with legal scholar Hozumi Yatsuka to warn of the dangers of socialism:

> An examination of the changes in popular sentiments in recent society shows that when the people make demands for political power, and when a redistribution of power is gradually carried out, they push further by demanding food and clothing. They desire an equal division of social wealth. Do they realize that such demands run counter to the current organization of state-society? Here lies the cause for the emergence of the so-called socialists who make every effort to destroy the foundations for state-society's existence. It appears that the immediate causes are the tremendous gap between rich and poor and the striking changes in ethical thought that have come with modern culture. To devise a policy for curing this disease at the root is now a matter of the greatest urgency. At the same time, for the preservation of state society, we must strictly regulate those people afflicted by it. We must defend against the outbreak of this disease. We must suppress it and stamp it out.[29]

As with national morality scholars, Yamagata and Hozumi viewed the dangers of "social destruction" as a moral problem. A "change in ethical thought" was one of the "immediate causes" for the emergence of socialism. The suppression of socialism, here represented as a disease to be stamped out, was necessary for stabilizing state-society, and such stability itself was in turn needed for "preserving the foundation of national morality." Eradicating the dangerous thought of socialism was to be coordinated with the cultivation of "healthy thought," which involved the promotion of "wholesome and beneficial reading."[30]

Fukasaku Yasubumi was also concerned by the "rampant violence" that he read of each day in the newspaper. He explained "dangerous actions" as stemming from dangerous thought. Drawing on the philosophy of Wang Yangming, "who identified knowledge and action," and Socrates, "who identified virtue and knowledge," Fukasaku asserted that "thought is a form of internalized action and action is a form of externalized thought." The "origin of the violent and dangerous action" that he witnessed in Japan was for him "the product of dangerous thought." He supported the legal measures for suppressing such thought, noting with approval that "those responsible for propagating the anarcho-communism of Petr Kropotkin have been imprisoned for a sentence of several months." But he also proposed the use of "wholesome thought" to "reform and subjugate" dangerous thought. According to Fukasaku, the struggle for existence that Herbert Spencer described extended to the world of thought, and the wholesome thought upheld by national morality was engaged in a struggle for existence with dangerous thought.[31]

The High Treason Incident mentioned above marked a high point of suppressive violence and violent reaction to suppression that had been taking place for some time. At the close of Japan's war with Russia in 1905, rioting broke out in the Hibiya District of Tokyo. Rioters (numbering ten thousand by some estimates) attacked and burned more than 350 buildings, including police stations and police boxes, the prime minister's residence, the foreign ministry, and private homes. More than one thousand people were injured and seventeen were killed (mostly by the police, armed with swords and attempting to restore order).[32] In 1907, called "the year of the strike," strikes at the Ashio copper mines, the coal mines of Koike, and the dockyards in Uraga led to violent rioting.[33] In June of the following year, with the release from prison of socialist activist Yamaguchi Kōken, his supporters took to the streets waving red flags and shouting "anarchism." Police moved in, charging demonstrators with violation of the Public Peace Police Law. Fourteen were arrested, including anarchists Arahata Kanson and Ōsugi Sakae. In his autobiography, Arahata described his treatment at the hands of the police: "The police stripped Ōsugi and myself naked and dragged us by our feet through the corridors. They kicked and beat us.... [F]inally, they were surprised when I lost consciousness and relented."[34] So intense were the social disruptions of this time that the entire period between the Russo-Japanese War and the rice riots of 1918 has been called "a period of urban mass riot."[35]

This dangerous thought that national morality scholars, bureaucrats, legal scholars, and others feared was the "evil" that Inoue spoke of in his definition of the good. It was "that which is not in accord" with the objective of complete personality. In other words, dangerous thought, inasmuch as it undermined the authority of the state, constituted an obstacle on the path toward the ideal of complete loyalty to the state. Only through its eradication could the good flourish. To "approach" the ideal therefore required violence—the suppression of the alterity of the other, the reduction of the other (dangerous thought) to the same (national morality). But what precisely was dangerous about "dangerous thought"? What steps were taken to increase the authority of the call for loyal subjects and to undermine that of dangerous thought? Finally, how did proponents of so-called dangerous thought respond?

National Morality's Strategies for
Self-Legitimation and Suppression

Proponents of national morality made use of a number of strategies intended to shore up the authority of their own position while serving to de-legitimize and eradicate the variety of alternative normative orientations they collectively termed "dangerous thought." These strategies included efforts to represent alternative moral views as dangerous, to establish the "timeless" (and therefore indisputable) features of national morality, and to disseminate national morality through lectures, moral training textbooks, and so forth.

Inoue's statements concerning the High Treason Incident were part of an effort to de-legitimize a collective other called "dangerous thought." For Inoue, anarchism was not the only danger to national morality. In the one epithet of dangerous thought, Inoue grouped together a wide variety of diverse views on society, the person, and nature. Individualism, socialism, anarchism, literary naturalism—all became, under Inoue's representation of them, the collective other of national morality. Treating these diverse modes of thought as a single, unitary object facilitated their de-legitimation. All became "harmful," "poisonous," and "dangerous." Indeed, the dangerous and destructive nature of one could be attributed to each of the others.

Inoue, Yoshida Seiichi, and other proponents of national morality made it clear that the claims of "other" modes of thought concerning society, the individual, and morality were not in any sense "Japanese"; rather, they were imports from "Western civilization." Yoshida, for example, in the preface to his *Essentials of National Morality* (*Kokumin dōtoku yōryō*, 1916), closely echoed the words of Inoue's writing four years before. In a section titled "The Disruption of the Intellectual World," Yoshida wrote, "[W]ithin Western civilization is included a great deal of unhealthy thought of the kind that destroys national morality."[36] The "unhealthy thought" referred to here included anarchism, socialism, and individualism, each, according to Yoshida, a product of Western civilization. To admit that any view prioritizing the individual or calling for the abolition of the state was "Japanese" would have inhibited national morality's own claims to speak for what was authentically Japanese.

Through this collective representation, all of Japan's social ills could be attributed to a single "foreign" other, a single obstacle to moral homogeneity and social stability. In national morality discourse, then, dangerous thought became, in the words of Slavoj Žižek, "an intruder who introduces from outside disorder, decomposition and corruption of the social edifice . . . appear[ing] as an outward positive cause whose elimination would enable us to restore order, stability and identity."[37] By representing anarchism, socialism, individualism, and literary naturalism in this way, Inoue and other proponents of national morality legiti-mized their suppression. Thus, the suppression of the "dangerous other" was of central importance to the national morality project. Yet it was equally impor-tant, of course, to secure the legitimacy of national morality itself.

The architects of national morality devoted a good deal of effort to estab-lishing the timeless values of the Japanese people. There are, they claimed, cer-tain unchanging moral sensibilities common to all Japanese, those living today and those of remote antiquity. By projecting contemporary constructions of national morality into Japan's past, that is, by rewriting the past so as to accord with the state's need for loyal subjects in the present, national morality dis-course sought to mask the contingency of its claims and enhance its authority.

This required the effort to essentialize Japan's past as well as its present. Relying on the national character discourse prevalent at the time, national morality scholars developed a series of oppositions between Japan and other countries, and between Orient and Occident, to create the unique moral char-acteristics of the Japanese. National morality, as a morality of the national folk, was configured as a unique attribute of Japan's national character. In defining Japan's own unique morality, national morality scholars relied on essentialized conceptions of the other, of the national character of China, Korea, England, France, and the like. In other words, explicit claims about national morality carried with them implicit claims about the other. To claim, for example, that the unique national morality of Japan was "instinctive," as Inoue Tetsujirō did, was to imply something about the moral outlooks of other nations. In this case, Inoue opposed the "instinctiveness" of Japan's national morality to the "intel-lectual" nature of "Western morality." Oftentimes the opposition was not merely implied, but explicitly stated. For example, Inoue stated that while the family system is a central feature of Japan's national morality, no such system exists in the countries of the West. Moreover, Inoue claimed that while in China there is of course the individual family system—that is, the "individual family"—there is no "composite" family system like that of Japan. In regard to the virtue of loy-alty, Inoue asserted that although China does know the teaching of loyalty-as-filiality, it lacks the actuality of it. China prioritizes filiality over loyalty, while in Japan it is the reverse. And in the "individualistic" West, loyalty and filiality are not attributed the same degree of importance as they are in "group-oriented" (dantaishugi) Japan.[38] In each case, then, essentialized conceptions of the other were used to assert the timeless features of a Japanese moral identity.

Fukasaku Yasubumi constructed an even more comprehensive set of oppo-sitions with which to define Japan's national morality and the morality of the "Orient" generally. He described the morality of the West as individualistic, theoretical, concerned primarily with universal moral truths, and emphasizing independence. National morality, on the other hand, he described by way of direct opposition to each of these characteristics of the West. It was group-centered, practical, concerned with the particular moral sensibilities of the Japanese, and emphasized selflessness. In addition, he opposed Western morality's intellectual quality to Japan's emotive nature. As an example, he stated, "[W]e must view the theory of utilitarianism, which has been called a morality of calculation, as an intellectual morality. And we must view our country's morality of loyalty and filiality as one of feeling."[39]

Within this national character discourse, the essentialization of the other went hand in hand with the essentialization of the self. While national morality scholars insisted upon a particular moral character of "the Japanese," they were constantly confronted by alternative moral positions within Japan that called their claims into question. Only through the annihilation of these alternative moralities could claims to universal status (within the localized space of Japan) for a unique Japanese moral sensibility be fully verified. The spirit of the Japanese people, the family system, and the values of the Japanese—each drew its authority from the idea that they were unique attributes of Japan and common to all Japanese. Contemporary narratives on Japanese culture often reassert and sustain these same essentialized attributes. But it is worth noting that many of the supposedly "timeless characteristics" of the Japanese and Japanese culture are here—in early twentieth-century Japan—being produced.

In addition to efforts to undermine the authority of "dangerous thought" through strategies of representation and measures for masking the contingency of national morality, national morality scholars worked closely with the state, particularly the Ministry of Education, to disseminate national morality widely. This involved a series of Ministry of Education–sponsored lectures on national morality, the establishment of state control over the production and dissemination of textbooks for the moral training of Japan's youth, and the promulgation of various government edicts associated with national morality.

In 1910 the Ministry of Education organized a special lecture series on national morality. Here, Inoue Tetsujirō presented his lectures that were published in his *Outline of National Morality*. Between July 1910 and July of the following year Inoue lectured on national morality to students, to middle-school teachers, and to the teachers of Japan's teachers—the instructors in charge of the departments of moral training at the Teachers' Colleges.[40] Legal scholar Hozumi Yatsuka also participated in this lecture series, where he discussed "The Main Points of National Morality" and moral training textbooks for use in the third year of higher-school education. In another such lecture series held the following year, Hozumi lectured on national morality and the ethics of the family-state before an audience of middle-school and women's high-school instructors.[41] These lectures and the audiences to which they were directed clearly reflect the state's awareness of the importance of education in the dissemination and legitimation of its own moral orientation. Such Ministry of Education–sponsored lectures were an effective means for disseminating national morality, particularly as they exerted a kind of hierarchical control over the education system through the indoctrination of both regular teachers and instructors at the Teachers' Colleges. Yet the state's most effective means for disseminating national morality was through the textbooks for moral training that were used by primary, middle, and high school students.

In 1897 state authorities announced that all school textbooks for moral training would be produced by the government rather than by private companies. Katō Hiroyuki was appointed to head a Ministry of Education committee to carry out this aim, and the new textbooks, the first set of "state-authorized textbooks," were completed in 1903. After Japan's victory in its war with Russia in 1905, however, and with increasingly vocal assertions of Japan's unique and distinctive national essence, or *kokutai,* dissatisfaction with these textbooks grew. Hozumi was among the more vocal of these critics who claimed that the current textbooks did not go far enough to emphasize the moral characteristics of Japan, in particular the "great moral principle of loyalty and filial piety *(chūkō no taigi).*" Siding with Hozumi, the Nihon Kōdōkai (the Japanese Society for the Expansion of the Way, a society for moral education established by Nishimura Shigeki), issued an "Opinion on State Moral Education Textbooks" in which was stated, "The Imperial House and the State in our country, of themselves, constitute one body. Since our national polity is one in which there is no State apart from the Imperial House and the Imperial House does not exist apart from the State, loyalty to the ruler is patriotism and patriotism is loyalty to the ruler."[42] The current textbooks, according to the Nihon Kōdōkai, did not make this identity clear.

In response to growing pressure, the Ministry of Education in 1908 set up an investigative committee to review textbooks used in schools. Hozumi was appointed to chair this committee and led the revisions that were carried out between 1908 and 1911.[43] In the end, the Ministry of Education authorized a comprehensive revision of textbooks on moral training. The revised textbooks placed greater emphasis on the notions of family-state, filiality as loyalty as patriotism, and ancestor worship and expanded the sections on the Sino-Japanese and Russo-Japanese wars.[44] Compared to the 1903 textbooks, the revised 1910 version de-emphasized personal and social ethics and placed greater emphasis on state and family ethics.[45]

According to Karasawa Tomitarō, a historian of Japan's education system, these Ministry of Education initiatives represented "an effort to replace the modern elements that thrived [in the moral training texts of previous years] with reactionary Confucian and feudalistic elements."[46] Such initiatives, however, were in fact quite modern in that they reflect the modern nation-state's efforts to create loyal subjects and to win consent for its rule by disseminating and naturalizing national morality throughout society. Of particular concern in these texts were the subject's obligations to the state. Inoue Tetsujirō, for example, made this quite clear in his Ministry of Education–authorized *Newly Edited Textbook for Moral Training* (*Shinhen shūshin kyōkasho*, 1911). Inoue explained that the subject *(shinmin)*, as an element of the state, shares the fate of the state. "The vitality of the state depends upon the prosperity of its subjects, and the prosperity of the subject depends upon the vitality of the state." In order to assure such vitality and prosperity, Inoue stressed, "subjects must first of all submit to the commands of the state. The state possesses an absolute and unlimited authority over the subject, and the subject may not defy it, whatever the situation might be."[47] Direct exhortations to obedience were supplemented by stories and images in textbooks. The story of Kiguchi Kohei the soldier, which appeared in textbooks for moral training at least from 1903, provided students with a model of dutiful moral action. A battle scene (see figure 4) accompanies a brief lesson that reads: "Although Kiguchi Kohei was

Figure 4. Kiguchi Kohei, a model of dutiful action. Illustration from *Primary School Textbook for Moral Training* (*Jinjō shōgaku shūshin sho*, Tokyo, 1918).

hit by the enemy's bullet and was about to die, he did not let the bugle fall from his lips."[48] Kiguchi fulfilled his duty to the end. Such assertions of the authority of the state and demands for the obedience of the subject were common to the state-authorized moral training textbooks of this time.[49] These textbooks were disseminated more widely than the previous state-authorized textbooks, becoming the first truly nationwide textbooks for moral education.[50]

Further efforts to disseminate national morality took the form of government edicts. Just several months after the Red Flag Incident of June 1908, Home Minister Hirata Tosuke drafted and issued the Boshin Edict (Boshin shōsho). According to the then vice minister of education Okada Ryōhei, the Boshin Edict was issued to combat the disunity brought about by "many undesirable phenomena...such as naturalism and extreme individualism."[51] The edict called upon the "loyal subjects" of Japan to follow the "teachings of Our revered Ancestors," which included frugal living, hard work, and diligence. Upon the careful adherence to these teachings rested the fate of the nation.[52] In his history of education in modern Japan, Karasawa Tomitarō linked this edict to sociomoral disorder and to the government's efforts to legitimize national morality. "From the time of the proclamation of the Boshin Edict in 1908," he observes, "the government viewed social uneasiness and confusion as the result of moral and ethical disorder, and consequently attempted to even more strongly compel compliance with the family-state morality of loyalty, filial piety, and so on."[53] Of course, the Boshin Edict was itself part of the state's efforts to authorize the "family-state morality" of kokumin dōtoku. Moreover, the Boshin Edict invariably appeared, together with the Imperial Rescript on Education of 1890, as a front-piece in moral training textbooks. These two key government statements on moral propriety, then, were not simply issued to state and local prefectural bureaucracies, but were efficiently disseminated so as to become central texts in the moral training of each Japanese student. Through various strategies, then, national morality proponents sought to de-legitimize "dangerous thought" while enhancing the authority of their own moral claims. Nevertheless, the national morality position was by no means unassailable.

Strategies for Resisting National Morality

Proponents of socialism, individualism, anarchism, and other forms of thought opposed to national morality resisted the state's effort to create a homogeneous moral space through a number of discursive strategies.[54] First, they sought to undermine national morality's authority to speak for the good by depicting it, as well as the state that sponsored it, as a moral failure. National morality, inasmuch as it was the moral vision of the state, could be attacked by calling attention to the state's disregard for the people. Although national morality scholars emphasized the subject's obligations to the state, the state itself was not without certain moral obligations to its subjects. National morality's justification for its demands for loyalty to the state lay, in part, in the role the state played in protecting the lives and property of its subjects. Inoue Tetsujirō, for example, wrote of this legal contract in his 1905 exposition on state and world morality. "The state protects us," Inoue wrote. "It keeps our lives, our property, and so on free from danger, and the inevitable result of this is that we in turn must carry out our proper duty to the state."[55] Fukasaku Yasubumi, Yoshida Kumaji, and other national morality scholars spoke of the state in similar terms.[56] Many claimed, however, that the state had failed to fulfill this obligation and as a result had no basis for its demands of absolute loyalty. Defiance was justified by calling attention to the moral failings of the state.

The pollution of the lands surrounding Yanaka Village in Tochigi Prefecture and the subsequent deaths due to copper poisoning caused by the Ashio copper mine provided critics of national morality with a vivid example of the moral failings of the state. Arahata Kanson, a proponent of socialism and editor of the anarchist journal *Modern Thought (Kindai shisō)*, wrote of the effect of the copper pollution in *A History of the Destruction of Yanaka Village (Yanaka mura metsubō shi,* 1907). "The power of the government and the wealth of capitalists have brought the ruin of this tiny village in what can only be called a well-organized crime."[57] Outraged by what he saw as "the government's merciless cruelty," Arahata wanted retribution. "Let us look to the day which will surely come," he wrote, "when we will revenge ourselves on them [the government], using exactly the same means and methods as they used on the people of Yanaka village."

Arahata believed that it was precisely through this kind of disregard for the people that the state created conditions for the growth of anarchism. "The government abuses people, mistreats them and oppresses them. It mocks the people, has nothing but contempt for them, and governs them badly. And, in doing this, it is producing many violent anarchists, whom we will always regard with affection."[58] In this way, Arahata redirected blame. The state itself was responsible for any disruption the anarchists had caused because it had failed in its moral obligation to the people. Other criticisms were directed at broader social conditions.

"Why are you poor?" asked Uchiyama Gudō, a Buddhist monk and socialist sympathizer. "Shall I tell you the reason why? Because the emperor, the wealthy, the large landowners—they are all blood-sucking ticks."[59] According to Uchiyama, here citing a popular song of the day, the powerful—the wealthy, those who governed, even the emperor—were concerned not with the well being of the people but only with their own further enrichment. Uchiyama was among the anarchist activists executed in the High Treason Incident. His statement was a critique not merely of the state, but of the broad intellectual space of state legitimacy of which national morality was a part.

Sharing many of Uchiyama's views, socialist Katayama Sen described the moral failings of Japanese society just after the turn of the century. "In the world of socialism," wrote Katayama in his 1903 *My Socialism (Waga shakaishugi)*, "true morality will prevail." In the world of capitalism, however, morality was sacrificed "for the benefit of the capitalist." Katayama asserted that the current society, characterized by severe economic competition for monetary gain, impeded the development of true morality. "To hope for the development of civic virtues in a society governed by selfishness is like searching for a fish in a tree." He believed that in a capitalist society it would be futile to expect any real development of a "true morality":

> The religionist, the moralist, and the scholar are mere tools for justifying the capitalist's position; their knowledge, truths and ideals are completely discarded and ignored. Their opinions and arguments are like those of the religionists and moralists of the slave states in the southern part of North America, who, during the American Civil War carried out to end slavery, taught soldiers in their camps that slavery is a fair and just institution.[60]

For Katayama, scholars of national morality were nothing more than tools for the legitimation of an immoral capitalist system. Instead of joining the battle to bring about "true morality," they merely reinforced the conditions that impeded it.

In addition, Katayama was highly critical of academic moral discourse and its theories, proposing instead a "simple morality" free from the Ministry of Education's intrusion. "We socialists are not ones who discuss the origins of the moral sentiments. We do not carry out critiques of the various thought on such matters. Rather, we simply speak of actual morality. The basis for this living morality, a morality that the people can practice on their own, is economics." By the 1908 national morality textbook revision ordered by the Ministry of Education, national morality had become formulaic and complicated. Textbooks were required to discuss a standard set of concepts: the family-state, ancestor worship, the unity of loyalty and filiality, patriotism, and so on. Each required a detailed explanation in school textbooks and oftentimes lengthy exegesis in scholarly works on the subject. By contrast, socialism put forward an extremely simple morality. "To have adequate food and clothing, to know courtesy—this is the foundation for the morality of socialism."[61] On this view, then, the state-sponsored national morality, for all its detailed attention to the family-state, loyalty, and filiality, had missed what was of true moral significance.

National morality was also criticized as an exploitative system of obligations. While *kokumin dōtoku* was upheld as "the people's morality," anarchists attacked it as a "morality created for the benefit of one certain class alone."[62] Economist Kawakami Hajime was equally critical. "Loyalty, courage, public service—this is the highest morality," he stated disapprovingly. While the people in the countries of the West have rights, Japan is "a country of obligations."[63] The well-known writer and proponent of individualism Natsume Soseki echoed this sentiment in a 1911 article on literature and morality. Soseki claimed that national morality was less a set of virtues as a set of duties, adherence to which was to the state's, but not necessarily to the individual's, advantage. "When we look closely at the old Confucian moral slogans—loyalty, filial piety, chastity— we realize that they were nothing but duties imposed solely for the benefit of those who possessed absolute power under the social system of the time."[64] This statement, written in August 1911 (shortly after Inoue's lectures on national morality at Tokyo Imperial University and about half a year after the executions associated with the High Treason Incident), was not merely a critique of the moral views of Japan's past; it was a thinly veiled critique leveled directly at national morality.

Central to the national morality conception of the state was the idea that completion or realization of the individual's potentiality could take place only in and through the state. Although national morality scholars maintained that to actualize or realize the personality of the state was in fact to actualize individual personality as well, critics emerged claiming that national morality placed undue emphasis on the individual's obligations to the state. For them, national morality merely used the individual as a means to attain state ends.

As early as 1901 Nakashima Rikizō, the spokesman for personalism discussed earlier, began to express concern regarding the possibility that the good of society may be unduly privileged over the good of the individual.

> [This theory of social realization] has the weakness of attaching too much importance to the social aspect of life, and neglecting the individual side. It has a tendency to argue that the individual exists merely for the sake of society. I believe that a complete theory for attaining the good is one that, while giving weight to the social aspect of life, at the same time does not take the individual side lightly. I believe an even clearer discussion of the relationship between individual and society is necessary.[65]

By 1911 Nakashima expressed this fear even more forcefully. "The theory of social realization which... Green developed and which many scholars of our country espouse today errs in regarding the individual merely as a machine to realize the will of the society."[66] Nakashima himself, drawing on Green's thought, had introduced this theory of social realization in his writings on personalism. Here, however, Nakashima's personalist version of social realization, which in no way regarded the individual as a means to achieve social ends, has been displaced by national morality. Other objections to national morality's neglect of the individual like those of Nakashima's came from proponents of individualism.

Economist Kawakami Hajime (1879–1946) attacked national morality from the standpoint of individualism. Kawakami is perhaps best known as a Marxist social philosopher whose life and intellectual development have been ably outlined by Gail Lee Bernstein. Bernstein calls attention to Kawakami's "patriotic nationalist consciousness" during the early twentieth century before his turn to Marxism.[67] But if Kawakami loved the nation of Japan, he harbored strong criticisms of the state. In 1911, before his association with Marxism, Kawakami (at this time a lecturer on economics at Kyoto University) developed a systematic and comprehensive critique of the ethics of "state-ism" *(kokkashugi),* a term he used to refer to national morality. He criticized national morality's emphasis on the state and its disregard for the individual. In describing the intellectual landscape of Japan at this time, Kawakami drew an opposition between the individualism of the West and the "state-ism" of Japan. "The most prominent characteristic of Japan today," Kawakami asserted, "is its state-ism."[68] This, Kawakami explained, meant that the state was taken as the end and the individual was to be the means. In a statement that sounds much like that of Nakashima's above, Kawakami drew attention to the state's use of the individual. "The value of the individual's existence lies simply in being a tool for planning the development of the state." Kawakami maintained that because the ethics of state-ism privileged the survival of the state over the needs—even the lives—of every individual, it was an absurd doctrine. "If there were a case in which killing every individual were necessary for maintaining the existence of the state, then the state would be kept alive even though all individuals be sacrificed. This is the inevitable and logical conclusion of state-ism."[69] The ethical view of state-ism, then, demanded patriotism, loyalty to the state, and a willingness to sacrifice oneself for the good of the state. Kawakami contrasted Japan's state-ism to the individualism he believed characterized Western countries. In the West, Kawakami explained, the individual is the end and the state the means; therefore, the state would be dismantled rather than allow the sacrifice of the individuals that it comprises.[70]

And while national morality proponents warned of the dangers of individualism, for Kawakami the ethics of state-ism and its authorizing strategies constituted "an extremely dangerous misunderstanding" because it allowed for the prioritization of state over individual.[71] Under such conditions "scholars sacrifice their truth to the state."[72] They conceive of the state as an "omnipotent" apparatus "for attaining the good." "But the state does not do good for the people," Kawakami insisted; "indeed, it cannot do good." The state, he argued, makes demands on the people and can do nothing else. The individual is unable to set his or her own existential ends; the state commands the sacrifice of the individual to whatever is of benefit to the state. "Of course, it is impossible for the people to absolutely oppose this kind of command for sacrifice, and there is no room for moral criticism of this command for sacrifice."[73] Here, Kawakami claims that moral criticism of national morality's demand for self-sacrifice is curtailed because national morality itself speaks for what is moral. But Kawakami exaggerates. There is "room for moral criticism" and it does indeed take place, not only here in Kawakami's article, but elsewhere, as the various forms of resistance to national morality discussed in this chapter show. A philosophical critique of national morality, also appearing in the eventful year of 1911 that began with the executions of Kanno Suga, Kōtoku Shūsui, and ten others, came from Nishida Kitarō.

Nishida, in his well-known *Inquiry into the Good (Zen no kenkyū)*, offered a cogent critique of national morality and its capacity to provide a satisfactory basis for morality. In a brief but incisive chapter Nishida outlined the shortcomings of what he called "authority theories" of ethics; the unmistakable target of his critique was national morality. Proponents of these authority theories, he stated, "hold that good and evil are determined by the commands of the authority figure." They proclaim that morality "derives from the commands of that which has absolute authority and power over us, and so we should follow the laws of morality not for the advantage of the self, but simply for the sake of following the orders of that absolute authority."[74] In short, morality is obedience to the authoritative command.

Here we may recall Ōnishi Hajime's critique of the Imperial Rescript on Education discussed in the preceding chapter and his assertion that obedience to the command of one's ruler or father (i.e., loyalty and filial piety) cannot serve as a moral foundation. Nishida's critique of national morality closely parallels Ōnishi's. Ōnishi pointed out that one is not permitted to ask why a particular action is deemed moral. Indeed, to do so runs counter to the demand for unthinking obedience. Nishida reached the same conclusion: "In strict authority theory," he stated, "morality amounts to blind subservience."[75] An action undertaken for any reason other than to obey the authoritative command is an immoral act.

But these theories, Nishida maintained, fail to provide a basis to explain why obedience is moral or why we must obey: "we cannot explain why we must do the good.... We obey the authority figure simply because it is authoritative." Here, there is no standard for distinguishing good from evil. Our actions cannot therefore be motivated by moral conviction; under authority theories of morality, Nishida argued, our "moral motive" is "meaningless fear." Moreover, given that moral action is rendered as unthinking obedience, "morality and knowledge are polar opposites, and the ignorant are the good."[76]

Finally, under such conditions, where moral inquiry and questioning are to be set aside, the title Nishida selected for his work is telling. *An Inquiry into the Good* issues a challenge to this demand for obedience. National morality discouraged such inquiry because, if pursued far enough, one might conclude, as did Nishida and Ōnishi before him, that mere obedience to an authoritative command cannot provide a satisfactory ground for morality.

These descriptions of the moral failings of the state—its disregard for the welfare of its subjects, its encouragement of the "exploitative capitalist system," its emphasis on duties and obligations, its general disregard for the individual, and the incoherence of the morality it sponsored—marked the limits of the state's ability to legitimize national morality discourse. From an emphasis on the state as a moral failure, critiques of national morality moved to a more sophisticated level of engagement—the struggle for the meaning of key terms in the moral discourse of the day.

National morality and the state did not have a monopoly on the meaning of morality and the terms closely associated with it. Resistance to efforts by the state to create a society of homogeneous subjects, all equally loyal to the state, took the form of redefining or inverting the meaning of terms deployed by the state for the purpose of instilling loyalty. It was when "dangerous thought," upon whose "otherness" national morality relied for its own legitimacy, began to openly assert its own configurations of moral action that it became particularly dangerous in the minds of national morality scholars.

Moral positions were attacked and defended on the basis of the extent to which they contributed to the well-being of society or the state. Moral positions that somehow benefited society or the state were considered "wholesome." Thus, the term *kenzen* (healthy, wholesome) and its opposite, *fukenzen*, appeared frequently in both national morality discourse and in the writings of proponents of dangerous thought. Inoue Tetsujirō and other national morality scholars deployed the term *fukenzen* time and again in reference to dangerous thought. In fact, the phrase "unhealthy *(fukenzen)* thought of the sort that destroys national morality" had become something of a fixture in this discourse. Both Inoue and Yoshida Seiichi, for example, used this phrase, identically worded, reflecting how mechanical national morality's reliance on this term had become.[77]

Komatsubara Eitarō, minister of education during the particularly repressive second Katsura administration (1908–1911), sought to suppress "the popularity of naturalism and the penetration of socialism" by encouraging "wholesome *(kenzen)* reading beneficial to public morals."[78] This was seen to be particularly urgent in the wake of the High Treason Incident. To this end, he appointed in 1911 a special committee on literature to promote "wholesome" values in literature. In this context, wholesome literature was the sort that incorporated the values espoused in national morality: loyalty, filiality, and patriotism. Literary naturalism, described by scholar of religion Anesaki Masaharu as "a bitter protest against every kind of authority," was the primary target of the Ministry of Education's committee.[79] This genre of literature emphasized the authority of the individual and regarded national morality "with defiance and disgust."[80] Upon hearing of the formation of this committee, naturalist writer Togawa Shūkotsu proclaimed, "The wolves are preparing to eat the lambs.... [T]hey are trying to annihilate literature; the committee will be nothing but a branch police station for thought control." Concerning the committee's stated purpose of "encouraging literature" (which of course referred only to those genres consistent with national morality), Togawa exclaimed, "So now the government dares to tell us they want to 'protect' and 'encourage' our literature after it has grown to maturity on its own despite their persecution! What gall! What blind stupidity!"[81]

While the Katsura regime sought to suppress naturalistic literature by emphasizing its "unwholesome" character, writer Natsume Soseki, inverting the term, defended it precisely for its "wholesomeness." Soseki observed that in recent years the term "naturalism" evoked fear (particularly among those in government) and had been seen only as a "depraved" and "licentious" form of literature. But he asserted that such fear and hatred were in no way warranted. Soseki urged people to see naturalism's "wholesome side" as a form of literature that engages with human failings and human blunders, allowing readers to reflect on their own weaknesses. In this sense, Soseki maintained, "the literature of naturalism is just as concerned with morality as the literature of romanticism."[82] Nevertheless, the state viewed literary naturalism as unwholesome and as a threat to its authority. Despite the efforts of Soseki and others, the popularity of naturalistic literature waned, a development that pleased Inoue Tetsujirō, who regarded it as good "for the sake of public morals."[83]

In another example of this strategy of reconfiguring or inverting terms, Uchiyama Gudō, the Buddhist socialist mentioned earlier, attempted to reconfigure the "treasonous" act of defying state and emperor into an act of "heroism" by questioning the emperor's divine status. Outraged by the government's response to the Red Flag Incident of 1908, Uchiyama in the same year published and distributed an article calling for the abolition of the government and the establishment of "a free country without an emperor." Justifying this to his readers, Uchiyama argued that such an act was not treasonous; rather, it was a just and heroic act. It would abolish an exploitative and oppressive system most had been tricked into accepting. The emperor, Uchiyama claimed, through the medium of primary school teachers, had tricked the people into believing he is the child of the gods.[84] Under Uchiyama's reasoning, treason became heroism and the divinity of the emperor became deception. This reconfiguration of treason—describing defiance of the state as "heroic"—carried with it the implication that the loyalty to the state that proponents of national morality were so concerned to instill ought to be replaced by a higher loyalty to the needs of the destitute. In this sense, Uchiyama's views clearly represented an obstacle to national morality's "approach" toward moral homogeneity.

Anarchism was another contested term. In 1908 Sakamoto Seima—among those convicted in the High Treason Incident—attempted to reconfigure the pejorative connotation of the term "anarchism" *(museifushugi)* by deflecting some of its negative characterizations.

> People say that anarchism is the poison that comes from the mouths of traitors and that it is an extremely evil and dangerous doctrine. I do not know what they mean by traitors and rebels, but let us consider whether the principles of anarcho-communism really are a violent and dangerous doctrine as they say. The society that the great doctrine and spirit of anarcho-communism points to is a society without the state and without government. Indeed, it is a society that denies all authority. It is also a society which, by striving for the happiness and advantage of everyone, will encourage the progress and improvement of humankind.... In such a society all the rampage of the present monstrous private property system will disappear and the houses, fields, factories and all the other components of the economy will become the common property of everyone. Under these circumstances... [humanity] should be able to reach the limits of ethical and moral development.[85]

For Sakamoto, the "poisonous" doctrine of anarchism was in reality a "great doctrine" devoted to the promotion of the happiness, equality, and welfare of the people. To bring about the society he envisioned, however, the capitalist system of his day had to be overthrown. To this end, he called for a general strike to initiate revolution, yet in the wake of the High Treason Incident, support for such activism waned.

Just as threatening to the aims of national morality scholars were anarchist efforts to reconfigure what constituted moral action. Two terms of particular importance in this effort were *jindō* (the Way of humanity) and of course *dōtoku* (morality). While Inoue lectured to Japan's instructors of moral training about the morality of the Japanese people, anarchists, socialists, and others put forward different views of morality. Anarchist thinkers, drawing on the writings of anarchist philosopher Petr Kropotkin, argued for the complete renovation of morality. In a short piece titled "The Creation of Morality" (Dōtoku no sōzō), carried in a 1913 issue of Arahata Kanson's journal *Modern Thought (Kindai shisō)*, Ōsugi Sakae argued,

> Among a certain minority in society, now is a time in which conceptions of morality are completely changing. This is truly a dangerous time. The most moral of activities have now, by contrast, come to be seen as the most immoral of activities. The practices, the learning, and the morality created for the benefit of one certain class alone, conventionally held in respect and regarded as sacred, have all been completely abandoned. People have emerged who recognize so-called immoral actions as the highest duty to themselves and to the world. Truly, these are dangerous people. But according to the teachings of historians, and according to these dangerous people living in this dangerous age, history is ever advancing. This is a matter of creating morality. How fortunate to be born into this time, to be counted among these people. Truly, this is the chance of a lifetime.[86]

Here "morality" is turned upside down. The "most moral of activities" becomes in this piece "the most immoral," while "so-called immoral actions" become one's "highest duty." This article was clearly meant as an attack on the state, and more specifically on national morality. The "so-called immoral actions" mentioned here included violent activism directed against the state. But they were only immoral from the standpoint of the state and national morality. Ōsugi was fully aware of the dangers in "creating" a new morality. Circumventing the "false morality" emphasizing one's duty to the state, and drawing upon a long tradition of self-sacrificing action for some higher good or ideal reminiscent of the "men of high purpose" *(shishi)* during the Meiji Revolution, this article emphasized a person's "highest duty to themselves and to the world." Finally, this statement on the creation of a new morality opposed national morality because it was not truly a "people's morality" *(kokumin no dōtoku).* Rather, it represented national morality in much the same way as Natsume Soseki did, that is, as "morality created for the benefit of one certain class alone."

The "Way of humanity" *(jindō),* though not as obviously central to moral discourse as the term "morality," was nevertheless similarly disputed. The concept of *jindō* was fundamental to national morality because it served as the universal counterpart to Japan's particular morality. *Jindō* was the "moral Way" of all humanity, while national morality was particular to the Japanese people. But in national morality discourse, the two were in no way at odds with one another. In a chapter on the relationship between national morality and *jindō,* Inoue not only asserted that the two are compatible, he also argued, "National morality and *jindō* form an inseparable relationship."[87] He further described national morality and *jindō* in terms of the Buddhist idea of identity-in-difference *(sabetsu-soku-byōdō),* associating the former with difference and particularity *(sabetsu)* and the latter with sameness and the universal *(byōdō).* In other words, national morality was a particular manifestation of universal "good"; without the one, the other could not exist.[88] Yet Inoue's emphasis on the compatibility of national morality and *jindō* was in part a response to contrary claims—that national morality was in fact inconsistent with the way of humanity.

Arahata Kanson, writing two and half years after the High Treason Incident, depicted state officials as completely opposed to *jindō.* In the text cited below, he contemplated the morality of terrorism. The following passage also provides an example of the reappropriation of the pre-Meiji *shishi* ideal of risk taking in the name of a higher good, a higher loyalty.

> As Kropotkin discusses in "The Morality of the Anarchist," doing away with tyrants who oppose civilization [*bunmei*] and the way of humanity [*jindō*] is not a soap bubble that vanishes when it ascends into the air [i.e., a utopian illusion], it is the morality of the terrorist [*terorisuto no dōtoku*]. It is the command of conscience. It is the victory of human feeling over cowardice.[89]

This "morality of the terrorist," according to Arahata, encourages the fight for "civilization and the way of humanity." Here, Arahata's article attempts to reconfigure the meaning of "the Way of humanity" *(jindō).* In national morality thought, adherence to *jindō* (because it was in the end fully consistent with national morality, at least according to those like Inoue) required obedience to the state and its laws. For Arahata, however, the defense of *jindō* required moral action against the state in the form of terrorism. Those seeking to abolish the state and/or to realize a socialist society put this kind of terrorist morality into practice in the High Treason Incident of 1910-1911.

The economist Kawakami Hajime's critique of national morality also made use of a strategy that contested and reconfigured its underlying terms. In this case, the focus was the term *jinkaku* (personality). In national morality discourse, *jinkaku* referred to the personality of both the individual and the state. Through the cultivation of *jinkaku,* the good of the state (synonymous with the good of the individual) is realized. But Kawakami criticized that in Japan the personality of the individual had been completely disregarded, and that the state's personality alone was valued. He coined the term *koku-kaku* (state-personality) to describe the "state-ism" of Japan and to undermine the national morality conception of *jinkaku,* or personality.

The term *jinkaku* played an important role in Kawakami's analysis of state-ism. Drawing on the vocabulary of personalism, he claimed that the prioritization of the state over the individual in Japan reflects a complete absence of concern for the personality of the individual. "Among Japanese, there is no essential conception of personality." While societies in the West attach great value to the personal character of the individual and stress the importance of each individual setting his or her own ends, Japan according to Kawakami values only the character of the state. "The only thing whose existence is of value, the only thing that can set ends, is the state." Japan, for Kawakami, was not a society that values personal character, but one that values only "state-character" or "state-personality" *(koku-kaku).* Although Inoue and other proponents of national morality spoke of the good as the completion of personality, according to Kawakami it is the emperor who possesses the most complete personality. And as the emperor was the embodiment of the state, the completion of personality, that is, the pursuit of the ideal, takes place for the state, but not for the individual. The result, according to Kawakami, is that "in the West, the state is the slave of the people, but in Japan, the people are the slaves of the state."[90]

One final example of a "contested term" in moral discourse was Ninomiya Sontoku (1787–1856), a proponent of practical agrarian reforms for increasing crop production whose collection of moral aphorisms (the *Evening Talks,* or *Yawa*) became the central text for the Hōtoku (repaying virtue) movement initiated by his followers. In his *Evening Talks,* Sontoku expounded on the importance of hard work, frugality, and self-sacrifice for the good of others. Although he was relatively unknown in the intellectual environment of early Meiji Japan, by 1890 Sontoku had become an important resource in moral discourse.[91]

A variety of Meiji thinkers upholding diverse intellectual positions drew upon Sontoku's thought to support their own moral views. Some hoped to establish a moral basis for the seemingly amoral realm of economics. Christian socialist Abe Jirō, for example, called attention to the growing gap between society's rich and poor and to corrupt business leaders in league with equally corrupt politicians. He criticized industrialists who took pride in their amoral, survival-of-the-fittest approach to economic competition. For Abe, Sontoku's thought provided the perfect example of the inseparability of economic endeavors, whether rural farming or urban industry, and morality.[92] Sontoku, in this example, was used to defend the urban poor and to attack high-level corruption.

Abe's views can be situated in a broader discourse at this time on the need for morality to guide industrializing Japan. Like Abe, Mishima Tsuyoshi also sought to link morality to economics, arguing that the two are in fact "one and the same thing."[93] In a discussion of the etymology of the modern term for economics *(keizai),* Mishima explained that it was derived from the term *kei-rin* (ordering or governing the world). The ideograph *sai/zai* (to save or offer aid) took the place of *rin,* creating the modern compound *keizai* (economics in modern Japanese, but literally "ordering the world so as to save the people").[94] The term for economics, then, was originally not merely concerned with money, Mishima stressed, but with helping "the people." Moreover, a *keizai* unconcerned with morality, he asserted, was not true *keizai.*[95] In this discourse on the need to link economic labor and moral action, Sontoku's thought linking labor with morality served as a useful resource.

Katō Hiroyuki also drew upon Sontoku's thought to support his own views. Sontoku's ethics, according to Katō, were similar to the moral philosophy of Hobbes. For Katō, Sontoku's thought supported the contention that the good is not a heaven-given principle but rather the creation of humanity based on the needs of the stronger. Thus Katō too made use of Sontoku to support his "ethics of the stronger" viewpoint that he first developed in the 1880s.[96]

But perhaps the primary application of Sontoku's thought concerned Japan's national character. Since the introduction of the notion of hierarchical civilization, Japan struggled with the inferior civilizational status (vis-à-vis the West) to which it had been assigned. Both Nakashima and Inoue sought to locate something in Japan's past that could be upheld as Japan's valuable and unique contribution to the world. For Nakashima, Sontoku's thought resembled the ethics of T. H. Green. He drew a close parallel, for example, between Sontoku's statements on sincerity and Green's views on "self-realization."[97] This had the effect of claiming that prior to the introduction of personalism (and the link between individuality and a highly developed and civilized society) the idea of "personality" already existed in Japan.

Inoue, who like Nakashima found some notion of personality or individuality in Sontoku's thought,[98] was instrumental in the use of Sontoku as a moral example in the education of Japan's youth. From about 1890 moral training textbooks began to use Sontoku as a moral example.[99] Sontoku's emphasis on frugality and hard work, the central values of the Home Ministry-issued Boshin Edict of 1908, undoubtedly accorded well with the industrialization programs of the Meiji government. In addition, Inoue sought to establish Sontoku's *Evening Talks* as the Japanese equivalent of the *Analects* of Confucius and the Gospels of Christianity.[100] Here again, then, is the use of Sontoku to depict Japan's national character.

Finally, Christian Uchimura Kanzō also made use of Ninomiya Sontoku. During the Russo-Japanese War, Kanzō wrote a biography of Sontoku, published in English in 1908 as *Ninomiya Sontoku: A Peasant Saint*. Through this work, intended for a Western audience, Kanzō hoped to show the outside world qualities of Japan aside from the "blind loyalty and bloody patriotism" with which some Western journalists characterized Japan during its conflict with Russia. The virtues of frugality and hard work that Sontoku upheld, according to Kanzō, were deeply rooted in "oriental thought and the spirit of the Japanese nation."[101] For Kanzō, Sontoku was "a genuine Japanese undefiled yet by the Greatest-Happiness-Philosophy of the Occidental importation."[102] Kanzō's representation of Sontoku questions the "national morality" emphasis on loyalty and patriotism while upholding a "Japanese morality" of hard work and frugality as well as his own form of patriotism.

Sontoku's thought was applied in a number of ways for various ends in the moral discourse of the 1890s and 1900s. Socialists drew upon Sontoku to attack the government and big business, the government used Sontoku to instill the virtues of industry and frugality in Japan's youths (the future labor force), and others upheld Sontoku as a representative model of Japan's national moral character. Perhaps the widespread application of Sontoku's thought in the Meiji period can be explained by its adaptability and its suitability to defend a variety of intellectual positions.

Thus, a struggle to define the terms of moral discourse was an integral part of efforts to legitimize moral views, both for those who disseminated and those who opposed national morality. And while proponents of national morality achieved a certain degree of success in establishing such terms as morality, the Way of humanity, treason, loyalty, wholesome or dangerous or poisonous thought, and so forth, as fixtures of early twentieth-century moral discourse, they were unable to control the way these terms were received and reconfigured.

Finally, the questioning of national morality's truth-claims provided a third strategy with which to undermine its dominance. For example, even as Inoue, with the backing of the Ministry of Education, struggled to establish the authority of national morality through lectures to the nation's teachers, scholarly articles, textbooks on moral training, and so on, others viewed this so-called "people's morality" of loyalty and filiality as anachronistic, false, and devoid of authority.

Lecturing in 1911, Natsume Soseki discussed national morality, referring to it as the "romantic morality" that was dominant prior to the Meiji Revolution of 1868. This morality, he claimed, "has by and large passed away." Linking the progress of knowledge with the decline of this romantic morality's credibility, he asserted that "although romantic morality was seen to be true originally, now...one cannot but think of it as lies. This is because [romantic morality] has completely lost its actual authority." Soseki thus viewed the national morality project as an attempt to impose outmoded values on a society that was no longer willing to accept them. "Even if people are coerced into following this romantic morality as in the past," he claimed, "no one will practice it because human knowledge has advanced."[103] While Soseki depicted national morality as an anachronism and as a collection of lies, socialist thinkers questioned national morality's claims to moral particularism.

Katayama Sen, a leading Christian socialist who spent time in prison between 1911 and 1912 for his role in organizing worker strikes, argued that morality in Japan is not a product of national character and a function of the spirit of the people *(minzoku seishin)* as national morality proponents asserted, but rather a product of socioeconomic conditions.

> The condition of the national economy determines the conditions of national morality. In the final analysis, economic life governs the thought of the people. And so the level of the economy's development and progress determines the level of the development and progress for the religion and morality of the nation. For this reason, we believe that without the world of socialism, we will not fully enjoy true religion and morality.[104]

This view, insisting that national morality was not tied to the character of a people, directly undermined national morality scholars' assertion of moral sensibilities unique to Japan. The danger in this type of thinking for national morality was that it conceived of morality as determined by factors that transcend national particularity. The morality of Japan, just like that of any other nation, was governed by universal economic principles. According to this view, then, if one wanted to understand morality in Japan, the study of economics rather than "the people's spirit" should be the focus of attention.

Even the sacred truths surrounding the emperor came under attack. National morality affirmed the divine status of the emperor and, moreover, held that the emperor and the state were "of one body."[105] The emperor, then, was the concrete manifestation of the abstract spirit of the state *(kokka shin)*. To disobey or plot against the one was a show of disloyalty to the other. For Kawakami, it was precisely through this identification of state and emperor that the ethics of state-ism derived its authority. Kawakami's critique was directed at those, like Hozumi Yatsuka and the Nihon Kōdōkai, who asserted that "the emperor *is* the state" *(tennō wa sunawachi kokka nari)*.[106] In short, love and reverence for the emperor and the deities was synonymous with love and reverence for the state, and according to Kawakami, this was an all too commonly held view.[107]

At the root of much anti-state activism during the late Meiji period, however, was an effort to strike precisely at this key symbol for state legitimacy, the divine status of the emperor. Miyashita Takichi, a machine operator at the Kamezaki iron factory in Aichi Prefecture, provides one example. After his arrest in 1910 in connection with the assassination plot (the High Treason Incident, 1910–1911), he is said to have stated in a preliminary hearing, "Because the people of our country hold this sort of superstition about the imperial family [i.e., the emperor's divinity], it was totally impossible to realize socialism. Hence, I made up my mind to first make a bomb and then throw it at the emperor. I had to show that even the emperor is a human being that bleeds just like the rest of us, and thus destroy the people's superstition."[108] Miyashita, an anarchist activist, believed that the representation of the emperor as divine was the greatest obstacle to the spread of socialism in Japan and helped to maintain what he viewed as an exploitative and immoral capitalist system. Miyashita was executed for high treason in 1911, but his opposition to the divinity of the emperor was taken up by others. Kaneko Fumiko, an anarchist activist imprisoned for treason in the mid-1920s, was just as outspoken in her views of the emperor: "We have in our midst someone who is supposed to be a living god, one who is omnipotent and omniscient.... Yet his children are crying because of hunger, suffocating to death in the coal mines, and being crushed to death by factory machines. Why is this so? Because, in truth, the emperor is a mere human being."[109] As for "the concepts of loyalty to the emperor and love of nation," they were "simply rhetorical notions that are being manipulated by the tiny group of the privileged classes to fulfill their own greed and interests."[110]

Thus, the strategy of attacking national morality's most central truth-claims, as with efforts to lay bare the moral failings of the state and to contest the meaning of the terms of moral discourse, disrupted the legitimacy of national morality. National morality discourse, then, was by no means merely abstract and philosophical; it was deeply intertwined with the thought and activities of anarchists, socialists, and others that threatened the state's own moral vision for society.

Conclusions: The Dangers of the Moral Ideal

The conception of the good at the root of national morality discourse was a product of its intellectual context. In his *Outline of National Morality,* Inoue Tetsujirō claimed that through his newly formulated moral theory, the question of good and evil could finally be settled. He believed he had revealed the essence of "the good." But Inoue's decisive solution to the problem of good and evil was in fact a contingent normative claim produced within a specific set of historical conditions. Contemporary accounts of national morality devote inadequate attention to the historical conditions out of which national morality emerged. These accounts represent national morality as a set of statements about loyalty, filiality, the family-state, and patriotism. Centering solely on these "elements," they abstract national morality discourse from its philosophical and sociopolitical contexts and consequently overlook national morality's connections with the philosophical movement known as personalism and the "dangerous thought" of anarchism, socialism, individualism, and literary naturalism.

Inoue's configuration of the good as the pursuit of an ideal, and the ideal itself as complete personality, reflects the appropriation of the language and concepts of personalism. But national morality scholars reconfigured the terms of personalism in such a way that the only "truly good" action was action that served the state. Unlike personalism's ideal of self-realization, the ideal of national morality was the perfection of the state. The good, in other words, was the attempt to universalize a contingent and highly local moral perspective, to create a state-directed moral homogeneity through the suppression of difference. Read as allegory, Inoue's ostensibly apolitical treatise on national morality was, in fact, a highly political effort to provide philosophical justification for the state's cultivation of loyal subjects and its suppression of what it deemed dangerous thought.

"Dangerous thought" was dangerous because both its existence and assertions undermined national morality's claim to speak for the good. While national morality proponents demanded the approach toward their moral ideal—the state of moral homogeneity in which all subjects faithfully served the state—the presence of dangerous thought served as testimony to national morality's failure to attain its ideal. In short, dangerous thought was viewed as an obstacle to the good and as the cause of social disorder. The pursuit of social order and the cultivation of loyal action that served the state required its eradication.

But why did this new configuration of national morality, one that began with Inoue's lectures in 1910–1911, emerge when it did? The formation of community works through exclusion, and the state's efforts to create a moral community produced various "other" moral communities (supporters of anarchism, individualism, etc.) that were unable to find a place for themselves in the national morality vision for society. As this chapter has shown, the process of creating community was oftentimes violent, and with the twelve executions in the High Treason Incident, neither the state nor the population in general could ignore the violence carried out by the state in the pursuit of its ideal. The violence of the national morality project had become apparent to its architects.

Attempting to justify the state's use of violence in the suppression of anarchism and other forms of dangerous thought, Inoue wrote, "Those who embrace destructive thought are, in history's judgment, in error."[111] Yet through their engagement with dangerous thought, Inoue and other national morality advocates were forced to confront the realization that national morality was itself a form of destructive and dangerous thought that worked to legitimize the open, physical violence the state used against its enemies. Moreover, its efforts to reduce various other normative orientations to a single homogeneous moral space must be viewed as a form of violence as well—the violence of the suppression of otherness.

Yet the discourse on national morality enabled, sustained, and reproduced dangerous thought even while seeking to annihilate it. In their quest to monopolize the authority to speak for the morality of the entire nation, national morality proponents brought the issue of "the moral ideal" to the center of public discourse, thereby enabling those excluded by this ideal to question it. In other words, national morality discourse opened up a space of dissent. It provided the discursive conditions for marginalized voices not merely to be feared, but also heard. Moreover, although national morality and modes of thought opposed to national morality posed a threat to one another, each needed the other to define and sustain itself. For national morality, the dangerous other helped to sustain its own vitality and urgency. In this sense, while national morality and the state actively sought the annihilation of dangerous thought, its complete eradication would have erased the significance of national morality. To invoke the dangerous and destructive character of socialism, anarchism, and individualism was therefore not merely a descriptive activity, but was performative as well. That is, it served to create and re-create the other as the dangerous object to be opposed, suppressed, and feared. This constant condemnation of the other worked to sustain it. Every assertion on behalf of national morality implicitly reinforced a negative conception of the other. To "approach" the moral ideal, then, was not to move forward or upward toward some "better" end, but to sustain the current heterogeneous social reality of conflict and dissension.[112] In other words, to approach was always to remain within the realm of violence and suppression; it meant the constant but incomplete annihilation of the other.

Epilogue

The Ethics of Humanism and Moral Particularism in Twentieth-Century Japan

> From the time of Japan's defeat in 1945, Japan's good traditions and customs have been disavowed and this situation continues to this day. Most striking is that, in politics, administration, education, and the whole of social life, morality has been lost.
> —The Society for the Promotion of Constitutional Justice, 2003

The discipline of ethics *(rinrigaku)* emerged in Japan not as an objective and value-neutral form of academic inquiry, but as one among many competing normative views on how society ought to be ordered. From the early Meiji period, when Inoue Tetsujirō and others established this discipline, to the late Meiji project to create a homogeneous moral space called "national morality," *rinrigaku* occupied a position in proximity to the state. As the state pursued "civilization," Inoue Tetsujirō and other *rinrigaku* scholars sought to universalize a morality in keeping with this aim—suppressing "superstition" and "foolishness" in the process. When religious thinkers protested state interference in the moral lives of its citizens, *rinrigaku* condemned religion and its moral position as irrational and socially divisive. For a brief period at the close of the nineteenth century, certain *rinrigaku* scholars came to champion the liberty and equality of individuals; however, the desire to assert the "moral spirit of the Japanese folk" *(minzoku no seishin)* to counter the universalizing force of "Occidental ethics" soon eclipsed this position. Thus, the brief turn to the humanistic ethics of personalism that prioritized the cultivation of the individual was redirected toward an identity of Japanese particularism. Participants in the discourse on the collective morality of the folk *(kokumin dōtoku)* appropriated and reconfigured notions of "individual" and "cultivation," aligning them with the cultivation of the state. Creating and enforcing this folk morality entailed the exclusion of competing moral views in the early years of the twentieth century, such as anarchism, socialism, individualism.

The discipline of ethics was largely successful in establishing the parameters of legitimate moral discourse; the importance of self-sacrifice for the social whole and the necessity of preserving the state and "traditional values" came to be widely naturalized. Moreover, by claiming universal status for their moral perspectives, *rinrigaku* scholars sought to overcome the historical contingency of their assertions and thereby enhance their authority. In short, this was an effort to recast "the good," as a contingent moral perspective, into a timeless truth or universal principle. But perfect moral hegemony was never attained. *Rinrigaku's* authority was used to justify the state-led, violent suppression of alternative moral positions (e.g., the High Treason executions) so as to promote a unitary moral outlook as a basis for a unified and well-ordered society and a powerful state. Maintaining an image of the state as moral, however, required that such state-sponsored displays of violence be concealed, or when this was impossible, that they be represented as consistent with (and not as transgressions of) "civilized conduct" or "folk morality." In part, because the state could not conceal the violence it carried out in the name of morality, its claims to universality opened up a space for dissent and encouraged a questioning of the content of this putatively universal morality.[1] Thus, far from creating moral unity, the discipline of ethics in Japan (in conjunction with various state institutions) and its claims to moral universalism engendered and sustained the very moral dissension and violence it sought to overcome.

This study of the formation of Meiji ethics, outlined in brief above, can be read as a kind of prehistory to the much-studied intellectual history of wartime Japan. Of course, the national morality of late Meiji was not the antecedent cause to the "inevitable" effect of Japan's interwar fascism. There was never a direct line of historical inevitability linking moral discourse of the 1910s to that of the first decades of the Shōwa period (1926–1989). Nevertheless, it was during the late Meiji that many of the key strategies, concepts, and presuppositions of 1930s intellectual discourse began to emerge. A morality of self-negation, the representation of "Western thought" as poisonous, and terms such as *kokumin* or *minzoku,* for example, figured prominently in early Shōwa intellectual exchanges. Though transformed since their emergence in the Meiji period, their re-conceptualization by Shōwa intellectuals was in part enabled and mediated by their prior usage in Meiji. A thorough understanding of their semantic variability and the specific ways in which they were tied to values and morality in early Shōwa requires familiarity with their status during the late Meiji period.

For example, the demand for individual self-negation, so prevalent in wartime Japan, is evident in late Meiji as well. Fukasaku Yasubumi's call for a national morality based upon "self-sacrificing action in which the individual extinguishes his egoistic self and brings to life his eternal higher self on behalf of the state" prefigures Nishitani Keiji's statements of 1942: "Why must the state demand public service from the people that extinguishes their private sense of self? It is, quite simply, because of the need to strengthen, as much as possible, its internal unity as a state."² Self-negation for both Fukasaku and Nishitani amounted to effective state regulation of the human interiority, which, in turn, depended upon the state's ability to naturalize the terms of moral discourse. The "egoistic" self was linked to individualism (denounced as dangerous and foreign) and to the pursuit of selfish desires, while the self that sacrifices on behalf of the state was "higher," "eternal," and almost divine.

Strategies of representation whereby "Western thought" becomes a foreign disease or poison threatening "Japanese values" are also common to both late Meiji and Shōwa. We see such a strategy clearly articulated in Inoue Tetsujirō's warnings of the "great poison" of anarchism, which he represented as foreign, dangerous, and subversive to Japan's national morality, and again in Hozumi Yatsuka's and Yamagata Aritomo's desire to stamp out the "disease of social-ism" and those afflicted by it.³ Decades later, those associated with the Japan Romantic School (Nihon Romanha), participants in the "Overcoming Moder-nity" symposium of the early 1940s, and others made use of a similar strat-egy. Kamei Katsuichirō, associated with both groups just mentioned, provides a representative example of depicting Western civilization as an illness. "The war that we are now fighting," he stated, "is externally a struggle to overthrow the power of England and America and internally to find the root cure for the sickness of the spirit brought on by modern civilization."⁴ Similarly, scholar of Islam Ōkawa Shūmei also spoke of a spiritual malaise brought on by the West and its materialistic values that threatened the spiritual values of Asia. Ōkawa believed that "the path of Europe and the path of Asia...must join together," but he was convinced that such a merging could come about only, "without exception," through war.⁵ In early 1942, with Japan now at war, philosopher Kōsaka Masaaki understood Japan's current struggle as "a war between the Ori-ental morality and the Occidental morality." The most pressing question to be addressed, he suggested, was "which morality will play a more important role in World History in the future."⁶ More attention is needed to clarify the way the Pacific War came to be viewed as a contest of competing moralities.

In addition, much intellectual discourse of the 1930s centered on the con-cept of the Japanese *minzoku,* or ethnicity. Yet the codification of an opposi-tion between *kokumin* ("the people who live together under the same state") and *minzoku* ("those who share the same race, religion, manners, customs, and language") began at the turn of the century, if not earlier.⁷ Late Meiji scholars of national morality spoke of the morality of the *kokumin,* not of the *minzoku.* Yet their depiction of this morality, linking it to Japan's *kokutai* and unique characteristics and differentiating it from the moralities of "the West" and China, often blurred the lines between these two categories. Indeed, as discussed in chapter 5, some argued that these two categories overlapped, that—in the case of Japan—the people under the state were the people sharing the same race, language, and customs. The term *minzoku* remained semantically unstable in early Shōwa, but continued to be intertwined with questions of value and morality. A study of early Shōwa *minzoku* discourse can benefit from an examination of the term's genealogy, its contested status during late Meiji, and the way in which ideologies and moralities of race and ethnicity came to be constructed.

A final example is the effort to ascribe to "the West" a subject-object opposition as fundamental to its knowledge, values, history, and so on, while upholding for Japan a predisposition to view subject and object (individual and social totality, finite and infinite spirit, etc.) as always already conjoined. Harry Harootunian notes philosopher Miki Kiyoshi's opposition to "the curse of Western philosophy and its unbending and baneful devotion to maintaining the subject/object dualism and its consequences for knowledge and power."[8] Ōkawa too, like many others of the early Shōwa, argued that "individual and society, grasped ethically, are two aspects of one body, an inseparable reality."[9] A parallel (but not identical) critique, discussed in chapter 4 as a shift to a hylomorphic epistemology unifying subject and object, emerged in the 1890s among Japan's philosophers of personalism. The assertion of a subject-object unity had important implications for ethical thought in both periods; it served as a basis for a morality of self-negation and self-sacrifice on behalf of the state. This, then, is another intellectual framework or feature of discourse that emerged in its own context in the late 1920s and early 1930s, but that had antecedent traces in the Meiji period. Thus, the concerns of late Meiji intellectual discourse broadly, and the specific articulation of these terms in the moral discourse of the time, prefigured much of what was to come and suggests that a greater familiarity with Meiji moral discourse and its key terms will enrich our interpretations of the moral landscape of interwar and wartime Japan.

The purpose of the foregoing paragraphs is not to put forward *kokumin*, *minzoku*, and other terms that figured so prominently in Japan's interwar and wartime periods as ahistorical concepts, but to call attention to their semantic fluidity by juxtaposing their status in the 1930s with their prehistory in the late Meiji period. Clearly, it is crucial to approach these terms through the intellectual context in which they are used. Moreover, the national morality movement of late Meiji was not part of a single discourse stretching from Meiji to the Pacific War; too much had changed—economically, internationally, intellectually—between these two points to make such an assumption.[10]

One of the key changes that sets the two apart was the emergence of a discourse on "culture." Tetsuo Najita and Harry Harootunian describe an "intellectual shift from 'cosmopolitanism' to 'culturalism'" that came to be articulated in the 1930s by a wide range of thinkers of diverse backgrounds: Watsuji Tetsurō, Yanagida Kunio, Tanizaki Junichirō, Nishida Kitarō, and others.[11] Culturalism centered on a critique of the materialism, mechanization, and alienation of modern society. By linking these conditions with the "West," culturalism functioned as a critique of Euro-Americanism. Inasmuch as these conditions now characterized Japan, culturalism was also a critique of what Japan itself had become. Above all, culturalism lamented a loss of "spiritual values" and, for some participants in this discourse, presaged a coming "cultural struggle," or *Kulturkampf* (a German term circulating in Japan at least since 1912), with the West, as noted in the above case of Ōkawa Shūmei.[12]

Just several years beyond the close of the Meiji period, Japan was in the midst of a different cultural struggle, World War I. By this time, national morality discourse was coming to be configured in terms of the "cosmopolitanism" discussed above. National morality was Japan's moral contribution to the world. This is clear in moral philosopher Yoshida Seiichi's *Essentials of National Morality* (*Kokumin dōtoku yōryō*, 1916). He described the then ongoing World War I as "a cultural struggle *(bunka teki kyōsō)* now taking place with Western countries." It was too late, he suggested, "to remove the long-standing influence of Western thought" from Japan and equally clear that Japan could not retreat from the international community behind its own borders. But Japan could still make its own unique contribution to the world. "Our people," Yoshida predicted, "will contribute to the advancement of the world by developing a new and unique civilization, earning them the reverence of all the peoples of the world." Japan's contribution, however, must be guided by its own values, its own "ideal of the good and the beautiful." Yoshida therefore called upon his countrymen to "exalt the sprit of our national morality."[13] In this work, culture, cosmopolitanism, Japanese values, and national morality are intertwined, but the cultural struggle Yoshida described is not what it later became—the powerful desire to cleanse Japan and the Orient of the West's inauthentic and harmful influence. This example reminds us that while attention to the conceptual vocabulary late Meiji shared with early Shōwa is crucial, our interpretations of this vocabulary must remain sensitive to the shifting intellectual, cultural, and social contexts in which it appeared.

Yoshida wrote widely not only on national morality, but on the humanistic moral philosophy of personalism as well. His works and those of Inoue Tetsujirō and others contributed to the gradual displacement of personalism by the national morality movement during the first decades of the twentieth century. But personalism was not erased altogether. Indeed, some kind of "humanistic" ethics has persisted in Japan alongside and in confrontation with an ethics of national particularism throughout the twentieth century.

During the early Taishō period (1912–1926), for example, women contested the dominant gender norms of their day by appropriating the term "personality" (jinkaku) and the broader ethics of self-realization expounded by personalism. Calling themselves "new women," Hiratsuka Raichō, Itō Noe, Yosano Akiko, Yamakawa Kikue, and others questioned the dominant assertion that women ought to be educated to become "good wives and wise mothers."

The "good wife wise mother" ideal held that women were to be educated as women; they were to cultivate the "womanly virtues" of chastity and obedience, to assist their husbands, and rear their children. But in addition to this they were to be educated as national subjects. According to a 1918 statement by a government committee on women's education, the cultivation of womanly virtues should not take precedence over the cultivation of "a sense of state." Moreover, it was not enough for women themselves to be good and faithful subjects of the state; they also had to be wise mothers who raise children who will in turn become good and faithful subjects. For this reason, the statement continued, "women's education must above all strengthen a woman's sense of national essence (kokutai) and strengthen the foundation of national morality (kokumin dōtoku)."[14] Thus, the cultivation of good wives and wise mothers blended with national morality discourse. And just as proponents of national morality emphasized the importance of "healthy thought," we see the same emphasis among those upholding the ideal of the good wife and wise mother. Okuda Yoshihito, education minister from 1913 to 1914, stated, "Whether a girl turns out good or not depends on the wisdom of the mother. The mother, therefore, must in all cases instill the child with healthy thought.... If the mother of a household, regardless of the schooling she may have received, lacks healthy thought, then it will be impossible to accomplish the true aim of education."[15] The true aim of education was to instill both women and men with the healthy thought of patriotic loyalty to the state.

While educators and state bureaucrats undertook to educate women as women (by cultivating virtues specific to their gender) and as national subjects (by instilling a "sense of state"), "new women" demanded that women be educated as persons. Their argument, in short, was that although gender differences are undeniable, they are not so important as the commonalities men and women share as human beings. To assert that women are persons was to make an ontological claim; it was an effort to affirm that women, like men, possessed "personality," a self-awareness of one's own individuality. For Raichō and other new women, good wife/wise mother education was far too narrow to allow for one's full development as a person. "This kind of women's education," Raichō insisted, "does not touch on those things that are of fundamental significance in life. Consequently, as a form of education that in no way supplies the fertilizer for the roots of personality, it is thus the greatest obstacle to the free development of today's women. I will therefore always maintain an unchanging spirit of defiance toward it."[16] Thus, as I have argued elsewhere, the concept of personality was reappropriated to provide the ontological basis both for contesting the good wife/wise mother ideal and for upholding the alternative moral ideal of the new woman.[17]

As persons, Raichō argued, women need "no longer tolerate silently and meekly walking the path that the oppressed women of the past have walked." The new woman will walk her own path; she will create the paths that she herself chooses to follow. For Raichō, this required "the destruction of the old morality and the old laws created for the convenience of men" so as to create a "new kingdom" ordered by a "new morality."[18] Precisely what this new morality was to be was never clearly explained, although it was clearly grounded in a reworked version of personality.[19] Yet this willingness to allow the new woman ideal to remain ambiguous reflects a greater openness to moral alterity. The carefully specified and rigid ideal of the good wife/wise mother closed off action and thought that obstructed its realization. The more open ideal of the new woman, on the other hand, while quite clear in its opposition to "the old morality," nevertheless afforded women greater latitude in deciding how to live as new women.

The legacy of personalism appears, as well, at a time of heightened attention to democratic government during the 1920s, referred to in historical narratives as "Taishō Democracy." Certain thinkers at this time continued to advocate many of the goals of personalism, oftentimes making use of the same moral vocabulary as did Nakashima Rikizō in the 1890s. Yoshino Sakuzō (1878–1933), political historian, social critic, and proponent of "government based on the people" *(minponshugi)*, was perhaps the foremost such thinker.

Although Yoshino formulated his arguments within the atmosphere of national character discourse (and his writings do reflect this discourse), his central concern was not to cultivate national or cultural particularism, but to promote the movement of Japanese society toward a universal ideal: a form of democracy in which the people controlled the direction of politics and where no individual was prevented from pursuing the realization of their potential self.

Like Nakashima, Yoshino prioritized the good of the individual over the social totality. The government's role was to promote the good of the individual, and this involved the facilitation of the individual's realization of his or her true self *(shinjitsu no jiga)*.[20] Moreover, Yoshino foresaw the eventual development of national societies into a world society, into a single and universal "unified spiritual whole."[21] This would necessarily involve a de-emphasis on the particularities of the nation, with attention being directed away from the national folk toward humanity in general and the realization of universal human potential. This was the ideal end Yoshino envisioned, one he hoped would guide politics in Japan. In short, Yoshino's ultimate concern, like Nakashima's before him, was "the universal" rather than national or cultural particularity. The pursuit of this universal ideal (problematized below) necessarily involved the cultivation of the individual, and in this sense, too, Yoshino appears intellectually close to Nakashima. Although Yoshino's position, again like Nakashima's, was fairly short-lived and proved unsustainable, there were those in his day or of subsequent generations—Nitobe Inazō, Suzuki Bunji, Abe Jirō, Kawai Eijirō—who drew inspiration either from Yoshino's *minponshugi* or Nakashima's humanistic personalism as they contested proponents of some form of "national morality."[22]

The idea of national morality has likewise remained a focus of moral discourse throughout the twentieth century. In the early 1930s the well-known moral philosopher Watsuji Tetsurō (1889–1960), who like Inoue Tetsujirō held the chair of ethics at Tokyo University, took up the issue of Japan's national morality in an open lecture held in 1930. Here, he strongly denounced prior conceptions of national morality, such as those of Inoue Tetsujirō, Yoshida Kumaji, and Fukasaku Yasubumi. These thinkers, he believed, failed to distinguish between national morality as "historical fact" (i.e., as it "actually existed" in the past) and as it ought to be, that is, as a "mission" to be realized in the future.[23] National morality scholars of late Meiji focused on the former, investigating various moral texts from Japan's past. But equally if not more important, according to Watsuji, was Japan's potential national morality. Here, Watsuji spoke of the realization of universal moral principles, principles inherent in all national moralities (i.e., in all the conceptions of morality held by all the *kokumin* of the world).[24] Such universal moral principles, however, could be realized only within the particular national-ethnic form.

> The morality of the *kokumin* is the realization of universal morality. The principle of human nature is made to take shape only within *kokumin* as the entirety of humanity. But, however universal the course that guides this realization of universal morality may be, what is in fact realized is always nothing other than the particular. So long as the structure of humanity remains subject to the burdens of history and climate, the universal cannot be realized universally.[25]

In this passage, Watsuji suggests that the universal moral principles common to all humanity can be manifested only within the particular *kokumin* or nation, because such principles and the way they are implemented are subject to the same historical and climatic conditions that shape the people of each nation. Thus, *kokumin dōtoku* for Watsuji was not the morality of the state; rather, it was the particular manifestation of the universal morality of humanity *(ningen)*.[26] It was the creation of the Japanese people *(minzoku)*. The formula expressed in the above citation allows Watsuji to uphold Japanese moral particularism even while grounding it in the authoritative universalism of humanity.[27]

National morality continues to be a central feature of Japanese moral discourse in more recent years as well. Ishihara Shintarō, elected as the governor of Tokyo in 1999, in 2003, and again in 2007 and known outside Japan for his provocative book *The Japan That Can Say No,* lamented Japan's moral decline in a short work titled "Japan's Morality" (Nippon no dōgi, 1974). "There is a spiritual void," he states, "at the core of the Japanese nation, a moral degeneration that characterizes everything that happens in this society" and that may ultimately destroy the nation. The loss of morality in Japan, Ishihara explains, stems from the loss of "the divine symbol necessary in any national morality." Japan's divine symbol of moral unity, the emperor, can no longer provide the basis for a national morality; meanwhile, nothing has emerged to take its place and unite the people. Political leadership, according to Ishihara, lacks the power on its own to produce a national morality in Japan, and yet "politics is, nevertheless, the most powerful tool to nurture and weld a moral philosophy into a living force." Ishihara's statements follow a common pattern: he calls attention to moral decline, attempts to diagnose its cause, and then begins to seek a remedy by calling on political leadership to address Japan's moral decline. In this text, he provides little in the way of specifics on what this much needed moral philosophy would be.[28] Others in the past decade, however, not only identify the cause but put forward clear solutions.

Upholding national morality in present-day Japan is the overriding concern of the Nihon Kōdōkai, an organization for the promotion of morality founded in 1887 by Nishimura Shigeki. According to its current administrators, the Nihon Kōdōkai's objectives have remained consistent from the time of its foundation in the Meiji period: "to pursue the ideal of promoting national morality *(kokumin dōtoku)* and establishing a moral state." In line with the aims of its founder, it seeks "to rectify the minds of the people, to improve customs, to cultivate national power, and thereby to promote the prestige of Japan." This begins with the cultivation of the self, but is then extended outward to the cultivation of others in society. The society's current president, Suzuki

Isao, describing a 2001 Kōdōkai symposium titled "Thinking about Home Education," called attention to the problems of discipline in the home during the
postwar period. Expressing a concern about moral decline similar to Ishihara's,
he warned that under today's conditions, there may be no "Japan of tomorrow"
for the young people of today. The symposium aimed to confront this issue by
contributing to the "nurturing of healthy youths."[29] The Kōdōkai's aims reflect a
commitment to the wide-scale dissemination of a national morality, expressed
here as the pursuit of an ideal to "rectify the minds of the people." Moreover,
the society's concern with "healthy youths" in the context of education and discipline in the home is reminiscent of the "healthy thought" national morality sought to inculcate a century ago. The same questions directed in the last
chapter at national morality might be usefully applied here as well. What is the
content of "healthy thought" and the national morality here advocated? Who
decides such an important issue? By delineating the boundaries for healthy
thought, has "unhealthy thought" come to be identified as well? Is unhealthy
thought to be regulated, and if so, by whom?

In a similar example, the Society for the Promotion of Constitutional Justice (Rikken Yōseikai) launched a campaign in 2003 to reinstitute the Imperial
Rescript on Education, the 1890 document calling for loyal and dutiful subjects in the name of the emperor, as a basis for Japanese morality. The postwar
"democratic morality," according to this society, has produced among the Japanese people "an unfilial attitude toward one's parents, disaffection toward one's
siblings, disharmony between husbands and wives, distrust between friends,
immodesty and extravagance." In short, Japan's current morality is the antith-
esis in every way to that espoused in the Imperial Rescript on Education. A
pamphlet distributed by this society titled "Let's Rescue Japan by Reviving the
Rescript on Education" begins,

> The Imperial Rescript on Education is the conscience of Japan. From the
> time of Japan's defeat in 1945, Japan's good traditions and customs have
> been disavowed and this situation continues to this day. Most striking is
> that, in politics, administration, education, and the whole of social life,
> morality has been lost.... This is because the Rescript on Education, the
> foundation of the morality of the Japanese people, is disavowed by the
> current constitution (the preamble and article nine) that was forced upon
> Japan by command of the occupying army (GHQ).... This great error must
> be corrected.

The Imperial Rescript is presented in this pamphlet as a benign statement on
virtues that any can accept—indeed, that all must defend. Filial piety (oya-

kōkō), for example, which holds a prominent place in the Imperial Rescript, is here upheld as a universal virtue containing a human truth that endures "now as in the past, in Japan as throughout the world." This statement thus mirrors the Imperial Rescript itself, which concludes, "The Way here set forth is...infallible for all ages and true in all places."[30] The Society for the Promotion of Constitutional Justice, then, provides yet another example of an assertion of moral decline to be resolved by a common Japanese morality.[31]

Perhaps the most thorough attention to "national morality" in Japan in recent years can be found in a popular work by Nishibe Susumu, a social critic, writer, and former lecturer at Tokyo University. In 2000 Nishibe published a lengthy work titled *National Morality (Kokumin no dōtoku).* In this text there is much that is reminiscent of the national morality thought of Inoue Tetsujirō, Fukasaku Yasubumi, Yoshida Kumaji, and others at the beginning of the twentieth century. But Nishibe's project is part of a new discourse with new objectives and new enemies. Unlike Inoue and others in the 1910s who sought to eradicate the "dangerous thought" of anarchism, socialism, and individualism, dangerous thought for Nishibe is what he understands as "civil society" and its values. Indeed, his work begins with a glossary of terms in which he defines *kokumin* (nation or national subject) in direct opposition to the term *shimin* (citizen, as in *shimin shakai,* or civil society). Nishibe's glossary of terms functions not unlike the dictionaries of Meiji *rinrigaku* scholars and their efforts to fix the meanings of terms so as to establish an authoritative and unitary moral vocabulary.

Nishibe's starting point in this text is the crime, political corruption, and disaffected youth in contemporary Japan. All are indications of moral decline brought on by the postwar diffusion of the values of American-style modernism. After the Meiji Revolution of 1868, and with close engagement with and then resistance to the West, Nishibe explains, Japan began to reexamine its unique identity. But with Japan's defeat in the Pacific War and with the postwar Americanization that followed, Japan suffered a "loss of spirit" that led to a decline in morality. Nishibe's national morality involves a nostalgia for the "spiritual predominance" of the prewar period.[32]

Specifically, progressivism, humanism, pacifism, and democracy are to blame for Japan's moral decline, says Nishibe, as these form the foundation for values that privilege not the public realm, but the realm of private benefit. In Nishibe's view, "liberty destroys morality," and the idea that "all are born equal" is an exaggeration and an "unproven proposition." And as for humanism, with its emphasis on the dignity of the individual, it is "nothing more than a rash, arrogant human narcissism."[33]

Nishibe calls for the rebuilding of morality in such a way as to restore public order. In this effort, he explains, history can serve as a guide. The history of the nation, together with common sense, will provide the perspective from which to identify the long-term values of the public sphere that have been handed down from the past. These values are not "universal"; they are particular to the nation's traditions and to its history. Hence, the study of Japan's past and its language, says Nishibe, is essential for moral education.

Nishibe is one of the directors of the Japanese Society for History Textbook Reform, the organization that published his work on national morality. Established in 1996, this society is committed to the reconstruction of history education in Japan. But if history is to reveal the particular values of Japan, as Nishibe believes, history education must de-emphasize or remove narratives that are inconsistent with those values. This is precisely the objective of the Society for History Textbook Reform: to radically rewrite Japan's activities during the Pacific War, refuting what they see as mistaken views about the actions of the Japanese army, "comfort women," and the Nanjing Massacre.[34] For Nishibe, this reconfigured past will help to cultivate national pride and an essentialized morality particular to the Japanese people.

If we are persuaded by these varied statements on the "loss of morality" from Inoue to Nishibe, then Japan has been in a perpetual state of moral decline, ever poised at a crucial historical moment when its values are under siege and in jeopardy of being swept away. Alternatively, sounding the alarm of moral decline may be viewed as a strategy to depict other moralities as immoral and to sanction one's own moral position. At issue then is not the decline or loss of "morality" per se (i.e., some essentialized set of natural and enduring values) but a marginalization of the particular moral positions of those who speak for a national or Japanese morality in the postwar period. Their concern is that a moral position other than their own will attain even greater hegemony.

Nishibe's struggle to resist the hegemonic claims of civil society and its putatively universal values led to the imposition of his own hegemonic claims about values common to all Japanese. His project is thus predicated upon essentializing, Nihonjin-ron-style assertions of Japanese identity. But, as with national morality discourse a century ago, will not the efforts of Nishibe and his supporters to universalize (within Japan) some formal conception of "Japanese values" involve the suppression of alternative moralities? Is this not true also of Watsuji, Ishihara, the Nihon Kōdōkai, and the Society for the Promotion of Constitutional Justice? It appears that the problematic notion of a "national morality" is as much in need of critical scrutiny today as it was in Japan a century ago.

This notion of the moral universal, then, though unquestionably useful for its tremendous legitimizing authority, has carried with it the danger of exclusion and violent suppression. And though the various statements on national morality outlined above center on a "particular" morality of Japan rather than the universal norms of civilization or humanity, they equally rely upon some sense of the universal; they, too, suppress and exclude. Each form of national morality (Inoue's, Watsuji's, Nishibe's), despite their differences, sought to universalize a single homogeneous moral vision within the space of the nation, thereby excluding alternative moral possibilities.

Equally problematic, of course, is what I have called a "humanistic ethics," an approach—like personalism or what Nishibe has dismissively called the values of civil society—that seeks to transcend the morality of the nation and to look to all of humanity as the foundation for morality. We see that for the "new women" of early Taishō, for Yoshino Sakuzō, and for contemporary critics of Nishibe, an ethics of humanism provided a powerful critique of (or at least a viable alternative to) moral particularism. Yet both of these broad approaches to morality have equally relied upon a problematic universalism and strategies of inclusion and exclusion, regardless of whether the moral starting point is the "Japanese person" or simply "the person."

Yet as we look back at Meiji moral discourse, it is necessary to go beyond the mere denunciation of the "false universal" (a claim to perfect inclusiveness while in fact excluding).[35] Indeed, much of the foregoing discussion in this work, from the early Meiji ethics of civilization to the late Meiji and early Taishō ethics of spirit, suggests that even as the universal excluded, it carried the potential to enable dissent. So long as the putative universal (civilization, the spirit of the kokumin, healthy thought, the Orient) constituted itself in opposition to what it excluded (barbarism or other ways of being human, other kokumin, dangerous thought, the West), it produced spaces from which resistance could be waged. This was as true for anarchists resisting national morality as it was for the architects of national morality resisting the universalizing claims of "Occidental ethics." Only ostensibly do we see in this protracted struggle to speak for the good the desire to make an "immoral" society "moral" and only from one perspective a desire for moral hegemony; from a different perspective we see the intense effort to obstruct and prevent moral hegemony, whatever its moral content.

Notes

Introduction

1. As opposed to my assertion that the good was a product (which suggests an ideological construction), I use the terms "reveal," "revelation," and "revelatory" in regard to early Meiji intellectuals' presupposition that the good was somehow always present awaiting discovery, that the good was revealed to the objective observer through empirical observation or the application of instrumental reason. I am suggesting that the faith that Meiji "enlightenment intellectuals" *(keimōsha)* had in the existence or presence of moral truths unmediated by their own methods and presuppositions bore a resemblance to the understanding of "revelation" *(keiji)* in Japan at this time. On the term *keiji*, see Tokutani Toyonosuke and Matsuo Yūshirō, eds., *Futsū jutsugo jii* (Tokyo: Keibunsha, 1905), 262.

2. I use the term "hegemony" not only to refer to the predominance the state desired for its own moral vision, but also to draw upon the rich intellectual history of this concept so as to think about and better understand how the state's moral vision became authoritative, how alternative moralities came to be suppressed as illegitimate, illegal, and immoral, and how resistance to the moral projects of the state was carried out.

3. Marx and Engels' claim is from their *German Ideology*. See Karl Marx and Frederick Engels, "Feuerbach: Opposition of the Materialist and Idealist Outlook," in *The German Ideology, Part One*, ed. C. J. Arthur (New York: International Publishers, 1970), 65–66. Marxist critic Fredric Jameson makes a similar observation: "In its narrowest sense, ethical thought projects as permanent features of human 'experience,' and thus as a kind of 'wisdom' about personal life and interpersonal relations, what are in reality the historical and institutional specifics of a determinate type of group solidarity or class cohesion. ... [A]ll ethics lives by exclusion and predicates certain types of Otherness." See Fredric Jameson, *The Political Unconscious: Narrative as a Socially Symbolic Act* (Ithaca, N.Y.: Cornell University Press, 1981), 59–60.

4. This explanatory framework, a shift from an ethics of civilization to an ethics of spirit, provides an alternative means to interpret Meiji intellectual history and supplements existing scholarship dealing with broader social changes of this time. For example,

Carol Gluck focuses on the political and social world of Meiji's "articulate elite" and on the emergence of "emperor system" *(tennōsei)* ideology. Tetsuo Najita's key explanatory framework is the tension between "bureaucratism" (efficient, measurable performance) and "idealism" (idealistic, selfless action). Douglas Howland approaches the creation of the modern Japanese state through a semiotic study of Japan's appropriation (and transformation) of Euro-American political concepts and the reaction of a "self-appointed elite" who privileged law and order over personal freedoms. See Carol Gluck, *Japan's Modern Myths: Ideology in the Late Meiji Period* (Princeton, N.J.: Princeton University Press, 1985); Tetsuo Najita, *Japan: The Intellectual Foundations of Modern Japanese Politics* (Chicago and London: University of Chicago Press, 1974); and Douglas Howland, *Translating the West: Language and Political Reason in Nineteenth-Century Japan* (Honolulu: University of Hawai'i Press, 2002).

Chapter 1: Civilization and Foolishness

1. In his careful study of political thought in Meiji Japan, Douglas Howland suggests that the term *bunmeikaika* (so often translated as "civilization and enlightenment") should be understood as expressing two competing views on civilization and its attainment: as the universal telos of social development and progress *(bunmei)* and as "the public cultivation of civilization through government policy" or as the "civilizing process" *(kaika)*. See Douglas Howland, *Translating the West: Language and Political Reason in Nineteenth-Century Japan* (Honolulu: University of Hawai'i Press, 2002), 42–43. Ōkubo Toshiaki presents the term *bunmeikaika* as a late Tokugawa/early Meiji neologism, the two terms coming together into a single compound only at this time. He also discusses the etymology of the term(s) in the context of Chinese documents. See Ōkubo, *Meirokusha* (Tokyo: Kōdansha, 2007), esp. 272–275.

2. Inoue Tetsujirō, *Rinri shinsetsu,* in *Meiji bunka zenshū,* vol. 23: *Shisō hen,* ed. Meiji Bunka Kenkyūkai (Tokyo: Nihon Hyōronsha, 1967), 414. All translations are my own unless otherwise indicated.

3. Elsewhere in this text Inoue wrote, "To be indulgent and idle, to be licentious in the way of manners, this is the detestable feature of humanity." Ibid., 424–425.

4. Tetsuo Najita, *Japan: The Intellectual Foundations of Modern Japanese Politics* (Chicago and London: University of Chicago Press, 1974), 78.

5. Peter Duus, *The Rise of Modern Japan* (Boston: Houghton Mifflin Company, 1976), 92.

6. Katō Hiroyuki, *Jinken shinsetsu,* in *Nihon no meicho,* vol. 34: *Nishi Amane and Katō Hiroyuki,* ed. Uete Michiari (Tokyo: Chūōkōronsha, 1972), 452. This translation is from Katō Hiroyuki, "A Reconsideration of Human Rights," trans. J. Victor Koschmann, in *From Japan's Modernity,* ed. Center for East Asian Studies (Chicago: CEAS, 2002), 35. Katō was citing Darwin from his *Descent of Man.*

7. Nishimura Shigeki, *Nihon dōtoku ron,* in *Hakuō Sōsho,* ed. Nihon Kōdōkai (Tokyo: Nihon Kōdōkai, 1976), 8. This translation is from Donald Shively, "Nishimura

Shigeki: A Confucian View of Modernization," in *Confucian Reponses to Modernization*, ed. Marius Jansen (Stanford, Calif.: Stanford University Press, 1959), 215.

8. Inoue Tetsujirō, "Meiji no tetsugaku kaisō roku," in *Tokubetsu kōza kōenran* (Tokyo: Kindaisha, 1926), 5.

9. This was the title of an essay by natural-right theorist Ueki Emori. See his "Ishingo dōtoku no taihai seshi koto o ronzu," in *Tōyō shinbun* no. 1064 (28 April 1886). This essay is also included in *Ishingo dōtoku no taihai seshi koto o ronzu*, ed. Sotozaki Mitsuhiro (Tokyo: Hōsei Daigaku Shuppankyoku, 1982), 162–164.

10. The Tokugawa regime relied upon syncretic ideological apparatuses for control, not merely upon Neo-Confucianism. Moreover, the level of uprisings, riots, and general popular discontent suggests a lack of any real social order. On these points, see Peter Nosco, ed., *Confucianism and Tokugawa Culture* (Honolulu: University of Hawai'i Press, 1984).

11. Nishimura Shigeki, "Shūshin jikoku hi ni michi ron," *Meiroku zasshi* 31 (1 March 1875), ed. Ōkubo Toshiaki (Tokyo: Rittaisha, 1976), 4–7; William Braisted, *Meiroku Zasshi: Journal of the Japanese Enlightenment* (Cambridge, Mass.: Harvard University Press, 1976), 379. Unless otherwise indicated, translations of selections from *Meiroku zasshi* in this chapter are from Braisted's text.

12. Fukuzawa Yukichi, *Bunmei ron no gairyaku* (Tokyo: Iwanami shoten, 1988), 24. This translation appears in Fukuzawa Yukichi, *An Outline of a Theory of Civilization*, trans. David Dilworth and G. Cameron Hurst (Tokyo: Sophia University, 1973), 13.

13. Fukuzawa lays out this hierarchy of "highly civilized" *(saijō no bunmei koku)*, "half-civilized" *(hankai no koku)*, and "barbaric" *(yaban no koku)* countries in his *Bunmei ron no gairyaku.*

14. Nishimura Shigeki, for example, spoke of civilization *(bunmeikaika)* as "advancing toward propriety" and as the "improvement of human character." See Nishimura Shigeki, "Seigo jūnikai," *Meiroku zasshi* 36 (May 1875): 6–9; Braisted, *Meiroku Zasshi*, 446.

15. Hane Mikiso, *Peasants, Rebels, Woman and Outcastes* (Lanham, Md.: Rowman and Littlefield, 2003), 62. Hane notes that such government exhortations had little effect.

16. Hane points out, however, that few could actually afford this new source of nutrition, even had they overcome their aversion to it. Ibid.

17. This image appeared in Kanagaki Robun, "Seiyō dōchū hizakurige," in *Meiji bungaku zenshū*, vol. 1: *Meiji kaikaki bungaku shū*, ed. Okitsu Kaname (Tokyo: Chikuma shobō, 1966), 107. This is one example of Robun's satire on civilization.

18. Sakatani Shiroshi, "Kitsune-setsu no gi," *Meiroku zasshi* 20 (November 1874): 4–5; Braisted, *Meiroku Zasshi*, 253–254.

19. Tsuda Mamichi, "Tengu," *Meiroku zasshi* 14 (July 1874), in *Meiroku zasshi*, vol. 2, ed. Yamamuro Shinichi (Tokyo: Iwanami shoten, 2008), 45–49; Braisted, *Meiroku Zasshi*, 186.

20. For an excellent examination of the folk knowledge of spirits and superstition during the Meiji period, see Gerald Figal, *Civilization and Monsters: Spirits of Modernity in Meiji Japan* (Durham, N.C., and London: Duke University Press, 1999).

21. Tsuda Mamichi, "Kaika o susumuru hōhō o ronzu," *Meiroku zasshi* 3 (undated), in *Meiroku zasshi,* vol. 1, ed. Yamamuro Shinichi (Tokyo: Iwanami shoten, 1999), 120; Braisted, *Meiroku Zasshi,* 38–39.

22. At stake here was the need for Japan to improve its image in the eyes of the West to further its diplomatic objectives. In the 1850s and 1860s, Japan had signed a number of treaties with America, England, France, and other Western powers. They contained extraterritoriality provisions (e.g., an American suspected of a crime in Japan would be tried by American, not Japanese, courts) that the Western nations refused to revise until Japan had a workable civil code and legislative structure in place. The persistence of "barbaric customs" did nothing to change Japan's uncivilized status in the eyes of the West. Nishimura Shigeki, for example, a key contributor to moral discourse throughout the Meiji period, was deeply concerned with "correcting customs and clarifying proprieties." Indeed, "whether countries are judged barbarian [*bankoku*] or enlightened [*bunmei koku*]," he argued, "depends on the people's customs." Until Japan advanced its level of civilization, Nishimura and others believed, it could not hope to revise its unequal treaties with the Western powers.

23. Sakatani Shiroshi, "Seikyō no gi: 2," *Meiroku zasshi* 25 (December 1874), in *Meiroku zasshi,* vol. 2, ed. Yamamuro Shinichi (Tokyo: Iwanami shoten, 2008), 311; Braisted, *Meiroku Zasshi,* 311.

24. Sakatani Shiroshi, "Seikyō no gi: 1," *Meiroku zasshi* 22 (December 1874), in *Meiroku zasshi,* vol. 2, ed. Yamamuro Shinichi (Tokyo: Iwanami shoten, 2008), 243–244; Braisted, *Meiroku Zasshi,* 279.

25. Monbushō, ed., *Gakusei hachi-jū nen shi* (Tokyo: Ōkurashō insatsukyoku, 1954), see esp. 720–721. Translations are from Herbert Passin, *Society and Education in Japan* (New York: Teachers College, Columbia University, 1965), 210–211.

26. Fukuzawa Yukichi, *Gakumon no susume* (Tokyo: Iwanami shoten, 1970), 11. Translation is from Passin, *Society and Education in Japan,* 206.

27. Ibid., 18–19; Passin, *Society and Education in Japan,* 209. Scholar of educational thought in Japan Horio Teruhisa discusses the relationship between education and governing during the early Meiji period and the dispute on education policy that emerged in the mid-1870s between Fukuzawa and Mori Arinori. See Horio, *Educational Thought and Ideology in Modern Japan: State Authority and Intellectual Freedom,* trans. Steven Platzer (Tokyo: University of Tokyo Press, 1989), 24–64.

28. Fukuzawa's phrase was "muchi no tokugi wa mutoku ni hitoshiki nari." Fukuzawa, *Bunmei ron no gairyaku,* 129.

29. Ibid., 113. This quote is from Fukuzawa, *An Outline of a Theory of Civilization,* 83.

30. Historian Tsuda Sokichi, in his preface to Dilworth's translation of *Bunmei ron no gairyaku,* wrote, "He [Fukuzawa] compares intelligence and virtue.... [H]is view that the former is more crucial to the progress of civilization...come[s] from Buckle." See Fukuzawa, *An Outline of a Theory of Civilization,* xxi.

31. Henry Thomas Buckle, *History of Civilization in England,* vol. 1 (New York: D. Appleton-Century Company, 1934), 125, 131, 132.

32. Fukuzawa, *Gakumon no susume*, 25.

33. Rekishigaku kenkyūkai, ed., *Nihonshi shiryō*, vol. 4, *Kindai* (Tokyo: Iwanami shoten, 1997), 82.

34. Nishimura, "Shūshin jikoku hi ni michi ron," 4–7; Braisted, *Meiroku Zasshi*, 382.

35. Ishii Ryōsuke, ed., *Japanese Legislation in the Meiji Era*, trans. William J. Chambliss (Tokyo: Pan-Pacific Press, 1958), 356–357.

36. Mori Arinori, "Saishōron: 3," *Meiroku zasshi* 15 (August 1874), in *Meiroku zasshi*, vol. 2, ed. Yamamuro Shinichi (Tokyo: Iwanami shoten, 2008), 53; Braisted, *Meiroku Zasshi*, 189.

37. Mori Arinori, "Saishōron: 1," *Meiroku zasshi* 8 (May 1874), in *Meiroku zasshi*, vol. 1, ed. Yamamuro Shinichi (Tokyo: Iwanami shoten, 1999), 278; Braisted, *Meiroku Zasshi*, 105. The "Outline of the New Criminal Law" of 1870 changed the status of concubines, elevating them to the position of "a relative of the second degree" and thus conferring upon them the same status as a wife.

38. See Nishimura Shigeki, *Nihon dōtoku ron*, 8; Motoyama Yukihiko, "Nishimura Shigeki no kyōiku shisō," in *Soritsu nijūgo shūnen kinen ronbun shū* (Kyoto: Kyoto University, 1954), 442.

39. Motoda Eifu, "Kyōgaku taishi," in Passin, *Society and Education in Japan*, 227.

40. Itō Hirobumi, "Kyōiku-gi," in *Kyōiku chokugo kampatsu kankei shiryō-shū*, vol. 1, ed. Kokumin seishin bunka kenkyūjo (Tokyo: 1940), 5–9; Passin, *Society and Education in Japan*, 229–233.

41. Yamagata Aritomo, "Imperial Precepts to Soldiers and Sailors," in *Sources of Japanese Tradition*, vol. 2, ed. Tsunoda Ryusaku et al. (New York: Columbia University Press, 1964), 199.

42. Yamagata Aritomo, "Kokkai kaisetsu ni Kansuru kengi," in *Yamagata Aritomo ikensho*, ed. Ōyama Azusa (Tokyo: Hara shobō, 1966), 85. Carol Gluck provides several translated lines from Yamagata on this point. See Gluck, *Japan's Modern Myths*, 119.

43. Nishimura, *Nihon dōtoku ron*, 16–17.

44. Nishimura, "Wakumon jūgojō," in Hakuō Sōsho, 991–992.

45. "Shōgakkō kyōsoku kōryō," in *Gakusei hachi-jū nen shi*, ed. Monbushō, 763.

46. Monbushō, ed., *Gakusei hachi-jū nen shi*, 763, 844–845.

47. The late 1870s and early 1880s provide numerous examples of this position. For a further example, see Sakatani Shiroshi, "Seikyō no gi: 1," *Meiroku zasshi* 22 (December 1874), in *Meiroku zasshi*, vol. 2, ed. Yamamuro Shinichi (Tokyo: Iwanami shoten, 2008), 243–247; Braisted, *Meiroku Zasshi*, 279–281. "Religion and law," Sakatani wrote, "can exert control by establishing restraints, but they cannot prevent disturbances because they cannot assure a balance." "Seikyō no gi: 1,"198; Braisted, *Meiroku Zasshi*, 256.

48. Fukuzawa Yukichi, "Nikushoku no setsu," in *Meiji bungaku zenshū*, vol. 8: *Fukuzawa Yukichi shū*, ed. Tomita Masafumi (Tokyo: Chikuma shobō, 1966), 334–335.

49. For this and other images by Kyōsai, see *Kawanabe Kyōsai to monjin tachi*, ed. Kawanabe Kyōsai kinen bijutsukan (Nikkō: Kosugi hōan kinen nikkō bijutsukan, 2001), 29. Also see Timothy Clark, *Demon of Painting: The Art of Kawanabe Kyōsai* (London:

British Museum Press, 1993), 126. The editors of *Shinbun zasshi,* the journal Fudō has in his hand, later praised Kyōsai's artistic talent. (See the 28 Sept 1874 issue.) Yet their description of this work as *shinki* and *myōan,* terms conveying strangeness and eccentricity, recalls Edo-period artwork that similarly contested an oppressive social structure through "strange" and "eccentric" representations. For an insightful discussion of this issue, see Katsuya Hirano, "Spaces of Dissent: Cultural Politics in Late Tokugawa Japan," Ph.D. diss., University of Chicago, 2003, esp. chapter 4, "Grotesque Realism: Politics of Chaos," 157–202. For a brief description of Fudō Myō-ō, see Yamasaki Taikō, *Shingon: Japanese Esoteric Buddhism* (Boston and London: Shambhala, 1988), 172–175.

  50. A charge made in 1875 in the *Choya shinbun.* See Okitsu Kaname, *Tenkanki no bungaku* (Tokyo: Waseda Daigaku shuppanbu, 1960), 109. Also see Donald Keene, *Dawn to the West: Japanese Literature in the Modern Era* (New York: Holt, Rinehart and Winston, 1989), 28.

  51. See Keene, *Dawn to the West,* 14. Of Robun, Keene writes, "Robun's only concern was with selling books" (16). And elsewhere, "If they [*gesaku* writers] could have made a living in some other, equally undemanding manner, they no doubt would cheerfully have abandoned their profession" (14).

  52. Okitsu Kaname, for example, writes "in terms of its content, this [Robun's text] is nonsense literature with absolutely no relation to Fukuzawa's *Kyūri zukai.*" See Okitsu Kaname's "Critique," in *Meiji bungaku zenshū,* vol. 1: *Meiji kaikaki bungaku shū,* 437.

  53. Kanagaki Robun, "Kyūri zukai," in *Meiji no bungaku,* vol. 1: *Kanagaki Robun,* ed. Tsubouchi Yuzō (Tokyo: Chikuma shobō, 2002), 352, 344–345.

  54. For the notion of "profaning the sacred" and its subversive implications, see Mikhail Bakhtin, *Rabelais and His World,* trans. H. Iswolsky (Bloomington and Indianapolis: Indiana University Press, 1984).

  55. G. B. Sansom, *The Western World and Japan* (New York: Vintage Books, 1973), 385.

  56. Kanagaki Robun, *Aguranabe,* ed. Kobayashi Chikahei (Tokyo: Iwanami shoten, 1967), 28–29. This translation appears in Donald Keene, *Modern Japanese Literature* (New York: Grove Press Inc., 1956), 32.

  57. This is Keene's observation in ibid., 31.

  58. Kanagaki, *Aguranabe,* 106.

  59. Writings that made use of the kana syllabary (as opposed to complex Chinese ideographs) were directed at those with less education. As a journalist, Robun wrote for the *Kana shinbun* and the *Iroha shinbun,* two newspapers that primarily used kana. The name "Kanagaki," then, implies a low-brow style of writing intended for the "foolish" and uneducated masses.

  60. Robun also wrote the title of his book, *Aguranabe,* using the character for foolishness. He wrote *"agura"* not with the usual characters that convey "sitting cross-legged" but with characters to convey "ease," "foolishness," and "enjoyment." Thus the title (as with many of the puns in his writings) conveys two meanings simultaneously: "sitting cross-legged before a pot of stew" and "a stew of ease, foolishness, and enjoyment."

61. Robert G. Henricks, trans., *Lao-Tzu Te-Tao Ching* (New York: Ballantine Books, 1989), 72. For another example, see Jien, "Gukanshō," in *Nihon koten bungaku taikei,* vol. 86: *Gukanshō,* ed. Okami Masao and Akamatsu Toshihide (Tokyo: Iwanami shoten, 1967), passim.

62. Mantei Ōga, "Tōsei rikō musume," in *Meiji bungaku zenshū,* vol. 1: *Meiji kai-kaki bungaku shū,* 182.

63. Discussing this kind of universalizing discourse, Judith Butler remarks, "Although they often appear as transcultural or formal criteria by which existing cultural conventions are to be judged, they are precisely cultural conventions." See Judith Butler et al., *Contingency, Hegemony, Universality: Contemporary Dialogues on the Left* (London and New York: Verso, 2000), 39.

64. See Okitsu, ed., *Tenkanki no bungaku,* 109.

65. It is important to distinguish between the positing of some "universal" foundation and its complete actualization or "universalization" in practice. Certainly Inoue and others recognized that "civilized" practice had not been universally realized in Japanese society. But because they held the normative claims of civilization to be rooted in a universal epistemological foundation true in all times and places, only the ignorant or foolish would think to dispute them. Thus, while foolishness presented an obstacle to the dissemination of civilized practice, it also called into question the universal status of civilization itself through subversive and parodic textual strategies.

66. Butler et al., *Contingency, Hegemony, Universality,* 24.

Chapter 2: The Epistemology of *Rinrigaku*

1. Neither Carter nor Blocker and Starling discuss these four ethical texts. Robert E. Carter, *Encounter with Enlightenment: A Study of Japanese Ethics* (Albany: State University of New York Press, 2001); H. Gene Blocker and Christopher I. Starling, *Japanese Philosophy* (Albany: State University of New York Press, 2001). Piovesana includes a brief discussion of Nishimura's *Nihon dōtoku ron,* which he describes as "vague eclecticism." See G. K. Piovesana, *Recent Japanese Philosophical Thought, 1862–1912* (Tokyo: Enderle Bookstore, 1963), 33. Specific critiques of Inoue's *New Theory of Ethics* by Kōsaka, Matsuzaki, and Piovesana are discussed below in this chapter.

2. Attacks on the Neo-Confucian conception of *ri* began long before Nishi's time. Harry Harootunian, for example, locates in the eighteenth century "a profound epistemological break" brought about by Ogyū Sorai and other thinkers of this period. Sorai and others called into question the dominant conceptions of *ri* of this time. Harootunian states, "The essential property of this intellectual shift was a notation of a break in the line; its path to resolution was marked by an attack on *ri*...." See Harry Harootunian, "Ideology as Conflict," in *Conflict in Modern Japanese History,* ed. Tetsuo Najita and J. Victor Koschmann (Princeton, N.J.: Princeton University Press, 1982), 31. Also see Maruyama Masao, *Studies in the Intellectual History of Tokugawa Japan,* trans. Mikiso Hane (Tokyo: University of Tokyo Press, 1974), 90.

3. Albert Craig argues that, prior to Nishi, one can locate an implicit assertion of two discrete types of principle in the works of Sakuma Shōzan, a proponent of Western learning and an advisor to the *bakufu* government in its final years. For Shōzan, the acquisition of knowledge was a matter of apprehending the *ri* (i.e., principle) inherent in all things. "I have received chiefly the teachings of the Ch'eng-Chu [Hsi] school," he stated, "and with this I [seek to] penetrate the *ri* of the 10,000 things and of heaven and earth." Shōzan, however, is well known for his "Western technique, Eastern morality" *(tōyō dōtoku, seiyō gei)* maxim, through which he admitted the West's superiority in terms of technology but retained for Japan (or the "East" generally) a privileged position from which to speak for virtue. His assertion that "with Western studies alone there is no consideration of virtue *[dōtoku giri]*" implied, Craig suggests, a distinction between a *ri* of virtue and a *ri* of material knowledge. By contrast, Harry Harootunian argues that Shōzan "did not think of anything so elaborate as the notion of two distinct cultures informed by two different principles *(ri)*. No more does his later slogan *Tōyō dōtoku, seiyō gei* ("Oriental ethics as base, Western technique as means") assume a radical cultural difference on the grounds that the *ri* of Japan was different from that of the West. See Albert Craig, "Science and Confucianism in Tokugawa Japan," in *Changing Japanese Attitudes toward Modernization*, ed. Marius B. Jansen (Princeton, N.J.: Princeton University Press, 1965), 133–160, 153, for quotations; Harry Harootunian, *Toward Restoration: The Growth of Political Consciousness in Tokugawa Japan* (Berkeley and Los Angeles: University of California Press, 1970), 144. If one assumes that Shōzan did begin to posit two different types of *ri,* nevertheless the split was not clearly articulated as a fact-value distinction until Nishi Amane.

4. Fung Yu-lan, *A History of Chinese Philosophy,* vol. 2 (Princeton, N.J.: Princeton University Press, 1983), 543.

5. As a concise definition of a complex and polysemous term, the above explanation is of course an essentialization. There was no unitary object we can unproblematically call a "Neo-Confucian epistemology" during the Tokugawa period. Similarly, there was not a single conception of *ri;* rather, we must speak of a single term with a plurality of shifting meanings. But perhaps an essentialized *ri* is appropriate at this point, not because we can only apprehend *ri* by denying its complexities, but because Nishi himself began with an essentialized representation of *ri* so as to facilitate his critique of Neo-Confucianism.

6. Nishi Amane, "Hyakuichi shinron," (Hereafter HISR) in *Nishi Amane Zenshū,* vol. 1, ed. Ōkubo Toshiaki (Tokyo: Munetaka shobō, 1960), 276–277.

7. Ibid., 277. This translation is from Thomas Havens, *Nishi Amane and Modern Japanese Thought* (Princeton, N.J.: Princeton University Press, 1970), 134. Nichiren, a thirteenth-century Buddhist monk, claimed that it was his prayers that brought about the typhoon (the divine wind) that destroyed the invading Mongol fleet in 1281.

8. Nishi, HISR, 277.

9. Ibid., 236.

10. Ibid., 277. Nishi's opposition roughly corresponds to the distinction between the human and natural sciences, or the *Geisteswissenschaften* and the *Naturwissenschaften.*

11. Ibid., 277–78. Translation is from Havens, *Nishi Amane,* 134.

12. Nishi equated "reason" and "law of nature" with the French *raison* and *loi de nature,* and with German and Dutch terms as well. He stated, "The meaning is the same in each language." See Nishi, "Shōhaku sakki," in *Nishi Amane Zenshū,* 1:169.

13. Nishi Amane, "Jōchi kankeiron," in *Nishi Amane Zenshū,* 1:473.

14. Nishi, as well as others at this time, actually used the term *dōri* in a number of different ways. *Dōri* was used as "reason" (as in a reason for doing something), as a synonym for *risei* (the human faculty of reason), and, as mentioned above, as the essence or principle making an object what it is. *Dōri* was also used in a Confucian context to indicate the "moral way."

15. "'Reason' in its general usage," Nishi explained, "is translated as *dōri,* in its narrow usage it is translated as *risei.*" *Dōri* meant "reason" as in a reason given to support one's opinion, a reason for making a particular decision. The more important term for Nishi was *risei,* i.e., the human faculty for rational thought. See Nishi, "Shōhaku sakki," in *Nishi Amane Zenshū,* 1:169

16. Nishi, "Jōchi kankeiron," in *Nishi Amane Zenshū,* 1:475. Here Nishi was drawing on the Kantian triad of intellect-emotion-will *(chi-jō-i).* Nishi equated intellect and reason in some passages.

17. Charles Taylor, *Human Agency and Language: Philosophical Papers 1* (Cambridge: Cambridge University Press, 1985), 4.

18. Julia Adeney Thomas, *Reconfiguring Modernity: Concepts of Nature in Japanese Political Ideology* (Berkeley and Los Angeles: University of California Press, 2001), 3. Thomas also provides an illuminating discussion of Katō Hiroyuki and his *Reconsideration of Human Rights (Jinken shinsetsu),* a work discussed below.

19. Nishi, HISR, 277.

20. Nishi called material principle or *butsuri* "a puriori" *(a priori)* and mental principle or *shinri* "a posuteriori" *(a posteriori).* See Nishi, HISR, 278. Although Nishi used the term *a priori* for material principles, he may have in fact had in mind empirical physical principles rather than truths independent of experience.

21. Sōgo Masaaki and Hida Yoshifumi, comps., *Meiji no kotoba jiten* (Tokyo: Tokyodō shuppan, 1986), 200.

22. Marius Jansen, ed., *Cambridge History of Japan,* vol. 5: *The Nineteenth Century* (New York: Cambridge University Press, 1989), 109.

23. Watanabe Kazan, "Shinkiron," trans. Katsuya Hirano, in *Readings in Tokugawa Thought,* 3rd ed., edited by University of Chicago Center for East Asian Studies (Chicago: CEAS, 1998), 187–195.

24. Takano Chōei, "Seiyō gakushi no setsu," in *Kazan Choei ronshū,* ed. Satō Shosuke (Tokyo: Iwanami shoten, 1994), 195. The original date for this work is uncertain. It was probably written shortly after 1832.

25. Jansen, ed., *Cambridge History of Japan,* 5:442.

26. Fukuzawa's term was *koshu no wakudeki.* See Maruyama Masao, "Fukuzawa ni okeru jitsugaku no tenkai," in *Kindai Nihon shisō taikei,* vol. 2: *Fukuzawa Yukichi shū,* ed. Ishida Takeshi (Tokyo: Chikuma shobō, 1974), 563–578.

27. Fukuzawa Yukichi, *Gakumon no susume* (Tokyo: Iwanami shoten, 2001), 12–13. This translation appears in Passin, *Society and Education in Japan*, 206–207.

28. Ibid., 13. Also see Wang Jia Hua, *Nihon no kindaika to jugaku* (Tokyo: Nōbunkyō, 1998), 147.

29. Tsuda Mamichi, "Kaika o susumuru hōhō o ronzu," *Meiroku zasshi* 3 (undated), in *Meiroku zasshi*, vol. 1, ed. Yamamuro Shinichi (Tokyo: Iwanami shoten, 1999), 117–118. This translation is from Braisted, *Meiroku Zasshi*, 38.

30. Maruyama, "Fukuzawa ni okeru jitsugaku no tenkai," 568; cited in Wang, *Nihon no kindaika*, 148. Also see Maruyama Masao, *Maruyama Masao shū*, vol. 3 (Tokyo: Iwanami shoten, 1995), 113, 115.

31. As conceptions of *jitsugaku* that "did not have ethics *(rinri)* at its core," Minamoto lists the following: the "empiricist view of *jitsugaku*" put forward by Ogyū Sorai, the "rational *jitsugaku*" of thinkers at the Kaitokudō merchant academy, the view of *jitsugaku* emphasizing *keisei saimin* ("ordering society so as to save the people") of Kaihō Seiran, Watanabe Kazan, and Takano Choei, the view of *jitsugaku* that allowed for a combination of Confucian and Western learning of Sakuma Shōzan, and Yoshida Shōin's notion of *jitsugaku* that demanded political revolution.

32. Minamoto Ryōen, *Kinsei shoki jitsugaku shisō no kenkyū* (Tokyo: Sōbunsha, 1980), 550–552.

33. Concerning the idea that all statements carry with them some kind of "evaluative accent," see V. N. Volosinov, *Marxism and the Philosophy of Language*, trans. Ladislav Matejka and I. R. Titunik (Cambridge: Harvard University Press, 1996). See especially chapter 4, "Theme and Meaning in Language."

34. My understanding of "representation" is based largely on the works of Richard Rorty and Charles Taylor. "Naturalism," as discussed by Taylor, shares many of these epistemological features as well. See Richard Rorty, *Philosophy and the Mirror of Nature* (Princeton, N.J.: Princeton University Press, 1979), passim; Taylor, *Human Agency and Language*, 4 and passim.

35. This was an ironic appropriation of the Buddhist term "three treasures," i.e., the Buddha, the dharma, and the *sangha*, or priesthood.

36. Nishi Amane, "Jinsei sambō," *Meiroku zasshi* 38 (June 1875), ed. Ōkubo Toshiaki (Tokyo: Rittaisha, 1976), 3.

37. Nishi Amane, "Jinsei sambō," *Meiroku zasshi* 40 (August 1875), 4. This translation is from Braisted, *Meiroku Zasshi*, 489.

38. Nishi, "Jinsei sambō," *Meiroku zasshi* 40 (August 1875), 4; from Braisted, *Meiroku Zasshi*, 490.

39. Nishi, "Jinsei sambō," *Meiroku zasshi* 40 (August 1875), 4; from Braisted, *Meiroku Zasshi*, 489.

40. Citations from this and the preceding paragraph in Nishi, "Jinsei sambō," *Meiroku zasshi* 38 (June 1875), 3–5; from Braisted, *Meiroku Zasshi*, 464–466.

41. For a history of the establishment of Tokyo University, the organization of its departments, and courses offered, see Tokyo Teikoku Daigaku, ed., *Tokyo Teikoku Daigaku 50 nen shi*, vol. 1 (Tokyo: Tokyo Teikoku Daigaku, 1932), 467.

42. While the law and sciences departments had antecedents in the former Kaiseigakkō, the Department of Letters was entirely new. By 1932 the Department of Letters comprised courses in philosophy, history, and literature; however, during the early years of Tokyo University the Department of Letters was of a broader scope. In addition to philosophy, history, and literature, it included politics and economics. Initially, no courses on Eastern philosophy were offered; however, by 1881 some courses on Indian and Chinese philosophy were being taught. See ibid., 685–686, 701.

43. For a discussion of courses on *dōgigaku* and *rinrigaku,* see Tokyo Teikoku Daigaku, ed., *Tokyo Teikoku Daigaku Jutsu Taikan: Bungakubu* (Tokyo: Tokyo Teikoku Daigaku, 1942), 386–395.

44. Scholar of Japanese intellectual history Koyasu Nobukuni makes a similar claim. He states that Inoue's *Rinri shinsetsu* was the first philosophical treatment of ethics in modern Japan. See his "Kindai 'rinri' gainen no seiritsu to sono yukue," *Shisō* 6: 912 (2000), passim and esp. 5, 7.

45. Inoue, *Rinri shinsetsu,* 414.

46. Inoue relied heavily on Sidgwick's *The Methods of Ethics,* in which Sidgwick distinguished intuitionism from hedonism, and further subdivided the latter into universalistic hedonism (also altruism) and individualistic hedonism (also egoism, Epicureanism). Sidgwick stated, "The two methods which take happiness as an ultimate end it will be convenient to distinguish as Egoistic and Universalistic Hedonism." See Henry Sidgwick, *The Methods of Ethics* (Indianapolis: Hackett Publishing Co., 1981), 11.

47. Inoue, *Rinri shinsetsu,* 416.

48. Ibid., 414. To this already extensive list, Inoue added "the Taikyoku of Confucius, the Nameless of Lao Tzu, the Negation of negation of Soshu... Kant's noumena, Spinoza's substance, the absolute of Schelling, Spencer's unknowable, Strauss's change, Hartmann's unconscious spirit, Arnold's power, and Huxley's natural order." See ibid., 422.

49. Inoue stated that these thinkers all referred to the phenomenal world as "universal existence." See ibid.

50. This and the passages cited above can be found in ibid., 420–425.

51. Ibid., 424. Inoue actually spelled out *soruwaiwaru obu fuitchisuto* (survival of the fittest) in *furigana* script next to the characters.

52. Ibid., 424–425.

53. See Kōsaka Masaaki, *Meiji shisōshi* (Kyoto: Tōeisha, 1999), 267; and David Abosch's translation of this work: Kōsaka Masaaki, *Japanese Thought in the Meiji Era* (Tokyo: Pan Pacific Press, 1958), 240–241. Kōsaka devotes less than two and a half pages to a discussion of *Rinri shinsetsu.* See also Shimomura Toratarō, "The Modernization of Japan, with Special Reference to Philosophy," in *The Modernization of Japan,* vol. 7. Compiled by Japanese National Commission for Unesco (Tokyo: Japan Society for the Promotion of Science, 1966), 15; Piovesana, *Recent Japanese Philosophical Thought,* 40–41; Matsuzaki Minoru, "Rinri shinsetsu kaitai," in *Meiji bunka zenshū,* vol. 23: *Shisō hen* (Tokyo: Nihon Hyōronsha, 1967), 19.

54. Inoue, *Rinri shinsetsu,* 415.

55. Ibid., 415. Italics added.

56. Koyasu, "Kindai 'rinri' gainen no seiritsu," 7.

57. The Japanese titles were *Kyōsha no kenri to dōtoku hōritsu no kankei,* 1888; *Kyōsha no kenri no kyōsō,* 1893; *Dōtoku hōritsu no shimpo,* 1894; *Dōtoku hōritsu shinka no ri,* 1900; *Shizen to rinri,* 1912.

58. Katō Hiroyuki, "Kyōsha no kenri to dōtoku hōritsu no kankei," *Tetsugaku zasshi* 2(21) (October 5, 1888): 522. Katō noted that because the needs among civilized societies are similar, their views of the good coincide. Yet to hold this up as evidence of some unchanging moral principle of heaven, Katō claimed, was to make a grave error.

59. Ibid., 524–525.

60. Ibid., 518–519, 525.

61. Here, Katō introduced a new term into Japanese moral discourse. His phrase *kyōsha no kenri* was based on the German "Das Recht des Staerkeren." See ibid., 512.

62. Ibid., 514–515. Katō had already developed this view in his *Jinken shinsetsu.* See Katō, *Jinken shinsetsu;* Katō Hiroyuki, "A Reconsideration of Human Rights," trans. J. Victor Koschmann, in *From Japan's Modernity,* ed. University of Chicago Center for East Asian Studies (Chicago: CEAS, 2002), 12.

63. Katō, "Kyōsha no kenri," 516.

64. Katō, "A Reconsideration of Human Rights," 41.

65. Ibid., 41. This translation is a slightly revised version of Koschmann's. Koschmann translates *shinjutsu dōgi* as "mental powers and morality." Although Katō does link moral rectitude with the mentally superior educated elite, "mental power" was not that which distinguished good and evil. I suspect Katō, whose foreign language sources were primarily from German texts, had the term *Gesinnungsethik* in mind, a term meaning "moral sentiments." See Inoue Tetsujirō, et al., comps., *Tetsugaku jii* (Tokyo: Tokyo Daigaku Sangakubu, 1881). Also see Katō, *Jinken shinsetsu,* 460.

66. Minamoto Ryōen, "Katō Hiroyuki no rinri shisō," *Rinrigaku nenpō* 8 (1959): 127–143. For this citation, see 128.

67. Katō, "A Reconsideration of Human Rights," 20.

68. Ibid., 1.

69. Nishimura Shigeki, *Nihon dōtoku ron,* in *Hakuō Sōsho,* ed. Nihon Kōdōkai (Tokyo: Nihon Kōdōkai, 1976), 5–6.

70. Ibid., 6. An extended analysis of Nishimura's critique of *segaikyō* follows in chapter 3.

71. Ibid., 21. The way in which his moral framework ties Confucianism to Western philosophy belies his doubt that Confucianism can stand alone without the support of the authority of Western philosophy. For more on this point, see Gluck, *Japan's Modern Myths,* 125.

72. Ibid., 23–24. The translations from this paragraph appear in Donald H. Shively, "Nishimura Shigeki: A Confucian View of Modernization," in *Changing Japanese Attitudes toward Modernization,* ed. Marius B. Jansen (Princeton, N.J.: Princeton University Press, 1965), 216–217, n. 38.

73. Nishimura, *Nihon dōtoku ron,* 26–27. There are several reasons why Western philosophy, according to Nishimura, despite its favorable qualities when compared with

religion, is inappropriate as a foundation for Japan's morality. First, while knowledge is emphasized, personal conduct is not given due attention. It lacks a "method for cultivating peace of mind." Philosophers engage in polemics, seeking to "excel over past philosophers." And finally, the many diverse schools of thought mean there can be no common ground of opinion to address morality. This list appears in Shively, "Nishimura Shigeki," 235.

74. For citations in this paragraph, see Nishimura Shigeki, *Hakuō goroku* (Tokyo: Nihon Kōdōkai, 1996), 9–10.

75. The question of whether Nishimura "exhibited a progressive or a conservative tendency" is one of the central questions raised in many of the secondary works on Nishimura. Ienaga Saburō may have been the first to raise this question. See Ienaga Saburō, "Nishimura Shigeki ron," in *Nihon kindai shisōshi kenkyū* (Tokyo: Tokyo Daigaku shuppan, 1980), 133–168. Okita Yukikazu responds to Ienaga's view in his "Nishimura Shigeki no shoki shisō—ōka to dentō," *Nihon shisōshi* 18 (1982): 50–64. In addition, there are quite a few secondary works that deal either with Nishimura's thought in general or with his *Nihon dōtoku ron* specifically. See Furukawa Tetsushi, *Hakuō Nishimura Shigeki: Tenkanki Nihon no daishisōka* (Tokyo: Bunka sōgō shuppan, 1976); Ienaga Saburō, *Nihon dōtoku shisōshi* (Tokyo: Iwanami shoten, 1975); Motoyama Yukihiko, "Meiji zenhanki ni okeru Nishimura Shigeki no kyōiku shisō," in *Sōritsu nijūgo shūnen kinen rombunshū* (Kyoto: Kyoto Daigaku jimbunkagaku kenkyūjo, 1954), 432–451; Yoshida Kumaji, "Nishimura Shigeki," *Nihon kyōiku sentetsu sōsho*, vol. 20 (Tokyo: Bunkyō shoin, 1942). For a work in English on Nishimura (perhaps the only one to treat Nishimura exclusively), see Shively, "Nishimura Shigeki," 193–241.

76. Nishimura, *Hakuō goroku*, 22.

77. Ibid., 25–26.

78. Inoue, *Rinri shinsetsu*, 424.

79. Inoue Tetsujirō, "Seishin gakka no yakugo," in *Meiji bunka zenshū, Bekkan: Meiji jibutsu kigen*, ed. Meiji bunka kenkyūkai (Tokyo: Nihon hyōronsha, 1969), 521–522.

80. Katō, *A Reconsideration of Human Rights*, 42.

81. Inoue Enryō, "Katō sensei no ichi daigimon ni kotaen to su," *Tōyō gakugei zasshi* 33 (1883): 65.

82. Ibid., 66. In *A People's History of the United States: 1492–Present*, Howard Zinn notes, "In 1820, 120,000 Indians lived east of the Mississippi. By 1844, fewer than 30,000 were left." Most, he says, were moved westward, but many were killed or died of disease. See Howard Zinn, *A People's History of the United States: 1492–Present* (New York: Harper Collins, 1980; and Harper Perennial, 1995), 124. Enryō drew attention to the plight of Native Americans because theirs was a case of "evolution" in action.

83. Inoue Enryō used the example of infanticide to argue that the savage form of selection would prove detrimental to "the character of the people" and inhibit evolution. He held that both infanticide and medicine are types of artificial selection and both may contribute to evolution. Only the latter, however, is civilized. "The law of selection through infanticide, as a matter of course, fosters a cruel and savage character.

The advance of medicine fosters a benevolent and humane sentiment. In regard to the advancement of a society and the independence of a country, the most necessary thing is the cooperation and unity of the people. For cooperation and unity, the most necessary thing is friendship, harmony, and tolerance for one another." Such things, Enryō believed, enabled medical advances. Cultivating "a cruel and savage character," however, would obstruct the high-level evolution of society. See Inoue Enryō, "Katō sensei no ichi daigimon," 66–67.

84. By several accounts, including Inoue's own, Inoue coined the term *rinrigaku*. See Inoue, et al., comps, *Tetsugaku jii* (1881), 31.

85. Inoue Tetsujirō, "Seishin gakka no yakugo," 521–522. Among the other terms Inoue discussed was the term used to translate "philosophy." He wrote, "The term *tetsugaku* was the translation first given by Nishi Amane, and it has continued to be used at the Imperial University. Today, China too has come to use the term *tetsugaku*. There were some who initially used *rigaku* as a translation."

86. Nishimura Shigeki, "Shūshin kyōkasho no setsu," in *Hakuō sōsho*, vol. 2 (Tokyo: Nihon kōdōkai, 1976), 543.

87. Ibid. The term *rinri* may well be a Ming period (1368–1662) neologism, as Nishimura argued. But the concept of the five relations is of course much older. See, for example, the "Doctrine of the Mean" in *A Source Book in Chinese Philosophy*, ed. and trans. Wing-tsit Chan (Princeton, N.J.: Princeton University Press, 1973), 105.

88. Pierre Bourdieu, *Language and Symbolic Power*, trans. Gino Raymond and Matthew Adamson (Cambridge, Mass.: Harvard University Press, 1991), 48.

89. These four definitions are included in the *Kyōiku shinri ronri jutsugo shōkai*, ed. Fukyūsha (Tokyo: Fukyūsha, 1885).

90. In *Tetsugaku jii*, Inoue and Ariga do not provide extended definitions; they simply list an English term and its Japanese "equivalent." The "Explanation of Terms for Education, Psychology and Logic" gives no names as authors of this work, yet it draws heavily upon Inoue's translation of Alexander Bain's *Mental and Moral Science*. Moreover, Inoue was closely associated with the publisher of this work, Fukyūsha, who also published Inoue's own dictionary of philosophy.

91. *Kyōiku shinri ronri jutsugo shōkai*, 127.

92. Sōgo and Hida, comps., *Meiji no kotoba jiten*, 590.

93. The 1885 *Kyōiku shinri ronri jutsugo shōkai* dictionary indicated that this translation of Inoue's was among the sources it drew upon in the compilation of the dictionary.

94. Ibid.

95. *The Great Learning (Daxue)* is one of the Confucian texts that outlines these stipulations: "When the mind is rectified, the personal life is cultivated; when the personal life is cultivated, the family will be regulated; when the family is regulated, the state will be in order; and when the state is in order, there will be peace throughout the world. From the Son of Heaven down to the common people, all must regard cultivation of the personal life as the root or foundation." See Chan, trans. and comp., *A Source Book in Chinese Philosophy*, 86–87.

96. Nishimura, *Nihon dōtoku ron*, 46.

97. Ibid., 79. The "Englishman Smiles" was of course Samuel Smiles, whose work *Self-Help* was widely read in Japan during the 1870s and 1880s in its translated version. Nishimura's repeated emphasis on Japan's reputation abroad reflects his concern with the pursuit of civilization.

98. Ibid., 43, 45.

99. Ibid., 90.

100. Ibid., 92. This translation appears in Shively, *Nishimura Shigeki,* 215, n. 37.

101. See Shively, *Nishimura Shigeki,* 233–234.

102. In his *Kyōgaku taishi,* Motoda asserted, "For morality, the study of Confucius is the best guide." See Monbushō, ed., *Gakusei hachi-jū nen shi* (Tokyo: Ōkurashō Insatsukyoku, 1954), 715; Herbert Passin, *Society and Education in Japan* (New York: Teachers College, Columbia University, 1965), 227.

103. Kaigo Tokiomi, ed., *Nihon kyōkasho taikei, Kindai hen,* vol. 2, *Shūshin II* (Tokyo: Kōdansha, 1962), 683. This work provides concise overviews of the moral training textbooks issued by the Ministry of Education during the Meiji period. Nishimura continued to call for the use of these Confucian classics in moral training texts. See Nishimura, *Shūshin kyōkasho no setsu,* esp. 537–538. For a discussion of Nishimura's *Moral Teachings for Primary School* and the growing influence of developmental education *(kaihatsushugi)* in the 1880s, see Mark E. Lincicome, *Principle, Praxis, and the Politics of Educational Reform in Meiji Japan* (Honolulu: University of Hawai'i Press, 1995), 208–210 and passim.

104. Nishimura Shigeki, "Shōgaku shūshin-kun," in *Nihon kyōkasho taikei, Kindai hen,* ed. Kaigo, 683. With no interpretation or explanation to accompany the proverb and the difficult language used, critics argued against this pedagogical theory, and it quickly dropped out of Ministry of Education textbooks after this.

105. Havens, *Nishi Amane,* 136.

106. Katō, *A Reconsideration of Human Rights,* 42.

107. The idea of *rinrigaku,* in its association with philosophy, acting as an arbiter of the good and the true first suggested itself to me upon a reading of Rorty's *Philosophy and the Mirror of Nature.* Rorty states "If we deny that there are foundations to serve as common ground for adjudicating knowledge-claims, the notion of the philosopher as guardian of rationality seems endangered." He also discusses how the philosopher in traditional philosophy "serves the cultural function of keeping the other disciplines honest, limiting their claims to what can be properly 'grounded.'" See Rorty, *Philosophy and the Mirror of Nature,* 317, 162.

Chapter 3: *Rinrigaku* and Religion

1. In this chapter, I confine my examination to the social ethics of academics and religious apologists—two not necessarily discrete groups. While I refer in this chapter to "academics," "Buddhists," and "Christians," I do not mean to imply these groups demonstrated any kind of monolithic unity of opinion among themselves. They did

not. Nevertheless, I have found it useful to discuss them as "groups," each comprising individuals who occupy a roughly common intellectual space. Some thinkers, of course, cannot properly be confined to only one of these groups. Buddhist philosopher Inoue Enryō (discussed below) provides an excellent example of this.

2. I use the term "collective moral subjectivity" to refer to the moral space of each of the "groups" under discussion (i.e., *rinrigaku*, Christians, and Buddhists). This is a fluid intellectual space determined by, but also constituting or determining, discourse and material practices. The moral space of each was of course internally fragmented, that is, there were conflicting views not only between, for example, *rinrigaku* scholars and Christian apologists, but among *rinrigaku* scholars and among Christians. Nevertheless, representatives of each group sought to speak on behalf of that group in their engagement with *rinrigaku* (e.g., Buddhist apologists usually spoke of a "Buddhist morality" rather than a "Shin" or a "Zen" morality). This reflects an effort to create a subject position from which to speak.

3. The term *gōriteki* (in accord with *ri*) was a Meiji neologism, first appearing in 1881. See Sōgo and Hida, comps., *Meiji no kotoba jiten*, 162.

4. I have not seen the term *higōriteki* (irrational) used at this time, but the expression *dōri ni kanawanu* (inconsistent with reason) was used in reference to Christianity in texts of the 1880s. *Ri ni au* (i.e., *kanau*) is an alternative reading of *gōri*. In this sense, we might understand *dōri ni kanawanu* as *higōriteki* and thus "irrational." Some texts from this period attempt to establish this kind of equivalence among terms, presupposing "reason" or "rationality" as a fixed essential concept.

5. Inoue Enryō, "Rinri tsūron," in *Inoue Enryō senshū*, vol. 11, ed. Inoue Enryō Kinen Gakujutsu Senta (Tokyo: Tōyō Daigaku, 1992), 20–21 (italics added), and 31–32.

6. Ibid., 217–225, for Enryō's views on natural selection. On the supposition of God, see ibid., 16, 46; on replacing *dōtokugaku* with *rinrigaku*, see ibid., 358–359; on the promotion of happiness, see ibid., 126, 137.

7. Katō's phrase was *eisei fuhen fueki no banbutsuhō naru mono*. Katō Hiroyuki, *Jinken shinsetsu*, 422.

8. Ibid., 423. This translation appears in Katō, "A Reconsideration of Human Rights," 11.

9. Inoue Tetsujirō, *Rinri shinsetsu*, 424.

10. Ibid., 424. For Inoue's comments on "falsehoods," see ibid., 421. In a similar fashion, Soeda Juichi also criticized religion. He likened believers in religion to animals hoping to attain the favor of the gods through meritorious deeds and described this as "a pitiable situation." The religious "steadfastly believe that the gods, through their good offices, will police humanity." See Soeda Juichi, "Dōtoku no taihon wa nani ni yorite sadamen ya," *Tōyō gakugei zasshi* 18 (1883): 258.

11. Inoue Tetsujirō, *Rinri shinsetsu*, 424.

12. Ibid., 421.

13. Robert S. Schwantes, "Religion and Modernization in the Far East: A Symposium. I. Christianity versus Science: A Conflict of Ideas in Meiji Japan," *The Far Eastern Quarterly* 12:2 (1953): 123–132. For this citation, see 126–127.

14. Inoue Enryō, "Bukkyō katsuron joron," in *Inoue Enryō senshū*, vol. 3, ed. Inoue Enryō Kinen Gakujutsu Senta (Tokyo: Tōyō Daigaku, 1987), 392.

15. Murakami Senshō, *Bukkyō dōtoku shinron* (Tokyo: Tetsugaku shoin, 1888), 60–61.

16. Ibid., 15.

17. Shaku Sōen, "The Law of Cause and Effect, as Taught by Buddha," in *The World's Parliament of Religions*, vol. 2, ed. John Henry Barrows (Chicago: Parliament Publishing Company, 1893), 829–831. These citations are from a reprint of Sōen's text appearing in *The Eastern Buddhist* 26:2 (Autumn 1993): 135–137.

18. Murakami, *Bukkyō dōtoku shinron*, 5.

19. Ibid., 112.

20. Altruistic (or universalistic) and individualistic hedonism, discussed in the preceding chapter, were utilitarian notions advanced by Henry Sidgwick in his *Methods of Ethics* and treated in Inoue Tetsujirō's *Rinri shinsetsu*.

21. Murakami, *Bukkyō dōtoku shinron*, 113.

22. Ibid., 106.

23. Ibid., 114.

24. Inoue Enryō, *Rinri tsūron*, 38.

25. Ibid., 32–38.

26. Murakami, *Bukkyō dōtoku shinron*, 22. This view closely parallels Inoue Tetsujirō and Katō Hiroyuki's critique of natural right theory and the popular rights movement of the early 1880s. For an examination of the popular rights movement in the context of early Meiji moral discourse, see Richard Reitan, "Ethics and Natural Right Theory: Competing Conceptions of Nature during the Meiji Period," *Nempō Nihon shisōshi* 8 (March 2009): 1–28.

27. Ibid., 22–24.

28. See Nishimura Shigeki, *Nihon dōtoku ron*, in *Hakuō Sōsho*, ed. Nihon Kōdōkai (Tokyo: Nihon Kōdōkai, 1976), 23–24. This translation appears in Donald Shively, "Nishimura Shigeki: A Confucian View of Modernization," in *Changing Japanese Attitudes toward Modernization*, ed. Marius B. Jansen (Princeton, N.J.: Princeton University Press, 1965), 216–217.

29. Inoue Enryō, "Shūkyō shinron," in *Inoue Enryō senshū*, vol. 8, ed. Inoue Enryō Kinen Gakujutsu Senta (Tokyo: Tōyō Daigaku, 1991), 43–44.

30. Ibid., 11. He went on to argue that all things that contribute to the advancement of human knowledge must be utilized, and consequently he declared, "[I]t is in fact the urgent duty of today's scholars to widen [their study of] Buddhism."

31. Nishimura, *Nihon dōtoku ron*, 6.

32. Ibid., 21. For more on this point, see Gluck, *Japan's Modern Myths*, 125.

33. Kozaki Hiromichi, *Seikyō shinron* (Tokyo: Keiseisha, 1886), 96.

34. Fujishima Ryō-on, *Yasokyō no mudōri* (Kyoto: Nunobe Tsuneshichi, 1881). The passage cited is from an excerpt of this text in Mihashi Takeo, ed., *Meiji zenki shisōshi bunken* (Tokyo: Meijidō shoten, 1976), 471.

35. Nishimura, *Nihon dōtoku ron*, 5–6.

36. Inoue Enryō, *Rinri tsūron*, 40–42.

37. Nishimura, *Nihon dōtoku ron*, 7.

38. Ibid., 20.

39. Although Hardacre maintains that Nishimura described Shinto as a Way *(dō)* and thereby distinguished it from religion, various statements in *Nihon dōtoku ron* suggest that he did indeed consider Shinto under the category *shūkyō*. Nishimura described both Shinto and Buddhism as "Ways" *(dō)*. He referred to both Christianity and Buddhism as religion *(shūkyō)* and he treated Shinto, Christianity, and Buddhism alike, placing all three under the same heading of *segaikyō*—which in places he said was synonymous with religion *(shūkyō)*. See Helen Hardacre, *Shinto and the State* (Princeton, N.J.: Princeton University Press, 1989), 178, n. 22. Also see Nishimura, *Nihon dōtoku ron*, 20.

40. Donald Shively, "Motoda Eifu: Confucian Lecturer to the Meiji Emperor," in *Confucianism in Action*, ed. David S. Nivison (Stanford, Calif.: Stanford University Press, 1959), 327.

41. Ibid., 310, 317.

42. Inoue Tetsujirō, "Yaso benwakujo," *Tōyō gakugei zasshi* 18 (1883): 248–250, 249–250.

43. For a description of this uprising, see James Ketelaar, *Of Heretics and Martyrs in Meiji Japan: Buddhism and Its Persecution* (Princeton, N.J.: Princeton University Press, 1990), 78–86.

44. Murakami, *Bukkyō dōtoku shinron*, 3.

45. Ibid., 124. Regarding *gokoku rimin*, see 123.

46. Ibid., 20. Regarding "cultural progress," see 16–17.

47. Inoue Enryō, *Rinri tsūron*, 38–40.

48. See Schwantes, "Religion and Modernization in the Far East," 127.

49. Irwin Scheiner, *Christian Converts and Social Protest in Meiji Japan* (Berkeley and Los Angeles: University of California Press, 1970), 159–160.

50. Watanabe Minoru, *Niijima Jō*, vol. 35 (Tokyo: Yoshikawa kōbunkan, 1959), 189.

51. See Schwantes, "Religion and Modernization," 124. Originally from "A Pretended Memorial to a Westerner," in *Shinbun zasshi*, August 1872.

52. Tsuda Mamichi, "Kaika o susumuru hōhō o ronzu," *Meiroku zasshi* 3 (undated), in *Meiroku zasshi*, vol. 1, ed. Yamamuro Shinichi (Tokyo: Iwanami shoten, 1999), 121; Braisted, *Meiroku Zasshi*, 39.

53. Inoue Enryō, "Bukkyō katsuron joron," 363. Kōsaka Masaaki also takes up this point in *Meiji shisōshi* (Kyoto: Toeisha, 1999), 270. Also see Kōsaka Masaaki, *Japanese Thought in the Meiji Era*, trans. David Abosch (Tokyo: Pan Pacific Press, 1958), 244.

54. Uemura Masahisa, "Shinri ippan," in *Meiji bungaku zenshū*, vol. 46, ed. Takeda Kiyoko and Yoshida Kyūichi (Tokyo: Chikuō shobō, 1957), 90–91.

55. Kozaki Hiromichi, "Yushin tetsugaku," *Tetsugaku zasshi* 1:8 (1887): 379. Cited in Funayama Shinichi, *Meiji tetsugakushi kenkyū* (Kyoto: Mineruba shobō, 1959), 132–134.

56. William Haver, *The Body of This Death: Historicity and Sociality in the Time of AIDS* (Stanford, Calif.: Stanford University Press, 1996), 19.

57. See Frederick Copleston, *A History of Philosophy: Modern Philosophy, Bentham to Russell*, vol. 8, *Part 1* (New York: Image Books, 1967), 133–134.

58. Inoue Tetsujirō, "Nichi nichi shinbun no shūkyō ron o hyōshi awasete Ibii shi ni kotau," *Tōyō gakugei zasshi* 20 (1883): 313. Emphasis is Inoue's.

59. Hikaku shisōshi kenkyūkai, ed., *Meiji shisōka no shūkyōkan* (Tokyo: Ōkura shuppan, 1975), 345.

60. Kozaki, *Seikyō shinron*. Citation is from Takeda Kiyoko, *Ningenkan no sokoku: Kindai Nihon no shisō to Kirisutokyō* (Tokyo: Kōbundo shinsha, 1967), 76–77.

61. Nishimura Shigeki, "Shūshin jikoku hi ni michi ron," 4; Braisted, *Meiroku Zasshi*, 379. Nishimura also pointed out that "Mencius also observed that the family is the foundation of the nation and that the individual person is the foundation of the family." Nishimura Shigeki, "Shūshin jikoku hi ni michi ron," 4.

62. Nishimura Shigeki, "Shūshin jikoku hi ni michi ron," 4–5; Braisted, *Meiroku Zasshi*, 380–381.

63. Sakatani Shiroshi, "Kitsune-setsu no kōgi," *Meiroku zasshi* 20 (Nov 1874): 5–7; Braisted, *Meiroku Zasshi*, 256.

64. Sakatani, "Seikyō no gi," *Meiroku zasshi* 22 (Dec 1874): 4–6; Braisted, *Meiroku Zasshi*, 279.

65. Sakatani, "Seikyō no gi," 5–6; Braisted, *Meiroku Zasshi*, 280–281.

66. J. S. Mill, "On Liberty." In *Utilitarianism, Liberty and Representative Government* (London: J. M. Dent and Sons, 1922), 65.

67. Inoue Tetsujirō, "Miru no Jiyu no ri o hakusu," *Tōyō gakugei zasshi* 9 (1883): 14–16.

68. James Fitzjames Stephen, *Liberty, Equality, Fraternity* (Cambridge: Cambridge University Press, 1967). Leslie Stephen (1832–1904), brother of James Fitzjames, also wrote on Mill in his work *Science of Ethics* (1882). This work, an effort to expound an evolutionary theory of morality, is concerned with Mill only in passing, while *Liberty, Equality, Fraternity* devotes the first four chapters (more than half the book) to a critique of *On Liberty*.

69. Ibid., 44.

70. Ibid., 90.

71. Douglas Howland, *Personal Liberty and Public Good: The Introduction of John Stuart Mill to Japan and China* (Toronto: University of Toronto Press, 2005), 42. For those interested in further exploring the status of Mill in Meiji Japan, Howland's work is an excellent resource.

72. Uemura Masahisa, "Shinri ippan," in *Uemura Masahisa chosakushū*, vol. 4: *Shingaku shisō*, ed. Kawamoto Tetsuo (Tokyo: Shinkyō Shupansha, 1966), 98–101.

73. Cited in Takeda, *Ningen kan no sokoku*, 98–99.

74. Inoue Tetsujirō, "Yaso benwakujo," 248–250.

75. Fujishima Ryō-on, "Yasokyō no mudōri," excerpt in *Meiji zenki shisōshi bunken*, ed. Mihashi Takeo, 471. For yet another example of this viewpoint, see Soeda Juichi, "Dōtoku no taihon wa nani ni yorite sadamenya," 258.

76. Sawa Wataru, ed., *Uemura Masahisa to sono jidai*, vol. 3 (Tokyo: Kyōbunkan, 1976), 422–423.

77. Kozaki Hiromichi, *Seikyō shinron;* citation is from Takeda, *Ningenkan no sokoku,* 79.

78. Kozaki stated that to maintain morality, "authority" *(ken-i)* and "the power to reform the people" *(kankaryoku)* are necessary. See ibid., 80. Also see Kozaki, *Seikyō shinron,* 101–102.

79. For a thorough overview of this issue, see Notto R. Thelle, *Buddhism and Christianity in Japan: From Conflict to Dialogue, 1854–1899* (Honolulu: University of Hawaiʻi Press, 1987).

80. Michel de Certeau, *The Practice of Everyday Life,* trans. Steven Rendall (Berkeley and Los Angeles: University of California Press, 1988), xviii. The actual passage reads, "Although they [the trajectories, i.e., that which is produced by the consumer through his or her signifying practices] are composed with the vocabularies of established languages... the trajectories trace out the ruses of other interests and desires that are neither determined nor captured by the systems in which they develop."

Chapter 4: Resisting Civilizational Hierarchies

1. See Fukuzawa Yukichi, *Bunmei ron no gairyaku.* In this work, Fukuzawa appropriates Buckle's assertion that civilization is a matter of knowledge and virtue. See Buckle, *History of Civilization in England,* 125, 131, 132.

2. See, for example, Aizawa Seishisai's "Shinron," in *Nihon shisō taikei,* vol. 53: *Mitogaku,* ed. Imai Usaburō (Tokyo: Iwanami shoten, 1977), 49–159.

3. Inoue Tetsujirō used the term *kokuminsei* to translate the German term *Volkstum* (nationality or national characteristic) in the 1912 version of his dictionary of philosophy, but the emergence of a discourse on folk spirit began to emerge by the early 1890s. See, for example, Kuga Katsunan, "Kinji seironkō," in *Nihon no meicho,* vol. 37: *Kuga Katsunan, Miyake Setsurei* (Tokyo: Chūōkōronsha, 1971), 119–120, and Inoue et al., eds., *Tetsugaku jii* (Tokyo: Maruzen, 1912), 171.

4. Johann Gottfried von Herder, *Reflections on the Philosophy of the History of Mankind,* trans. T. O. Churchill, abridged version edited by Frank E. Manuel (Chicago and London: University of Chicago Press, 1968), 7.

5. See Matti Bunzl, "Franz Boas and the Humboldtian Tradition: From *Volksgeist* and *Nationalcharakter* to an Anthropological Concept of Culture," in *Volksgeist as Method and Ethic: Essays on Boasian Ethnography and the German Anthropological Tradition,* ed. George W. Stocking, Jr. (Madison: University of Wisconsin Press, 1996), 20.

6. The term *Kulturkampf,* translated as *bunka tōsō,* appears in Inoue Tetsujirō's 1912 edition of his *Tetsugaku jii.* By 1916 *Kulturkampf* and a new conception of civilization *(shin bunmei)* became central ideas in the discourse on national morality, discussed in the next chapter.

7. Percival Lowell, *The Soul of the Far East* (Boston and New York: Houghton, Mifflin and Company, 1888). For Lowell's statement on the Orient's lack of personality, see 202. Concerning the "march of mind," see 195, and see 213 on imagination.

8. Nakashima Rikizō, "Mr. Percival Lowell's Misconception of the Character of the Japanese," *New Englander and Yale Review* 14:2, New Series (February 1889): 97–102. Nakashima's quoted passages below are from this text. Italics are Nakashima's.

9. For Hegel's use and definition of the term "personality," see T. M. Knox, trans., *Hegel's Philosophy of Right* (London: Oxford University Press, 1967), 37, §35. Hegel's assertions about the Orient in his *Philosophy of History* targeted China rather than Japan. He argued that the Chinese lacked "free reason and imagination" while "the postulates of subjectivity" in China "are entirely ignored." He found the Chinese people to be "in a state of nonage, in virtue of the principle of patriarchal government," and concluded "free sentiment—the moral standpoint generally—is thereby thoroughly obliterated." Lowell applied this reasoning, the positing of imagination and subjectivity as requisites for morality, to the "Far East" generally. See G. W. F. Hegel, *The Philosophy of History,* ed. C. J. Friedrich (New York: Dover Publications, 1956), 123, 127–128, 131.

10. These are the assertions of Nishi Amane in his article "The Three Human Treasures" and Inoue Enryō in *Outline of Ethics.* These texts are addressed in chapters 2 and 3.

11. For an elaboration on Mill's utilitarianism, see Alasdair MacIntyre, *A Short History of Ethics* (New York: Simon and Schuster, 1996), 235; and see J. S. Mill, *Utilitarianism* (Boston: Willard Small, 1899), 17–20, where Mill discusses the higher pleasures and states, "[S]ome kinds of pleasure are more desirable and more valuable than others."

12. Nakashima Rikizō, "Eikoku shin kanto gakuha ni tsuite," *Tetsugaku zasshi* 69, 70 (1892): 411–421; 493–501; 71:581–584; 72:647–650.

13. "Related appearances," Green maintained, "are impossible apart from the action of intelligence." See T. H. Green, *Prolegomena to Ethics* (New York: Thomas Y. Crowell Co., 1969), 28.

14. Ibid., xiv. Although it may be that each finite consciousness constitutes nature to the extent that it apprehends this system of relations, Green argued that only some absolute, eternal consciousness (i.e., God) can account for the existence of our own finite consciousness.

15. Nakashima, "Eikoku shin Kanto gakuha ni tsuite," passim.

16. Nakashima viewed the good as the realization of the self *(jiga jitsugen),* and he described the self as personality *(jinkaku).* See Hirai Atsuko, "Self-Realization and Common Good: T. H. Green in Meiji Ethical Thought," *Journal of Japanese Studies* 5:1 (Winter 1979): 107–136, where Hirai explains that Nakashima changed the term *jiga* to *jinkaku,* apparently to avoid the connotation of "selfishness" associated with the former term.

17. Nakashima, "Eikoku shin Kanto gakuha ni tsuite," 583.

18. See Nishida Kitarō, "Gurin-shi no rinrigaku to ninshikiron," *Kyōiku jiron,* 362, 363, 364 (1895). This article is also included in *Nishida Kitarō zenshū,* vol. 13 (Tokyo: Iwanami shoten, 1966), 21–41.

19. Hirai Atsuko notes that Nakashima used Green's *Prolegomena to Ethics* as a classroom text. See Hirai, "Self-Realization and Common Good," 108.

20. Nakajima Tokuzō, "Gurin-shi chishiki tetsugaku o yomu," *Tetsugaku zasshi* 9:94 (1894): 899–930. See esp. 905–906.

21. Takayama Chogyū, *Chogyū zenshū,* vol. 4, ed. Anesaki Masaharu (Tokyo: Hakubunkan, 1927), 101.

22. Ibid., 102. He explained society's ideal with the idea of *higa teki byōdō shin* (roughly, no-self identity). One is at once differentiated *(sabetsu teki)* from society and at one with *(byōdō teki)* society. One is both individual *(kotai teki)* and universal *(fuhen teki)*. The term *sabetsu,* in Buddhist thought, signifies the distinctiveness of all phenomenal objects. *Byōdō,* a term used in opposition to *sabetsu,* refers to the oneness of all things. The concept of *byōdō soku sabetsu,* then, does not simply posit an equivalence; rather, it relates the oneness of all objects even in their difference. From the standpoint of the individual person, the perceiving subject (the one who sees) is distinct from the object perceived (the seen). But from the standpoint of *byōdō,* that is, from the standpoint at which the individual self is negated, all is one.

23. Nishida Kitarō, *Zen no kenkyū* (Tokyo: Iwanami shoten, 1999), 202. Abe Masao and Christopher Ives, in their translation of this work, use the term "actualization" for *jitsugen,* but note that this term can be rendered as "realization" and "fulfillment" as well. "Realization" is the term first translated as *jitsugen* by personalist philosophers. For comparison, see Nishida Kitarō, *An Inquiry into the Good,* trans. Abe Masao and Christopher Ives (New Haven, Conn.: Yale University Press, 1987), 142.

24. This unity of subject and object, or the effort to instill nature with its own subjectivity, would later become quite pronounced in the philosophy of such thinkers as Nishida Kitarō, Miki Kiyoshi, and Watsuji Tetsurō. It is here, with the introduction of personalism, that this view first gained legitimacy.

25. Nakashima Rikizō, *Rinri to kyōiku* (Tokyo and Osaka: Moriyoshikan, 1902), 98–99.

26. Ibid., 182.

27. John Crump, *The Origins of Socialist Thought in Japan* (New York: St. Martin's Press, 1983), 21.

28. See Ryōsuke Ishii, ed., *Japanese Legislation in the Meiji Era,* trans. William J. Chambliss (Tokyo: Pan-Pacific Press, 1958), 556–557.

29. Nakashima Rikizō, *Shihan gakkō shūshin shin kyōkasho* (Tokyo: Bungakusha, 1911), 39–41. This textbook was approved by the Ministry of Education for use in moral training courses at the teachers' colleges.

30. Ibid., 78–82. This discussion was in a chapter on "personality" *(jinkaku)*. With this focus on equality, liberty, and respect for the individual, Nakashima's moral textbook in places sounds as though it could have been written by a proponent of popular rights several decades before. But perhaps the real inheritors of the popular rights legacy were Kōtoku Shūsui and other anarchist thinkers, a subject addressed in the following chapter.

31. Nakashima, *Rinri to kyōiku,* 100.

32. Ibid., 101.

33. Ibid. Inoue Tetsujirō was one of those who criticized Nakashima's "Western" style of moral theorizing, asserting that his ethics was simply translated directly from the West with no consideration of the ethics of Japan. See Inoue Tetsujirō, "Meiji tetsugaku kai no kaiko," in *Iwanami kōza tetsugaku,* vol. 12, no. 4 (Tokyo: Iwanami shoten, 1932), 66. Also see Hirai, "Self-Realization and Common Good," 119.

34. Inoue Tetsujirō, "Meiji tetsugaku kai no kaiko," 66.

35. A translation of the Imperial Rescript on Education appears in Tsunoda et al., eds., *Sources of Japanese Tradition,* 139–140.

36. Inoue Tetsujirō, "Chokugo engi," in *Kindai Nihon shisō taikei,* vol. 31: *Meiji shisōshū II,* ed. Matsumoto Sannosuke (Tokyo: Chikuma shobō, 1977), 115.

37. Ibid., 89.

38. Ibid., 116.

39. Ibid.

40. Ōnishi Hajime, "Shiken issoku," in *Kindai Nihon shisō taikei,* vol. 31: *Meiji shisōshū II,* ed. Matsumoto Sannosuke (Tokyo: Chikuma shobō, 1977), 144–150. These translations appear in Sharon H. Nolte, "National Morality and Universal Ethics: Ōnishi Hajime and the Imperial Rescript on Education," *Monumenta Nipponica* 38:3 (Autumn 1983): 289–294.

41. Ōnishi Hajime, "Rinrigaku," in *Ōnishi Hakushi zenshu,* vol. 2: *Rinrigaku* (Tokyo: Keiseisha, 1903–1904), 265.

42. Ibid., 203.

43. Ōnishi Hajime, "Chūkō to dōtoku no kihon," in *Meiji bungaku zenshū,* vol. 80: *Meiji tetsugaku shisōshū,* ed. Senuma Shigeki (Tokyo: Chikuma shobō, 1974), 112–116.

44. Nolte, "National Morality and Universal Ethics," 290.

45. Ōnishi, "Chūkō to dōtoku no kihon," 114.

46. Nolte, "National Morality and Universal Ethics," 290.

47. Ōnishi, "Chūkō to dōtoku no kihon," 114.

48. Ōnishi Hajime, "Kokkashugi no kaishaku," in *Kindai Nihon shisō taikei,* vol. 31: *Meiji shisōshū II,* ed. Matsumoto Sannosuke (Tokyo: Chikuma shobō, 1977), 156.

49. Ibid., 155.

50. Inoue Tetsujirō, *Nihon Yōmeigakuha no tetsugaku* (Tokyo: Fusanbō, 1900), 4. Inoue used the term *todoku* (here translated as "eat away") to express the insidious nature of utilitarian morality. This term carries the connotation of something that is gradually eaten away by worms, and also of a poison that eats away at something.

51. Ibid., 4. Inoue's unusual term, the "virtue of the heart," combined *kokoro* with the *toku* of *dōtoku,* or morality.

52. Ibid., 4–5.

53. Inoue Tetsujirō, *Rinri shinsetsu,* 416, 419.

54. Inoue Tetsujirō and Kanie Yoshimaru, *Nihon rinri ihen,* vol. 1 (Kyoto: Rinsen shoten, 1970), 1.

55. Inoue Tetsujirō, *Nihon Yōmeigakuha no tetsugaku,* 2.

56. Ibid., 3.

57. Ibid. A decade and a half earlier, Nishimura Shigeki had already discussed the crucial role of morality in warfare. This was a time, however, when utilitarian thought still dominated moral discourse.

58. Inoue Tetsujirō, "Meiji no tetsugaku kaisō roku," 15–18. For Fukuzawa's views on the "tools of civilization," see Fukuzawa Yukichi, "Nisshin no sensō wa bunya no sensō nari," in *Nihonshi shiryō*, vol. 4: *Kindai*, ed. Rekishigaku kenkyūkai (Tokyo: Iwanami shoten, 1997), 221–222. Here, Fukuzawa describes the Sino-Japanese conflict as "a war between a country that planned for the progress of civilization and one that obstructed it."

59. For an excellent discussion of the conception of *wénmíng* at the close of the nineteenth century, see Douglas Howland, *Borders of Chinese Civilization: Geography and History at Empire's End* (Durham, N.C., and London: Duke University Press, 1996), 7, 13–15, and passim. Irokawa Daikichi also addresses the changing views of civilization during late Meiji. See Irokawa, *The Culture of the Meiji Period*, trans. Marius Jansen (Princeton, N.J.: Princeton University Press, 1985), 212–218.

60. Okakura Kakuzō, *The Book of Tea* (New York: Dover Publications, Inc., 1964), 2–3. Fukuzawa Yukichi, "Datsu-A ron," in *Kindai Nihon shisō taikei*, vol. 2: *Fukuzawa Yukichi shū*, ed. Ishida Takeshi (Tokyo: Chikuma shobō, 1975), 510–512. Nakae Chōmin also called attention to civilization's violence in order to question "the god of evolution" and civilization's promise of an eventual world of peace among democratic societies. See Nakae, *Sansuijin keirin mondō* (Tokyo: Iwanami shoten, 1998), 16–17, 60–70, and passim. For an English translation, see Nakae Chōmin, *A Discourse by Three Drunkards on Government*, trans. Nobuko Tsukui (New York and Tokyo: Weatherhill, 1992), 52, 91–100, and passim.

61. Inoue Tetsujirō, *Nihon Yōmeigakuha no tetsugaku*, 6.

62. Thus, moral discourse played an integral role in the creation of *tōyō*. Stefan Tanaka's views concerning the discourse on *tōyōshi* (Oriental history) are helpful here. In *Japan's Orient: Rendering Pasts into History*, Tanaka convincingly argues that in its construction of *tōyōshi*, Japan rejected the inferior position assigned to it by Western historiography. Declaring its origins as distinct from the West, that is, as situated in the Orient rather than the Occident, Japan was able to locate itself at the pinnacle of an Asian hierarchy to become the West's differentiated but equal other. See Stefan Tanaka, *Japan's Orient: Rendering Pasts into History* (Berkeley and Los Angeles: University of California Press, 1993).

63. Inoue Tetsujirō, *Nihon Yōmeigakuha no tetsugaku*, 2.

64. Ibid., 630–631.

65. Inoue Tetsujirō, *Nihon Shushigakuha no tetsugaku* (Tokyo: Fusanbō, 1905), 601. By "vices," Inoue referred to this school's tendency to produce "worthless scholars" who "like bookworms" were concerned only with theories and texts.

66. *Tokyo Asahi shinbun* (Tokyo), February 7, 1911. Also see Ōhashi Kenji, *Ryōshin to shisei no seishin shi: Nihon Yōmeigaku no kingendai* (Tokyo: Bensei shuppan, 1999), 84.

67. Inoue Tetsujirō, *Nihon Shushigakuha no tetsugaku*, 598–599.

68. Inoue Tetsujirō, "Ōyōmei no gaku o ronzu," *Yōmeigaku* 2 (July 20, 1896): 13. Inoue uses the neologism *rinrigaku* even for the philosophy of ancient China.

69. Certain of Wang Yang-ming's (Japanese: Ōyōmei) statements explain why Inoue took this view. In his "Questions on the Great Learning," Wang (for whom this school of Confucianism is named) discussed the investigation of things *(kowu)*. "*Ko* (investigating) means *cheng* (rectifying).... To rectify what is unrectified means to get rid of evil. To restore it to rectitude means to practice goodness." Here, the very investigation of the world was ethical practice. See Fung Yu-lan, *A History of Chinese Philosophy*, vol. 2, trans. Derk Bodde (Princeton, N.J.: Princeton University Press, 1953), 602. Fung cites Wang's "Questions on the Great Learning."

70. Tengaisei (pseudonym), "Inoue senshi no 'Ōyōmei no gaku o ronzu' o yomu," *Yōmeigaku* 4 (August 20, 1896). Cited in Okada Takehiko, "Kaisetsu," in *Fukkoku Yōmeigaku*, vol. 1, ed. Okada Takehiko (Tokyo: Mokujisha, 1984), 7.

71. Inoue Tetsujirō, *Nihon Yōmeigakuha no tetsugaku*, 2–4. Ōhashi Kenji also addresses Inoue's comparison of Shushi and Yōmei Confucianism. See Ōhashi, *Ryōshin to shisei no seishin shi*, 76–77.

72. Inoue Tetsujirō, *Nihon Yōmeigaku no tetsugaku*, 630–631.

73. Inoue Tetsujirō, *Nihon Kogakuha no tetsugaku* (Tokyo: Fusanbō, 1902), 744–746.

74. Inoue Tetsujirō, *Nihon Shushigakuha no tetsugaku*, 602–603.

75. Inoue's textbooks for moral training stressed the particularities of Japan, the timeless quality of the Japanese people as a "single family," and the unique quality of Japan's *kokutai* (national essence or body). Like Nakashima, he too began with a discussion of the individual's sociality and called attention to the need for cooperation. And again, like Nakashima, he asserted that the individual has a duty not only to others but to him or herself. But while Nakashima spoke of the cultivation of self-respect, Inoue maintained that "to fulfill one's duty in regard to oneself is to complete the Way in regard to one's ancestors and descendants, past, present and future, and in regard to society and the state." He devoted an entire chapter to "spirit" *(seishin)*, in which he urged not only the cultivation of the body and mind, but of the spirit as well. Moreover, he spoke of the "cultivation of the heart *(kokoro)*" as a means to foster filial conduct. See Inoue Tetsujirō, *Chūgaku shūshin kyōkasho*, vol. 3 (Tokyo: Kinkō tosho, 1902), 2–3.

76. Okada, *Fukkoku Yōmeigaku*, 5.

77. Inoue and Kanie, *Nihon rinri ihen*, 1–2.

78. Inoue Tetsujirō, *Nihon Yōmeigakuha no tetsugaku*, 630–631.

79. Ibid.

80. Inoue and Kanie, *Nihon rinri ihen*, 3.

81. Here I am drawing upon Richard Rorty's idea of "hylomorphism." He describes a "hylomorphic conception of knowledge" as "a conception according to which knowledge is not the possession of accurate *representations* of an object but rather the subject's becoming *identical* with the object." See Rorty, *Philosophy and the Mirror of Nature*, 45.

82. Knowledge *(chi)* of course referred to "intuitive knowledge" of the human heart. Thus *chikō goitsu* implied a unity of the internal realm of the heart/mind and the external realm of materiality, the body, and action.

83. Murakami Senshō, "Bukkyō muga ron," *Tetsugaku zasshi* 109 (March 10, 1896): 183.

84. Ibid., 192. While Murakami conceded that there are certain theories of the self within Buddhism, these he argued are quite different from "ordinary theories of the self."

85. Uchida Kanehira, "Hito to taikyoku," *Tōyō tetsugaku* 1 (1894): 55.

86. Oyanagi Shiketaka, "Jiga jitsugen setsu to jukyō no rinri," *Tetsugaku zasshi* 20 (1905): 241–250.

87. Okada, *Fukkoku Yōmeigaku*, "Sōron" 6–11; "Kaisetsu," 1, 9.

88. Nishida Kitarō, *Zen no kenkyū*, 117. This translation, with slight revisions on my part, appears in Nishida Kitarō, *An Inquiry into the Good*, 77–78.

89. Partha Chatterjee, *The Nation and Its Fragments: Colonial and Postcolonial Histories* (Princeton, N.J.: Princeton University Press, 1993), 6.

90. Japanese thinkers in mid-Meiji drew not only upon the past in the formation of "folk spirit" *(minzoku seishin),* but also upon the thought of J. G. Herder, Hegel, Joseph de Maistre, J. F. Herbart, and others.

91. This citation appears in Kōsaka Masaaki, *Meiji shisōshi* (Kyoto: Tōeisha, 1999), 248. The translation is from Kōsaka, *Japanese Thought in the Meiji Era,* 220.

Chapter 5: Approaching the Moral Idea

1. Henricks, trans, *Lao-Tzu Te-Tao Ching,* 222–223. I have translated *guojia* (Japanese *kokka*) as "state" and *zhenchen* (Japanese *teishin*) as "faithful subjects." If this were a text from Meiji Japan, these translations would evoke little comment. But of course, as a text of China of the first or second century BCE, *guojia* and *zhenchen* are probably best translated as "country" and "virtuous officials." I have therefore taken certain liberties with this translation, but my concern here is not to offer an "accurate" interpretation of this passage in its original context, but to use it as a heuristic device for illustrating the relationship between the state and its subjects in Meiji Japan.

2. For a list of works on national morality beginning with Inoue's *Outline of National Morality,* see Inoue Tetsujirō, *Waga kokutai to kokumin dōtoku* (Tokyo: Kōbundō, 1925), 492–497.

3. Is there such a thing as "discursive violence" or must violence be defined only in terms of its material effects? In this chapter, I consider the suppression of otherness, even when this remains on the level of discourse, a form of violence.

4. Regarding *minzoku no seishin,* see Inoue Tetsujirō, *Kokumin dōtoku gairon* (Tokyo: Sanseidō, 1912), 4. As mentioned in the preceding chapter, the idea that each nation possesses its own unique "national character" shaped late nineteenth- and early twentieth-century moral discourse in Japan. Inoue, in his 1912 edition of *Philosophy*

Dictionary (Tetsugaku jii), translated *minzoku seishin* as *Volksgeist*. The German notion of *Volksgeist* (i.e., spirit or genius of the *Volk*/folk/nation) was central to national character discourse of this time. In short, national morality was understood as an expression of the "folk spirit." Regarding the blurring of the lines between *kokumin* and *minzoku*, see, for example, Soeda Juichi, *Hōsei kyōkasho* (Tokyo: Kinkōdō, 1901), 7–9. Soeda, a legal scholar, sought to clarify the distinctions between an ethnicity *(minzoku)* and the national community *(kokumin)*, yet suggested that in the case of Japan the two overlapped. In 1901 he wrote,

> In our country, the *kokumin* and the *minzoku* are of the same body. *Kokumin* are the people who live together under the state. *Minzoku* are those who share the same race, religion, manners, customs and language, and whether they live under the same state or not is not at issue. For example, the British and Americans have different states, but they are one and the same *minzoku*. Although Austria has a unified state, there are different *minzoku* living there.

His point was that Japan's unique circumstances (its single body of *kokumin* and *minzoku*) provided greater homogeneity and therefore less potential for social disruption. But neither *kokumin* nor *minzoku* was a semantically stable term during the late Meiji period or in the decades that followed. National morality scholar Fukasaku Yasubumi understood the term *kokumin* much as Soeda. He described *kokuminsei* (roughly "national character"), for example, as "the common character of the people governed by the same governmental authority." In this sense, he argued that Japan's *kokuminsei* differed from that of China. Also like Soeda, he explained *minzoku* in racial terms. But because he placed Japanese and Chinese into the same broad racial category ("our *kokumin* of Japan and the *kokumin* of China," he stated, "are of the Mongolian race") he relied on the category of *kokumin* rather than *minzoku* for his construction of Japanese moral particularity. Fukasaku's national morality, then, is not one of the racial folk, but of the Japanese folk. See Fukasaku Yasubumi, *Kokumin dōtoku yōgi* (Tokyo: Kōdōkan, 1916), 23, 250–251. Still others, again showing the polysemy of these terms, argued for a "Yamato *minzoku*" distinct from Ainu and the peoples of Japan's colonies. Psychologist Ōmichi Uichi asserted, "The Ainu are not Yamato *minzoku*. Former Chinese now called Taiwanese are not Yamato *minzoku*, they are Japanese *kokumin*; they are not Japanese *minzoku*. The aboriginal people of Taiwan are likewise not Japanese *minzoku*." Ōmichi explained that the Ainu and aboriginal people of Taiwan are people "without a culture" *(mibunka)* and that such people are not called *minzoku*, which for Ōmichi applied to a "cultural grouping" *(bunka kyōdō)*. See Ōmichi Uichi, *Shakai shinrigaku* (Tokyo: Kinkōdō, 1913), 38. For a detailed elaboration and analysis of these terms, see Kevin Doak, *A History of Nationalism in Modern Japan: Placing the People* (Leiden and Boston: Brill, 2007), esp. chapters 5 and 6.

   5. Inoue Tetsujirō, *Kokumin dōtoku gairon*, 12. For a translation and discussion of the Imperial Rescript on Education, see Gluck, *Japan's Modern Myths*, 120–127. For an English translation of the preface to Inoue's *Kokumin dōtoku gairon*, see Inoue, "An

Outline of National Morality, excerpt," trans. Richard Reitan, in *From Japan's Modernity: A Reader.* Chicago: Center for East Asian Studies (Chicago: CEAS, 2002), 57–63.

6. Funayama Shinichi, *Nihon no kannen ronja* (Tokyo: Eihōsha, 1956), 109.

7. See Fukasaku, *Kokumin dōtoku yōgi*, 17–18; and Yoshida Kumaji's "Commentary" on Nishimura's text in Nishimura, *Nihon dōtoku ron* (Tokyo: Iwanami shoten, 1974), 120. Also see Nishimura, "Nihon dōtoku ron," in *Hakuō sōsho*, 7, 9, 94.

8. See Hozumi Yatsuka, *Kempō teiyō*, vol. 1 (Tokyo: Yūhikaku, 1910). Hozumi's views on ancestor worship are discussed in Richard Minear, *Japanese Tradition and Western Law* (Cambridge, Mass.: Harvard University Press, 1970), 71–76. Hozumi provided a circuitous line of reasoning that invoked the name of Amaterasu to legitimize loyalty to the throne. Weaving together the concept of loyalty-as-filiality, the family-state, and ancestor worship with a neo-nativist assertion of racial unity, he wrote, "The ancestor of my ancestors is the Sun Goddess. The Sun Goddess is the founder of our race, and the throne is the sacred house of our race.... Father and mother are ancestors living in the present; the emperor is the Sun Goddess living in the present. For the same reason, one is filial to his parents and loyal to the throne; and the national teaching which connects these two is the worship of ancestors." See Hozumi, *Kokumin kyōiku: Aikokushin* (Tokyo: 1897), 4–5. Cited in Minear, *Japanese Tradition and Western Law*, 73.

9. Carol Gluck, for example, in her work on Meiji ideology, devotes a chapter to a discussion of "civil morality" but does not mention personalism. Watsuji and Kaneko, in their brief overview of ethics at Tokyo University, discuss both national morality and personalism as "the two major pillars" of academic ethics at the turn of the century, but fail to show the interconnectedness of the two. See Gluck, *Japan's Modern Myths*, 102–156; Tokyo Teikoku Daigaku, ed., *Tokyo Teikoku Daigaku gakujutsu taikan*, vol. 1: *Sōsetsu Bungakubu* (Tokyo: Tokyo Teikoku Daigaku, 1942), 391.

10. T. H. Green, *Principles of Political Obligation* (Ann Arbor: The University of Michigan Press, 1967), 110.

11. Ibid., 147. Concerning "legal channels," see ibid., 111.

12. The problem arises, of course, when there are conflicting understandings of what this ideal is or ought to be. This was at the root of the conflict between national morality and "dangerous thought." This issue will be taken up below.

13. Of course, these two positions were not at all incompatible for T. H. Green and Nakashima Rikizō.

14. Yoshida Seiichi, *Rinrigaku yōgi* (Tokyo: Tokyo Hobunkan, 1907), 546.

15. Inoue Tetsujirō, *Kokumin dōtoku gairon*, appendix, 74–75.

16. The term Inoue used for "complete" (*kansei* or *kanzen*) can also be read as "perfect."

17. Inoue Tetsujirō, *Kokumin dōtoku gairon*, appendix, 85.

18. Fukasaku, *Kokumin dōtoku yōgi*, 21–22.

19. Inoue Tetsujirō, *Kokumin dōtoku gairon*, appendix, 85.

20. Fukasaku, *Kokumin dōtoku yōgi*, 20–23.

21. Ibid., 637–638.

22. Ibid., 19–20.

23. Ibid., 638, 640.

24. Inoue Tetsujirō, *Kokumin dōtoku gairon,* appendix, 75.

25. Regarding the trial for those accused in the High Treason Incident, see Itoya Toshio, *Taigyaku jiken* (Kyoto: San'ichi shobō, 1960), 51–92, 125–195.

26. Inoue Tetsujirō, *Kokumin dōtoku gairon,* 10.

27. Ibid., 10–11.

28. Katō Hiroyuki, "Shizen to rinri," cited in Kaneko Takezō, *Rinrigaku jiten* (Tokyo: Kobundō, 1957), 234.

29. Yamagata Aritomo and Hozumi Yatsuka, "Shakai hakaishugiron," in *Yamagata Aritomo ikensho,* ed. Ōyama Azusa (Tokyo: Hara shobō, 1966), 315. For an alternative, partial translation of this same passage, see Gluck, *Japan's Modern Myths,* 176.

30. Yamagata and Hozumi, "Shakai hakaishugiron," 318. Also see Gluck, *Japan's Modern Myths,* 177.

31. Fukasaku, *Kokumin dōtoku yogi,* 537–540.

32. The causes of this riot are a matter of some debate. The Hibiya Riot has been characterized as a protest over the terms of the Portsmouth Treaty concluding Japan's war with Russia by those calling for continued fighting, or as "a people's struggle against despotic ruling powers," or, again, simply as "a blind outburst." See Tetsuo Najita and J. Victor Koschmann, eds., *Conflict in Modern Japanese History* (Princeton, N.J.: Princeton University Press, 1982), 264, 275.

33. Gluck cites a Yokohama magazine: "Beginning with the Ashio copper mine riot, the disturbances at the Koike coal mines and the Uraga docks have followed one upon the other, and now there is the violence at the Horonai mines.... [T]here is no doubt that this year [1907] is the year of the strike." Gluck, *Japan's Modern Myths,* 175.

34. Arahata Kanson, *Kanson jiden,* vol. 1 (Tokyo: Iwanami shoten, 1999), 278.

35. Najita and Koschmann, eds., *Conflict in Modern Japanese History,* 268.

36. Yoshida Seiichi, *Kokumin dōtoku yōryō* (Tokyo: Hōbunkan, 1916), 353.

37. Slavoj Žižek, *The Sublime Object of Ideology* (London and New York: Verso, 1989), 127–128.

38. Inoue Tetsujirō, *Kokumin dōtoku gairon,* chapter 7. Regarding loyalty-as-filiality in China, see chapter 10.

39. Fukasaku, *Kokumin dōtoku yogi,* 37–38.

40. The Teachers' Colleges (Shihan Gakkō) were part of Japan's educational system from 1872 until 1945, when they were replaced by the departments of education within universities. They were established to train teachers for positions in primary and secondary schools. By 1886 there was just one Teachers' College in Tokyo under the management of the Minister of Education (the Upper Level Teachers' College), and there was one Teachers' College in each prefecture (the Ordinary Teachers' College). By 1897, in addition to the Upper Level Teachers' College, the Women's Upper Level Teachers' College was established in Tokyo. See Monbushō, ed., *Gakusei hachi-jū nen shi* (Tokyo: Ōkurashō insatsukyoku, 1954), 134–137, 195.

41. Inoue and Hozumi lectured for one week at the Ministry of Education's Center for the Study of Arts and Sciences in December 1910 and for one week in the lecture

hall of Tokyo Imperial University (as part of a training course for middle school teachers) in July 1911. See the preface to Inoue's *Outline of National Morality,* where he discusses the location and dates of his lectures. Inoue Tetsujirō, *Kokumin dōtoku gairon,* preface.

42. See Karasawa Tomitarō, *Kyōkasho no rekishi* (Tokyo: Sōbunsha, 1960), 278. This translation appears in Kōsaka Masaaki, *Japanese Thought in the Meiji Era,* 387.

43. Kōsaka, *Japanese Thought in the Meiji Era,* 387

44. Revised texts included chapters on "The Glory of the National Polity," "The Unity of Loyalty and Filial Piety," "Guard and Maintain the Imperial Prosperity," "The Teachings of Our Imperial Ancestors," etc. See Karasawa, *Kyōkasho no rekishi,* 286. Also see Wilbur M. Fridell, "Government Ethics Textbooks in Late Meiji Japan," *Journal of Asian Studies* 29 (1969–1970): 826–827; and Kōsaka, *Japanese Thought in the Meiji Era,* 387–388.

45. The declines and increases in the 1903 texts and 1910 revised texts were: personal ethics (41.7 percent down to 37.9 percent); social ethics (27.6 percent down to 23.6 percent); state ethics (14.7 percent up to 18 percent); and family ethics (10.4 percent up to 14.3 percent). These figures are from Karasawa, *Kyōkasho no rekishi,* 228. Also see Fridell, "Government Ethics Textbooks in Late Meiji Japan," 827.

46. Karasawa, *Kyōkasho no rekishi,* 277.

47. Inoue Tetsujirō, *Shinhen shūshin kyōkasho* (Tokyo: Kinkōtōshoseki kabushiki gaisha, 1911), 20–21.

48. Ministry of Education, ed., *Jinjō shōgaku shūshin sho* (Tokyo: Monbushō, 1918), 10. Historian Ienaga Saburō states that this same story appeared in a moral training textbook published in 1903. See Ienaga Saburō, *The Pacific War, 1931–1945: A Critical Perspective on Japan's Role in World War II* (New York: Pantheon Books, 1978), 24.

49. For additional examples, see Yoshida Seiichi, *Shūshin kyōkasho* (Tokyo and Osaka: Hōbunkan, 1912); and Nakashima Rikizō, *Shihan gakkō shūshin shin kyōkasho* (Tokyo: Bungakusha, 1911).

50. On this point, see Imai Seiichi, *Nihon kindai shi* II (Tokyo: Iwanami shoten, 1977), 62–63.

51. *Teikoku kyōiku* 323 (November 1908): 118–119, cited in Jay Rubin, *Injurious to Public Morals: Writers and the Meiji State* (Seattle: University of Washington Press, 1984), 109.

52. The text of the Boshin Edict is included in Monbushō, ed., *Gakusei hachi-jū nen shi,* 716.

53. Karasawa, *Kyōkasho no rekishi,* 288.

54. Obviously nondiscursive strategies were carried out as well. A number of examples have been mentioned above, such as the Red Flag Incident, strikes, riots, and assassination plots.

55. Inoue Tetsujirō, "Kokka teki dōtoku to sekai teki dōtoku," *Teiyū rinrikai rinri koenshū* (February 20, 1905), 62.

56. See, for example, Fukasaku, *Kokumin dōtoku yogi,* 18–24; Yoshida Kumaji, *Waga kokumin dōtoku* (Tokyo: Kōdōkan, 1918), 285–288.

57. Arahata Kanson, *Yanaka mura metsubō shi* (Tokyo: Iwanami shoten, 1999), 24. Also see Nimura Kazuo, *The Ashio Riot of 1907: A Social History of Mining in Japan,* trans. Terry Boardman and Andrew Gordon (Durham, N.C., and London: Duke University Press, 1997), 19-21.

58. Ibid. Concerning the government's cruelty, see ibid., 172. See ibid., 124, regarding government abuse. These translations appear in Crump, *The Origins of Socialist Thought in Japan,* 308.

59. Akiyama Kiyoshi, *Nihon no hangyaku shisō* (Tokyo: Buneisha, 1968), 33. Crump also touches on this statement by Gudō. For his alternative translation, see Crump, *The Origins of Socialist Thought in Japan,* 310.

60. This and the preceding citations are from Katayama Sen, "Waga shakaishugi," in *Nihon shakai undō shisōshi,* vol. 5, ed. Kishimoto Eitarō (Tokyo: Aoki shoten, 1968), 112–113.

61. Ibid., 113.

62. See Ōsugi Sakae, "Dōtoku no sōzō," *Kindai shisō* 1:5 (February 1913): 1.

63. Kawakami Hajime, "Nihon dōkutoku no kokkashugi," in *Kawakami Hajime chosakushū,* vol. 8 (Tokyo: Chikuma shobō, 1964), 185–210, 192.

64. Natsume Soseki, "Bungei to dōtoku," in *Natsume Soseki zenshū,* vol. 11 (Tokyo: Iwanami shoten, 1985), 384. This translation is from Soseki, *Kokoro: A Novel, and Selected Essays,* trans. Edwin McClellan (New York: Madison Books, 1992), 245.

65. Nakashima Rikizō, *Genkon no rinrigaku mondai* (Tokyo: Fukyūsha, 1901), 149.

66. Nakashima Rikizō and Shinoda Toshihide, *Shihan gakkō yō shūshin kyōkasho* (Tokyo: Bungakusha, 1911), 107. Cited in Hirai, "Self-Realization and Common Good," 126.

67. Gail Lee Bernstein, *Japanese Marxist: A Portrait of Kawakami Hajime, 1879–1946* (Cambridge, Mass.: Harvard University Press, 1990), 77 and passim.

68. Kawakami Hajime, "Nihon dōkutoku no kokkashugi," 189.

69. Ibid.

70. Clearly, the effectiveness of Kawakami's argument relied on the essentializing effect of the discourse on national character. In other words, both Kawakami and national morality theorists operated within this discourse on national character, but their descriptions of Japan's character were very different. Kawakami maintained that state-ism was the "most prominent characteristic" of Japan, while individualism is the key characteristic of all the nations of "the West." But unlike national morality proponents who treated national character as an inherent fixture based largely on unalterable factors of geography, history, and race, Kawakami viewed Japan's state-ism as something that could be contested and overcome.

71. Kawakami Hajime, "Nihon dōkutoku no kokkashugi," 194. Cf. Inoue Tetsujirō's use of the term *kiken* (dangerous). See Inoue, *Kokumin dōtoku gairon,* preface.

72. Kawakami Hajime, "Nihon dōkutoku no kokkashugi," 193. Compare this statement with that of socialist Katayama Sen in 1903: "The religionist, the moralist, and the scholar...their knowledge, truths, and ideals are completely discarded and ignored." Katayama, "Waga shakaishugi," 113.

73. Kawakami Hajime, "Nihon dōkutoku no kokkashugi," 192.

74. Nishida, *Zen no kenkyū*, 156. This translation is from Nishida, *An Inquiry into the Good*, 107.

75. Nishida, *Zen no kenkyū*, 159; Nishida, *An Inquiry into the Good*, 109.

76. Nishida, *Zen no kenkyū*, 157–159; Nishida, *An Inquiry into the Good*, 108–109.

77. The phrase was *kokumin dōtoku o hakai suru yō na fukenzen na shisō*. See Inoue Tetsujirō, *Kokumin dōtoku gairon*, 10; Yoshida Seiichi, *Kokumin dōtoku yōryō*, 353.

78. Gluck, *Japan's Modern Myths*, 171.

79. Anesaki Masaharu, *History of Japanese Religion* (Tokyo: Charles E. Tuttle Company, 1983), 387.

80. Koboshi [pseudonym], "Bungei jihyō," *Nihon oyobi Nihonjin* (January 1, 1908): 55–57. Cited in Rubin, *Injurious to Public Morals*, 62.

81. Togawa Shūkotsu, "Bungei iinkai shi-ken," in *Chūō kōron* (June 1911): 87–89. Cited in Rubin, *Injurious to Public Morals*, 207–209.

82. Natsume, "Bungei to dōtoku," 382–383.

83. Inoue Tetsujirō, "Gendai shisō no keikō ni tsuite," *Taiyō* (November 1910): 67.

84. Akiyama, *Nihon no hangyaku shisō*, 33.

85. Sakamoto Seima, "Nyusha no ji," *Kumamoto hyōron* (May 20, 1908): 1. This translation is from Crump, *The Origins of Socialist Thought in Japan*, 333.

86. Ōsugi, "Dōtoku no sōzō," 1. This text was almost certainly based on the anarchist thinker Petr Kropotkin's *Anarchist Morality* and reflects the impact of his thought in Japan. Kropotkin writes, "There are epochs in which the moral conception changes entirely. A man perceives that what he had considered moral is the deepest immorality. In some instances it is a custom, a venerated tradition, that is fundamentally immoral. In others we find a moral system framed in the interests of a single class. We cast them over-board and raise the cry 'Down with morality!' It becomes a duty to act 'immorally.'" Petr Kropotkin, "Anarchist Morality," in *Kropotkin's Revolutionary Pamphlets*, ed. Roger N. Baldwin (New York: Dover Publications, Inc., 1970), 112.

87. See Inoue Tetsujirō, *Kokumin dōtoku gairon*, 305–310.

88. Ibid., 310–311.

89. Arahata Kanson, "Nakagi no kyōmuto geki," *Kindai shisō* 1:10 (July 1913): 20. The phrase "utopian illusion" is from Crump's translation: "the overthrowing of the tyrants who set themselves up against civilisation and humanity is not a utopian illusion." See Crump, *The Origins of Socialist Thought in Japan*, 317.

90. Kawakami, "Nihon dōkutoku no kokkashugi," 190–191.

91. See, for example, Kenjō Teiji, "Kindai hōtoku undō no seiritsu," *Edo no shisō* no. 7, 65.

92. Abe Jirō, *Risō no hito* (Tokyo: Kaneo bunkandō, 1906), 12–13.

93. Mishima Tsuyoshi, "Dōtoku keizai gōitsu setsu," *Tetsugaku zasshi* 24 (1909): 135.

94. According to Mishima, *keisei* and *keirin* meant the same thing. Mishima did not refer to the often used Edo-period phrase *keisei saimin* (ordering the world to save

the people) in his article, but the term *sai* (to save) can be understood as *saimin* (saving the people). The modern compound for economics *(keizai)* may also have been formed from the first characters of the words *keisei saimin*. See Tetsuo Najita's informative discussion of political economy *(keisei saimin)* in *Visions of Virtue in Tokugawa Japan: The Kaitokudō Merchant Academy of Osaka* (Honolulu: University of Hawai'i Press, 1987), 8–10.

95. Mishima, "Dōtoku keizai gōitsu setsu," 135.

96. See R. L. Armstrong, *Just Before the Dawn: The Life and Work of Ninomiya Sontoku* (New York: The Macmillan Co., 1912), 66; Thomas R. H. Havens, "Religion and Agriculture in Nineteenth-Century Japan: Ninomiya Sontoku and the Hōtoku Movement," *The Japan Christian Quarterly* 38:2 (Spring 1972): 102.

97. Armstrong, *Just Before the Dawn,* 64.

98. In his works on national morality in the 1910s, Inoue was highly critical of the ethics of individualism. But here, it is important to distinguish individualism from "individuality" or "personality" *(jinkaku),* understood not as the egoistic pursuit of individual desires but as a self-conscious awareness of one's own individuality.

99. Kenjō, "Kindai hōtoku undō no seiritsu," 64.

100. Armstrong, *Just Before the Dawn,* 65–66.

101. Uchimura Kanzō, "Ninomiya Sontoku: A Peasant Saint," in *Ninomiya Sontoku: His Life and "Evening Talks,"* ed. Ishiguro Tadaatsu (Tokyo: Kenkyūsha, 1955), 72.

102. Ibid., 17.

103. Natsume, "Bungei to dōtoku," 383–384.

104. Katayama, "Waga shakaishugi," 113.

105. Fukasaku, for example, makes such an assertion. See Fukasaku, *Kokumin dōtoku yōgi,* 233. Also see Karasawa, *Kyōkasho no rekishi,* 278.

106. This is the assertion of Hozumi in texts he wrote in 1889 and 1910, but the Nihon Kōkdōkai made much the same assertion. See Minear, *Japanese Tradition and Western Law,* 57.

107. Kawakami, "Nihon dōkutoku no kokkashugi," 191, 193.

108. Akiyama, *Nihon no hangyaku shisō,* 41. This translation, with only slight revision on my part, is Crump's. See his *Origins of Socialist Thought in Japan,* 312.

109. Mikiso Hane, trans., *Reflections on the Way to the Gallows: Rebel Women in Pre-War Japan* (Berkeley: University of California Press, 1988), 124.

110. Ibid.

111. Inoue Tetsujirō, *Kokumin dōtoku gairon,* 10. Compare Yamagata's views on social destruction in Yamagata and Hozumi, "Shakai hakaishugiron," 315–316.

112. Does this mean then that the ideal, moral or otherwise, is necessarily harmful in all its forms? John Dewey, for example, maintained that the ideal in an abstract form is invariably harmful. Given the historically specific complexities surrounding the moral ideal of national morality scholars in early twentieth-century Japan—its philosophical articulation, the sometimes ineffective strategies for approaching it, the suppression of

moral alterity associated with the approach, the violent resistance to this ideal, etc.—I would hesitate to offer any ahistorical claim about the harmful nature of "the moral ideal" in general. I do, however, suggest that the *approach* toward a moral ideal has at least the potential for violence and danger, provided that we understand "approach" as the effort to establish a hegemonic position for any given contingent ethical claim. See John Dewey, "Changed Conceptions of the Ideal and the Real," in *Reconstruction in Philosophy* (Boston: Beacon Press, 1957), 103–131.

Epilogue

1. On the issue of the universal itself enabling dissent, see Slavoj Žižek, "Class Struggle or Postmodernism? Yes, Please!" in *Contingency, Hegemony, Universality: Contemporary Dialogues on the Left,* ed. Judith Butler (New York: Verso, 2000), 90–135, esp. 101. I return to this idea below.

2. See Fukasaku, *Kokumin dōtoku yōgi,* 638, 640; Nishitani Keiji, "'Kindai no chōkoku' shiron," in *Kindai no chōkoku,* ed. Kawakami Tetsutarō (Tokyo: Fusanbō, 2006), 27. I have slightly altered this translation of Nishitani's statement as it appears in Kevin Doak's "Nationalism as Dialectics: Ethnicity, Moralism, and the State in Early Twentieth-Century Japan," in *Rude Awakenings: Zen, the Kyoto School, and the Question of Nationalism,* ed. James W. Heisig and John C. Maraldo (Honolulu: University of Hawai'i Press, 1995), 193. See also, in the same edited volume, Jan Van Bragt's claim that "the self-negation demanded by (religious) nothingness is conveniently aligned to the self-negation that the totalitarian state demands of its citizens." Jan Van Bragt, "Kyoto Philosophy—Intrinsically Nationalistic?" in *Rude Awakenings,* ed. Heisig and Maraldo, 252.

3. Inoue Tetsujirō, *Kokumin dōtoku gairon,* 10; Yamagata and Hozumi, "Shakai hakaishugiron," 315.

4. Kawakami Tetsutarō, ed., *Kindai no chōkoku* (Tokyo: Fusanbō, 2006), 294; Harry Harootunian also references this statement by Kamei. See Harry Harootunian, *Overcome by Modernity: History, Culture, and Community in Interwar Japan* (Princeton, N.J.: Princeton University Press, 2000), 35.

5. Ōkawa Shūmei, "Nihon oyobi Nihonjin no michi," in *Ōkawa Shūmei zenshū* (Tokyo: Iwasaki shoten, 1961), 75.

6. Kōsaka Masaaki et al., "Tōakyōeiken no rinrisei to rekishisei," in *Chūō kōron* (April 1942), 121. For this passage in translation and for a discussion of this text, see Naoki Sakai, *Translation and Subjectivity: On "Japan" and Cultural Nationalism* (Minneapolis and London: University of Minnesota Press, 1997), 168.

7. These definitions of *minzoku* and *kokumin* are from Soeda Juichi, *Hōsei kyōkasho* (Tokyo: Kinkōdō, 1901), 7–9.

8. Harootunian, *Overcome by Modernity,* 42. Also see Miki Kiyoshi, "Dentō ron," in *Miki Kiyoshi zenshū* (Tokyo: Iwanami shoten, 1968), 307–317; and David Dilworth, ed., *Sourcebook for Modern Japanese Philosophy* (Westport, Conn.: Greenwood Press,

1998), 296. Dilworth et al. note that Miki described "the flow of tradition...as a 'contradictory unity' of subjective and objective, particular and universal, passionate and rational, dimensions of human life."

9. Ōkawa, "Nihon oyobi Nihonjin no michi," 5.

10. For a detailed overview of the dramatic changes Japan underwent during the interwar period, see Harootunian, *Overcome by Modernity.*

11. Tetsuo Najita and H. D. Harootunian, "Japan's Revolt against the West," in *Modern Japanese Thought,* ed. Bob Tadashi Wakabayashi (Cambridge: Cambridge University Press, 1998), 231. Historian Satō Hirō also describes a shift to "culture." "From the beginning of the Taishō period, the concept of culture *(bunka)* came to be widespread." He associates its emergence with the increased attention in Japan to neo-Kantianism and Kantian philosophy, which he describes as "philosophy of culture." See Satō Hirō, *Gaisetsu Nihon shisōshi* (Kyoto: Mineruba shobō, 2005), 252.

12. Inoue Tetsujirō's 1912 edition of the *Tetsugaku jii* lists *Kulturkampf* as *bunka tōsō,* i.e., "culture struggle." See Inoue Tetsujirō et al., comps, *Ei-doku-futsu-wa tetsugaku jii* (Tokyo: Maruzen, 1912), 84.

13. Yoshida Seiichi, *Kokumin dōtoku yōryō,* 1–2.

14. Fukaya Masashi, *Ryōsai-kenbo shugi no kyōiku* (Nagoya: Reimei shobō, 1981), 257.

15. Okuda Yoshihito, "Gendai joshi kyōiku no konpon hōshin," *Chūō kōron* (July 1913): 74.

16. Hiratsuka Raichō, "Inoue Tetsujirō shi no ryōfu kenbu o nanzu," in *Hiratsuka Raichō chosakushū,* vol. 2, ed. Hiratsuka Raichō chosaku shū henshū iinkai (Tokyo: Ōtsuki shoten, 1983), 344.

17. Richard Reitan, "Claiming Personality: Reassessing the Dangers of the 'New Woman' in early Taishō Japan," *positions: east asia cultures critique* (forthcoming).

18. Hiratsuka Raichō, "Atarashii onna," in *Hiratsuka Raichō hyōronshū,* ed. Kobayashi Tomie and Yoneda Sayoko (Tokyo: Iwanami shoten, 2005), 41–42.

19. In her essay "The New Woman," Raichō asked, "What will this new morality be?" Her answer was that "the new woman does not yet know." Similarly, Itō Noe, another contributor to *Seitō,* made repeated references to "opening up new paths" in her essay on the "new woman's road," but admitted "where this new road begins and where it will lead, I do not know." See Hiratsuka, "Atarashii onna," 43; and Itō Noe, "Atarashiki onna no michi," in *"Seitō" Josei kaihō ronshū,* ed. Hariba Kiyoko (Tokyo: Iwanami shoten, 2002), 93–95.

20. Yoshino Sakuzō, "Gendai shikō," in *Minponshugiron: Yoshino Sakuzō Hakushi minshushugi ronshū,* vol. 2 (Tokyo: Shin kigensha, 1948), 24–26. Also see Tetsuo Najita, "Some Reflections on Idealism in the Political Thought of Yoshino Sakuzō," in *Japan in Crisis: Essays on Taishō Democracy,* ed. Bernard S. Silberman and Harry D. Harootunian (Princeton, N.J.: Princeton University Press, 1974), 54.

21. Moriya Masamichi, "Yoshino Sakuzō," in *Nihon jimbutsushi taikei,* vol. 7: *Kindai III,* ed. Inoue Kiyoshi (Tokyo, Asakura shoten, 1960), 107–109; Najita, "Some Reflections on Idealism," 37.

22. See also Hamabayashi Masao, ed., *Tettei hihan: "Kokumin dōtoku"* (Tokyo: Ōtsuki shoten, 2001). Also see Kyoko Inoue, *Individual Dignity in Modern Japanese Thought: The Evolution of the Concept of* Jinkaku *in Moral and Educational Discourse* (Ann Arbor: Center for Japanese Studies, University of Michigan, 2001).

23. Watsuji Tetsurō, "Kokumin dōtoku ron," in *Watsuji Tetsurō zenshū, Bekkan II* (Tokyo: Iwanami shoten, 1992), 51.

24. See Yuasa Yasuo, "Kaisetsu," in *Watsuji Tetsurō zenshū, Bekkan I,* 479.

25. Watsuji, "Kokumin dōtoku ron," in ibid., 433.

26. This, at any rate, is Watsuji's position on the relationship between *minzoku* and the state in his texts on *kokumin dōtoku.* Elsewhere he develops different views of the state, e.g., the state as a conception that guides ethical self-consciousness. See Watsuji, *Ningen no gaku toshite no rinrigaku* (Tokyo: Iwanami shoten, 1999). And in his *Rinrigaku,* Watsuji describes the state as something that establishes itself through war. The state, he says here, is a sacred object; the sovereignty of the state is an expression of the absolute within the realm of finite human existence. See the appendix to *Rinrigaku* (chapter 7: "Kokka") in Watsuji, *Watsuji Tetsurō zenshū,* vol. 11 (Tokyo: Iwanami shoten, 1992).

27. The particular and the universal are brought together in Watsuji's conception of *kokumin,* which he describes as a "living totality." The ultimate unification of the social totality's personality *(zentai no jinkaku)* and the personality of the individual *(kojin no jinkaku)* is realized within the conception of *kokumin.* For elaboration on these points, see Yuasa, "Kaisetsu," 478. For additional studies of Watsuji's ethical thought, particularly in regard to his *kokumin dōtoku,* see Tsuda Masao, *Watsuji Tetsurō kenkyū: Kaishakugaku, kokumin dōtoku, shakaishugi* (Tokyo: Aoki shoten, 2001); Yamada Kō, *Watsuji Tetsurō ron* (Tokyo: Kadensha, 1987); and Satō Yasukuni, ed., *Yomigaeru Watsuji Tetsurō: Jinbun kagaku no saisei ni mukete* (Kyoto: Nakanishiya shuppan, 1999). For an English translation of Watsuji's major ethical work, see Watsuji Tetsurō, *Watsuji Tetsurō's Rinrigaku: Ethics in Japan,* trans. Yamamoto Seisaku and Robert E. Carter (Albany: State University of New York Press, 1996).

28. Ishihara Shintarō, "Nippon no dōgi," *Jiyū* (April 1974): 18–20, 32; Wayne R. Root and Takechi Manabu's translation appears in *The Japan Interpreter* 9(3) (Winter 1975): 276–291.

29. The information and translations concerning the Nihon Kōdōkai come from their brochure titled "Nihon Kōdōkai," which outlines its history and objectives. Nihon Kōdōkai, ed., "Nihon Kōdōkai" (Tokyo: Nihon Kōdōkai, n.d.).

30. For a complete translation of the Imperial Rescript on Education, see Gluck, *Japan's Modern Myths,* 121.

31. The statement on "democratic morality" is in Kyōiku chokugo undō jimu-kyoku, ed., *Nihon no Ryōshin* (Tokyo: Kyōiku chokugo undō jimukyoku, n.d.; preface dated 2003), 38. For the statement on the Imperial Rescript as the conscience of Japan, see Rikken Yōseikai's information pamphlet, "Kyōiku chokugo no fukkatsu de Nihon o sukuō!" (Tokyo: Rikken Yōseikai, 2003), 4.

32. Nishibe Susumu, *Kokumin no dōtoku* (Tokyo: Sankei shinbun nyūsu sābisu, 2000), 79.

33. See ibid., 212, and Hamabayashi, ed., *Tettei hihan: "Kokumin dōtoku,"* 17.

34. See Japanese Society for History Textbook Reform, ed., *The Restoration of a National History* (Tokyo: Society for History Textbook Reform, 1998).

35. See Žižek's discussion of "the standard historicist denouncing of each universality as 'false.'" Žižek, "Class Struggle or Postmodernism? Yes, Please!" 101.

Bibliography

Japanese Journals and Newspapers

Chūō kōron
Edō no shishō
Iroha shinbun
Kana shinbun
Kindai shisō
Kumamoto hyōron
Kyōiku jiron
Meiroku zasshi
Nihon oyobi Nihonjin
Nihon shisōshi
Rikugō zasshi
Rinrigaku nempō

Seitō
Shinbun zasshi
Shisō
Shushigaku
Taiyō
Teiyū rinrikai rinri kōenshū
Tetsugaku zasshi
Tokyo Asahi shinbun
Tōyōgakugei zasshi
Tōyō shinbun
Tōyō tetsugaku
Yōmeigaku

Japanese Sources

Abe Jirō. *Risō no hito*. Tokyo: Kaneo bunkandō, 1906.

Akiyama Kiyoshi. *Nihon no hangyaku shisō*. Tokyo: Buneisha, 1968.

Arahata Kanson. *Kanson jiden*. Tokyo: Iwanami shoten, 1999.

———. *Yanaka mura metsubō shi*. Tokyo: Iwanami shoten, 1999.

Asukai Masamichi. *Bunmei kaika*. Tokyo: Iwanami shoten, 1985.

Baba Tatsui. "Tempu jinken ron." In *Baba Tatsui zenshū*, vol. 2. Tokyo: Iwanami shoten, 1988, 79–120.

Fujishima Ryō-on. *Yasokyō no mudōri*. Kyoto: Nunobe Tsuneshichi, 1881.

Fukasaku Yasubumi. *Kokumin dōtoku yōgi*. Tokyo: Kōdōkan, 1916.

Fukaya Masashi. *Ryōsai-kenbo shugi no kyōiku*. Nagoya: Reimei shobō, 1981.

Fukuzawa Yukichi. *Bunmei ron no gairyaku*. Tokyo: Iwanami shoten, 1988.

———. "Datsu-A ron." In *Kindai Nihon shisō taikei*, vol. 2: *Fukuzawa Yukichi shū*, ed. Ishida Takeshi. Tokyo: Chikuma shobō, 1975, 510–512.

———. *Gakumon no susume*. Tokyo: Iwanami shoten, 2001.

————. "Nikushoku no setsu." In *Meiji bungaku zenshū,* vol. 8: *Fukuzawa Yukichi shū,* ed. Tomita Masafumi. Tokyo: Chikuma shobō, 1966, 334–335.

Fukyūsha, ed. *Kyōiku shinri ronri jutsugo shōkai.* Tokyo: Fukyūsha, 1885.

Funayama Shinichi. *Meiji tetsugakushi kenkyū.* Kyoto: Mineruba shobō, 1959.

————. *Nihon no kannen ronja.* Tokyo: Eihōsha, 1956.

Hamabayashi Masao, ed. *Tettei hihan "Kokumin dōtoku."* Tokyo: Ōtsuki shoten, 2001.

Hariba Kiyoko. *"Seitō" Josei kaihō ronshū.* Tokyo: Iwanami shoten, 2002.

Hikaku shisōshi kenkyūkai, ed. *Meiji shisōka no shūkyōkan.* Tokyo: Ōkura shuppan, 1975.

Hiratsuka Raichō. "Atarashii onna." In *Hiratsuka Raichō hyōronshū,* ed. Kobayashi Tomie and Yoneda Sayoko. Tokyo: Iwanami shoten, 2005, 41–43.

————. "Inoue Tetsujirō shi no ryōfu kenbu o nanzu." In *Hiratsuka Raichō chosakushū,* vol. 2, ed. Hiratsuka Raichō chosaku shū henshū iinkai. Tokyo: Ōtsuki shoten, 1983.

Ienaga Saburō. *Nihon dōtoku shisōshi.* Tokyo: Iwanami shoten, 1975.

————. *Nihon kindai shisōshi kenkyū.* Tokyo: Tokyo Daigaku shuppan, 1980.

Imai Seiichi. *Nihon kindai shi II.* Tokyo: Iwanami shoten, 1977.

Inoue Enryō. "Bukkyō katsuron joron." In *Inoue Enryō senshū,* vol. 3, ed. Inoue Enryō Kinen Gakujutsu Senta. Tokyo: Tōyō Daigaku, 1987, 327–393.

————."Katō sensei no ichi daigimon ni kotaen to su." *Tōyō gakugei zasshi* 33 (1883): 65–70.

————. "Rinri tsūron." In *Inoue Enryō senshū,* vol. 11, ed. Inoue Enryō Kinen Gakujutsu Senta. Tokyo: Tōyō Daigaku, 1992, 17–137.

————. "Shūkyō shinron." In *Inoue Enryō senshū,* vol. 8, ed. Inoue Enryō Kinen Gakujutsu Senta. Tokyo: Tōyō Daigaku, 1991, 11–48.

Inoue Kiyoshi, ed. *Nihon jimbutsushi taikei,* vol. 7: *Kindai III.* Tokyo, Asakura shoten, 1960.

Inoue Tetsujirō. "Chokugo engi." In *Kindai Nihon shisō taikei,* vol. 31: *Meiji shisōshū II,* ed. Matsumoto Sannosuke. Tokyo: Chikuma shobō, 1977, 85–116.

————. *Chūgaku shūshin kyōkasho,* vol. 3. Tokyo: Kinkō tosho, 1902.

————. "Kokka teki dōtoku to sekai teki dōtoku." *Teiyū rinrikai rinri koenshū* (February 1905).

————. *Kokumin dōtoku gairon.* Tokyo: Sanseidō, 1912.

————. "Meiji no tetsugaku kaisō roku." In *Tokubetsu kōza kōenran.* Tokyo: Kindaisha, 1926, 1–50.

————. "Meiji tetsugaku kai no kaiko." *Iwanami kōza tetsugaku.* Tokyo: Iwanami shoten, 1932.

————. "Miru no Jiyū no ri o hakusu." *Tōyō gakugei zasshi* 9 (1883): 13–17.

————. *Nihon Kogakuha no tetsugaku.* Tokyo: Fusanbō, 1902.

————. *Nihon Shushigakuha no tetsugaku.* Tokyo: Fusanbō, 1905.

————. *Nihon Yōmeigakuha no tetsugaku.* Tokyo: Fusanbō, 1900.

————. "Rinri shinsetsu." In *Meiji bunka zenshū,* vol. 23: *Shisō hen.* Tokyo: Nihon Hyōronsha, 1967, 412–430.

————. "Ryōfukenbu." *Yomiuri shinbun* (January 31, 1918): 4.

————. *Shinhen shūshin kyōkasho.* Tokyo: Kinkōtōshoseki kabushiki gaisha, 1911.

————. *Waga kokutai to kokumin dōtoku.* Tokyo: Kōbundō, 1925.

————. "Yaso benwakujo." *Tōyō gakugei zasshi* 18 (1883): 248–250.

Inoue Tetsujirō et al., comps. *Tetsugaku jii.* Tokyo: Tokyo Daigaku Sangakubu, 1881.

Inoue Tetsujirō and Ariga Nagao, comps. *Kaitei zōho tetsugaku jii.* Tokyo: Tokyo Daigaku Sangakubu, 1884.

Inoue Tetsujirō and Kanie Yoshimaru. *Nihon rinri ihen,* vol. 1. Kyoto: Rinsen shoten, 1970.

Inoue Tetsujirō, Motora Yujirō, and Nakashima Rikizō, comps. *Ei-doku-futsu-wa tetsugaku jii.* Tokyo: Maruzen, 1912.

Inoue Tetsujirō and Takayama Rinjirō. *Shinhen rinri kyōkasho.* Tokyo: Kinkōtōshoseki kabushiki gaisha, 1897.

Ishihara Shintarō. "Nippon no dōgi" *Jiyū* (April 1974): 18–32.

Itō Noe. "Atarashiki onna no michi." In *"Seitō" Josei kaihō ronshū,* ed. Hariba Kiyoko. Tokyo: Iwanami shoten, 2002, 93–95.

Itoya Toshio. *Taigyaku jiken.* Kyoto: San'ichi shobō, 1960.

Kaigo Tokiomi, ed. *Nihon kyōkasho taikei. Kindai hen,* vol. 2: *Shūshin II.* Tokyo: Kōdansha, 1962.

Kanagaki Robun. *Aguranabe.* Tokyo: Iwanami shoten, 1967.

————. "Kyūri zukai." In *Meiji no bungaku,* vol. 1: *Kanagaki Robun,* ed. Tsubouchi Yūzō. Tokyo: Chikuma shobō, 2002, 343–368.

Kaneko Takezō. *Rinrigaku jiten.* Tokyo: Kobundō, 1957.

Karasawa Tomitarō. *Kyōkasho no rekishi.* Tokyo: Sōbunsha, 1960.

Katayama Sen. "Waga shakaishugi." In *Nihon shakai undō shisōshi,* vol. 5, ed. Kishimoto Eitarō. Tokyo: Aoki shoten, 1968.

Katō Hiroyuki. "Jinken shinsetsu." In *Nihon no meicho,* vol. 34: *Nishi Amane and Katō Hiroyuki,* ed. Uete Michiari. Tokyo: Chūōkōronsha, 1972, 409–462.

————. "Kyōsha no kenri to dōtoku hōritsu no kankei." *Tetsugaku zasshi* 2(21) (1888): 511–525, and 2(22) (1888): 593–604.

Kawakami Hajime. "Nihon dōkutoku no kokkashugi." In *Kawakami Hajime chosakushū,* vol. 8. Tokyo: Chikuma shobō, 1964, 185–210.

————. *Kawakami Hajime chosakushū.* Tokyo: Chikuma shobō, 1964, 12 vols.

Kawakami Tetsutarō, ed. *Kindai no chōkoku.* Tokyo: Fusanbō, 2006.

Kawanabe Kyōsai kinen bijutsukan, ed. *Kawanabe Kyōsai to monjin tachi.* Nikkō: Kosugi hōan kinen nikkō bijutsukan, 2001.

Kazue Koichi. *Nihon no rinri shisōshi.* Tokyo: Gakugei shobō, 1963.

Kenjō Teiji. "Kindai hōtoku undō no seiritsu." *Edo no shisō* no. 7, 65.

Kiyohara Sadao. *Kaishū Nihon dōtokushi.* Tokyo: Chūbunkan, 1937.

Kobayashi Tomie and Yoneda Sayoko. *Hiratsuka Raichō hyōronshū.* Tokyo: Iwanami shoten, 2005.

Kojima Shimaseki et al., comps. *Bukkyō jiten.* Tokyo: Shirogumo shoja, 1895.

Kōsaka Masaaki. *Meiji shisōshi.* Kyoto: Tōeisha, 1999.

Kōsaka Masaaki et al. "Tōakyōeiken no rinrisei to rekishisei." In *Chūō kōron* (April 1942).

Koyasu Nobukuni. "Kindai 'rinri' gainen no seiritsu to sono yukue." *Shisō* 6(912) (June 2000): 4–24.

Kozaki Hiromichi. *Seikyō shinron*. Tokyo: Keiseisha, 1886.

Kuga Katsunan. "Kinji seironkō." In *Nihon no meicho*, vol. 37: *Kuga Katsunan, Miyake Setsurei*. Tokyo: Chūō kōronsha, 1971.

Kyōiku chokugo undō jimukyoku, ed. *Nihon no ryōshin*. Tokyo: Kyōiku chokugo undō jimukyoku, n.d.; preface dated 2003.

Mantei Ōga. "Tōsei rikō musume." In *Meiji bungaku zenshū*, vol. 1: *Meiji kaikaki bungaku shū*, ed. Okitsu Kaname. Tokyo: Chikuma shobō, 1966, 181–183.

Maruyama Masao. "Fukuzawa ni okeru jitsugaku no tenkai." In *Kindai Nihon shisō taikei*, vol. 2: *Fukuzawa Yukichi shū*, ed. Ishida Takeshi. Tokyo: Chikuma shobō, 1974.

Matsuzaki Minoru. "Rinri shinsetsu kaitai." In *Meiji bunka zenshū*, vol. 23: *Shisō hen*. Tokyo: Nihon hyōronsha, 1967, 18–20.

Meiji Bunka Kenkyūkai, ed. "Jinken shinsetsu bakuronshū." In *Meiji bunka zenshū*, no. 2. Tokyo: Nihon hyōronsha, 1967, 389–438.

Mihashi Takeo, ed. *Meiji zenki shisōshi bunken*. Tokyo: Meijidō shoten, 1976.

Minamoto Ryōen. "Katō Hiroyuki no rinri shisō." *Rinrigaku nenpō* 8 (1959): 127–143.

———. *Kinsei shoki jitsugaku shisō no kenkyū*. Tokyo: Sōbunsha, 1980.

Mishima Tsuyoshi. "Dōtoku keizai gōitsu setsu." *Tetsugaku zasshi* 24 (1909): 135.

Miura Tōsaku. *Nihon rinrigaku shi*. Tokyo: Chūkōkan shoten, 1939.

Monbushō, ed. *Gakusei hachi-jū nen shi*. Tokyo: Ōkurashō insatsukyoku, 1954.

———, ed. *Jinjō shōgaku shūshin sho*. Tokyo: Monbushō, 1918.

Murakami Senshō. *Bukkyō dōtoku shinron*. Tokyo: Tetsugaku shoin, 1888.

———. "Bukkyō muga ron." *Tetsugaku zasshi* 109 (March 10, 1896): 183–192.

Muraoka Tsukasa. "Nihon rinri shishōshi jō seiyō shisō to no kōshō." *Rinrigaku* 8 (1941): 3–46.

Nakae Chōmin. *Sansuijin keirin mondō*. Tokyo: Iwanami shoten, 1998.

Nakajima Tokuzō. "Gurin-shi chishiki tetsugaku o yomu." *Tetsugaku zasshi* 9:94 (1894): 899–930.

Nakashima Rikizō. "Eikoku shin kanto gakuha ni tsuite." *Tetsugaku zasshi* 7:69 (1892): 411–421; 7:70 (1892): 493–501; 8:71 (1893): 581–584; 8:72 (1893): 647–650.

———. *Genkon no rinrigaku mondai*. Tokyo: Fukyūsha, 1901.

———. *Rinri to kyōiku*. Tokyo and Osaka: Moriyoshikan, 1902.

———. *Shihan gakkō shūshin shin kyōkasho*. Tokyo: Bungakusha, 1911.

———. *Tokuiku to rinri*. Tokyo: Meguro shoten, 1907.

Nakashima Rikizō and Shinoda Toshihide. *Shihan gakkō yō shūshin kyōkasho*. Tokyo: Bungakusha, 1911.

Natsume Soseki. *Soseki zenshū*. Tokyo: Iwanami shoten, 1985.

Nihon Kōdōkai, ed. "Nihon Kōdōkai." Tokyo: Nihon Kōdōkai, n.d.

Nihon shisōshi kenkyūkai, ed. *Nihon ni okeru rinri shisō no tenkai*. Tokyo: Yoshikawa kōbunkan, 1965.

Nishi Amane. "Jinsei sambō." *Meiroku zasshi* (1875), ed. Ōkubo Toshiaki. Tokyo: Rittai-sha, 1976, 38: 1–5; 39: 1–4; 40: 1–5; 42: 5–7.

———. *Nishi Amane zenshū*, ed. Ōkubo Toshiaki. Tokyo: Munetaka shobō, 1960.

Nishibe Susumu. *Kokumin no dōtoku.* Tokyo: Sankei shinbun nyūsu sābisu, 2000.

Nishida Kitarō. *Nishida Kitarō zenshū.* Tokyo: Iwanami shoten, 1966.

———. *Zen no kenkyū.* Tokyo: Iwanami shoten, 1999.

Nishimura Shigeki. *Hakuō goroku,* ed. Nihon Kōdōkai. Tokyo: Nihon Kōdōkai, 1996.

———. *Nihon dōtoku ron.* In *Hakuō sōsho,* ed. Nihon Kōdōkai. Tokyo: Nihon Kōdōkai, 1976.

———. *Nishimura Shigeki zenshū*, ed. Nihon Kōdōkai. Kyoto: Shibunkaku, 1976, 3 vols.

———. *Shōgaku shūshin-kun.* Tokyo: Monbushō, 1880.

———. "Shūshin jikoku hi ni michi ron." *Meiroku zasshi* 31 (March 1, 1875), ed. Ōkubo Toshiaki (Tokyo: Rittaisha, 1976), 4–7.

Nishitani Keiji. "'Kindai no chōkoku' shiron." In *Kindai no chōkoku,* ed. Kawakami Tetsutarō. Tokyo: Fusanbō, 2006, 18–37.

Ogiwara Hiyoshi. "Nihon dōtoku shisōshi no kenkyū hō." *Nihon seishin bunka* 1(5–8) (1934): 53–63.

Ōhashi Kenji. *Ryōshin to shisei no seishin shi: Nihon Yōmeigaku no kingendai.* Tokyo: Bensei shuppan, 1999.

Okada Takehiko, ed. *Fukkoku Yōmeigaku,* vol. 1. Tokyo: Mokujisha, 1984.

Ōkawa Shūmei. "Nihon oyobi Nihonjin no michi." In *Ōkawa Shūmei zenshū,* vol. 1. Tokyo: Iwasaki shoten, 1961, 3–76.

Okita Yukiji. "'Rikugō zasshi' ni okeru Inoue Tetsujirō." *Kirisutokyō shakai mondai kenkyū* 30 (1982): 200–219.

Okitsu Kaname. *Tenkanki no bungaku.* Tokyo: Waseda Daigaku shuppanbu, 1960.

Ōkubo Toshiaki. *Meirokusha.* Tokyo: Kōdansha, 2007.

Okuda Yoshihito. "Gendai joshi kyōiku no konpon hōshin." *Chūō kōron* (July 1913): 74–76.

Ōmichi Uichi. *Shakai shinrigaku.* Tokyo: Kinkōdō, 1913.

Ōnishi Hajime. "Chūkō to dōtoku no kihon." In *Meiji bungaku zenshū,* vol. 80: *Meiji tetsugaku shisōshū,* ed. Senuma Shigeki. Tokyo: Chikuma shobō, 1974, 112–116.

———. "Kokkashugi no kaishaku." In *Kindai Nihon shisō taikei,* vol. 31: *Meiji shisōshū II,* ed. Matsumoto Sannosuke. Tokyo: Chikuma shobō, 1977, 155–157.

———. "Rinrigaku." In *Ōnishi Hakushi zenshū,* vol. 2: *Rinrigaku.* Tokyo: Keiseisha, 1903–1904.

———. "Shiken issoku." In *Kindai Nihon shisō taikei,* vol. 31: *Meiji shisōshū II,* ed. Matsumoto Sannosuke. Tokyo: Chikuma shobō, 1977, 144–150.

Ōsugi Sakae. "Dōtoku no sōzō." *Kindai shisō* 1(5) (February 1913): 1.

Ozawa Tomio, ed. *Nihonjin no rinri shisō.* Tokyo: Tōsen shuppan, 1970.

Rekishigaku kenkyūkai, ed. *Nihonshi shiryō,* vol 4: *Kindai.* Tokyo: Iwanami shoten, 1997.

Rikken Yōseikai. "Kyōiku chokugo no fukkatsu de Nihon o sukuō!" Tokyo: Rikken Yōseikai, 2003.

Sakatani Shiroshi. "Seikyō no gi." *Meiroku zasshi,* ed. Yamamuro Shinichi. Tokyo: Iwanami shoten, 2008, 243–247; 311–319.

Sako Junichirō. *Kindai Nihon shisōshi ni okeru jinkaku kannen no seiritsu.* Tokyo: Chōbunsha, 1995.

Satō Hirō. *Gaisetsu Nihon shisōshi.* Kyoto: Mineruba shobō, 2005.

Satō Yasukuni, ed. *Yomigaeru Watsuji Tetsurō: Jinbun kagaku no saisei ni mukete.* Kyoto: Nakanishiya shuppan, 1999.

Sawa Wataru, ed. *Uemura Masahisa to sono jidai.* Tokyo: Kyōbunkan, 1976.

Soeda Juichi. "Dōtoku no taihon wa nani ni yorite sadamenya." *Tōyō gakugei zasshi* 17 (1883): 227–229; 18 (1883): 258–261.

———. *Hōsei kyōkasho.* Tokyo: Kinkōdō, 1901.

Sōgo Masaaki and Hida Yoshifumi, comps. *Meiji no kotoba jiten.* Tokyo: Tokyodō shuppan, 1986.

Sotozaki Mitsuhiro, ed. *Ishingo dōtoku no taihai seshi koto o ronzu.* Tokyo: Hōsei Daigaku shuppankyoku, 1982.

Takano Chōei. "Seiyō gakushi no setsu." In *Kazan Choei ronshū,* ed. Satō Shosuke. Tokyo: Iwanami shoten, 1994.

Takayama Chogyū. *Chogyū zenshū,* vol. 4, ed. Anesaki Masaharu. Tokyo: Hakubunkan, 1927.

Take Kuniyasu. "'Rikugō zasshi' ni arawareta Harada Tasuku: Sono kindaika rinri ni furete." *Kirisutokyō shakai mondai kenkyū* 30 (1982): 147–165.

Takeda Kiyoko. *Ningenkan no sōkoku: Kindai Nihon no shisō to Kirisutokyō.* Tokyo: Kōbundō shinsha, 1967.

Tokutani Toyonosuke and Matsuo Yūshirō, eds. *Futsū jutsugo jii.* Tokyo: Keibunsha, 1905.

Tokyo Teikoku Daigaku, ed. *Tokyo Teikoku Daigaku gojūnen shi,* vol. 1. Tokyo: Tokyo Teikoku Daigaku, 1932.

———. *Tokyo Teikoku Daigaku gakujutsu Taikan,* vol. 1: *Sōsetsu Bungakubu.* Tokyo: Tokyo Teikoku Daigaku, 1942.

Tsuda Masao. *Watsuji Tetsurō kenkyū: Kaishakugaku, kokumin dōtoku, shakaishugi.* Tokyo: Aoki shoten, 2001.

Uemura Masahisa. "Shinri ippan." In *Meiji bungaku zenshū,* vol. 46, ed. Takeda Kiyoko and Yoshida Kyūichi. Tokyo: Chikuō shobō, 1957, 58–121.

———. *Uemura Masahisa chosakushū,* vol. 4: *Shingaku shisō,* ed. Kawamoto Tetsuo. Tokyo: Shinkyō shupansha, 1966.

Wang, Jia Hua. *Nihon no kindaika to jugaku.* Tokyo: Nobunkyō, 1998.

Watanabe Kazuyasu. "Kirisutokyō to jukyō to no kanren: Meiji jidai o chūshin toshite." *Nihon shisōshi* 6 (1978): 111–129.

———. "Meiji chūki no shisōteki kadai (part 2): Inoue Tetsujirō to Ōnishi Hajime." *Nihon bunka kenkyūjo kenkyū hōkoku* 11 (1975): 71–93.

Watanabe Minoru. *Niijima Jō,* vol. 35. Tokyo: Yoshikawa kōbunkan, 1959.

Watsuji Tetsurō. "Kokumin dōtoku ron." In *Watsuji Tetsurō zenshū, Bekkan I and II.* Tokyo: Iwanami shoten, 1992.

———. *Ningen no gaku toshite no rinrigaku.* Tokyo: Iwanami shoten, 1999.

————. *Rinrigaku.* In *Watsuji Tetsurō zenshū,* vol. 11. Tokyo: Iwanami shoten, 1992.

Yamada Kō. *Kindai Nihon dōtoku shisōshi kenkyū: Tennōsei ideorogi hihan.* Tokyo: Miraisha, 1972.

————. *Watsuji Tetsurō ron.* Tokyo: Kadensha, 1987.

Yamada Takao, ed. *Kindai Nihon no rinri shisō.* Tokyo: Daimeidō, 1981.

Yamagata Aritomo. *Yamagata Aritomo ikensho,* ed. Ōyama Azusa. Tokyo: Hara shobō, 1966.

Yamagata Aritomo and Hozumi Yatsuka. "Shakai hakaishugiron." In *Yamagata Aritomo ikensho,* ed. Ōyama Azusa (Tokyo: Hara shobō, 1966): 315–323.

Yamamuro Shinichi, ed. *Meiroku zasshi,* vols. 1 and 2. Tokyo: Iwanami shoten, 1999, 2008.

Yoshida Kumaji. "Kaisetsu." In Nishimura Shigeki's *Nihon dōtokuron.* Tokyo: Iwanami shoten, 1974, 107–121.

————. *Waga kokumin dōtoku.* Tokyo: Kōdōkan, 1918.

Yoshida Seiichi. *Kokumin dōtoku yōryō.* Tokyo: Hōbunkan, 1916.

————. *Rinrigaku kiso gainen kōwa: Jinkaku no tetsugaku.* Tokyo: Dōbunkan, 1908.

————. *Rinrigaku yōgi.* Tokyo: Tokyo Hōbunkan, 1907.

————. *Shūshin kyōkasho.* Tokyo and Osaka: Hōbunkan, 1912.

Yoshikawa Tetsushi. *Nihon rinri shisōshi gaisetsu.* Osaka: Osaka kyōiku tosho, 1960.

Yoshino Sakuzō. "Gendai shikō." In *Minponshugiron: Yoshino Sakuzō Hakushi minshushugi ronshū,* vol. 2. Tokyo: Shin kigensha, 1948.

Yuasa Yasuo. "Kaisetsu." In *Watsuji Tetsurō zenshū, Bekkan I.* Tokyo: Iwanami shoten, 1992.

English Sources

Anesaki, Masaharu. *History of Japanese Religion.* Tokyo: Charles E. Tuttle Company, 1983.

Armstrong, R. L. *Just Before the Dawn: The Life and Work of Ninomiya Sontoku.* New York: The Macmillan Co., 1912.

Bernstein, Gail Lee. *Japanese Marxist: A Portrait of Kawakami Hajime, 1879–1946.* Cambridge, Mass.: Harvard University Press, 1990.

Bourdieu, Pierre. *Language and Symbolic Power.* Translated by Gino Raymond and Matthew Adamson. Cambridge, Mass.: Harvard University Press, 1995.

Bowen, Roger W. *Rebellion and Democracy in Meiji Japan: A Study of Commoners in the Popular Rights Movement.* Berkeley and Los Angeles: University of California Press, 1980.

Braisted, William R. *Meiroku Zasshi: Journal of the Japanese Enlightenment.* Cambridge, Mass.: Harvard University Press, 1976.

Buckle, Henry Thomas. *History of Civilization in England,* vol. 1. New York: D. Appleton-Century Company, 1934.

Bunzl, Matti. "Franz Boas and the Humboldtian Tradition: From *Volksgeist* and *Nationalcharakter* to an Anthropological Concept of Culture." In *Volksgeist as Method and Ethic: Essays on Boasian Ethnography and the German Anthropological Tradition*, ed. George W. Stocking, Jr. Madison: University of Wisconsin Press, 1996.

Butler, Judith, et al., eds. *Contingency, Hegemony, Universality: Contemporary Dialogues on the Left*. London and New York: Verso, 2000.

Center for East Asian Studies, ed. *Readings in Tokugawa Thought*. Chicago: CEAS, 1998.

Chan, Wing-tsit, ed. and trans. *A Source Book in Chinese Philosophy*. Princeton, N.J.: Princeton University Press, 1973.

Clark, Timothy. *Demon of Painting: The Art of Kawanabe Kyōsai*. London: British Museum Press, 1993.

Crump, John. *The Origins of Socialist Thought in Japan*. New York: St. Martin's Press, 1983.

de Certeau, Michel. *The Practice of Everyday Life*. Translated by Steven Rendall. Berkeley and Los Angeles: University of California Press, 1988.

Dilworth, David, et al., eds. *Sourcebook for Modern Japanese Philosophy: Selected Documents*. Westport, Conn.: Greenwood Press, 1988.

Doak, Kevin. *A History of Nationalism in Modern Japan: Placing the People*. Leiden and Boston: Brill, 2007.

———. "Nationalism as Dialectics: Ethnicity, Moralism, and the State in Early Twentieth-Century Japan." In *Rude Awakenings: Zen, the Kyoto School, and the Question of Nationalism*, ed. James W. Heisig and John C. Maraldo. Honolulu: University of Hawai'i Press, 1995.

Figal, Gerald. *Civilization and Monsters: Spirits of Modernity in Meiji Japan*. Durham, N.C., and London: Duke University Press, 1999.

Fridell, Wilbur M. "Government Ethics Textbooks in Late Meiji Japan." *Journal of Asian Studies* 29 (1969–1970): 823–833.

Fukuzawa, Yukichi. *An Outline of a Theory of Civilization*. Translated by David Dilworth and G. Cameron Hurst. Tokyo: Sophia University, 1973.

Fung, Yu-lan. *A History of Chinese Philosophy*. Princeton, N.J.: Princeton University Press, 1983.

Gluck, Carol. *Japan's Modern Myths: Ideology in the Late Meiji Period*. Princeton, N.J.: Princeton University Press, 1985.

Green, T. H. *Principles of Political Obligation*. Ann Arbor: The University of Michigan Press, 1967.

———. *Prolegomena to Ethics*. New York: Thomas Y. Crowell Co., 1969.

Hane, Mikiso. *Peasants, Rebels, Woman and Outcastes: The Underside of Modern Japan*. Lanham, Md.: Rowman and Littlefield, 2003.

———, trans. *Reflections on the Way to the Gallows: Rebel Women in Pre-War Japan*. Berkeley: University of California Press, 1988.

Hardacre, Helen. *Shinto and the State*. Princeton, N.J.: Princeton University Press, 1989.

Harootunian, Harry. *Overcome by Modernity: History, Culture, and Community in Interwar Japan*. Princeton, N.J.: Princeton University Press, 2000.

———. *Toward Restoration: The Growth of Political Consciousness in Tokugawa Japan.* Berkeley and Los Angeles: University of California Press, 1970.

Havens, Thomas. *Nishi Amane and Modern Japanese Thought.* Princeton, N.J.: Princeton University Press, 1970.

Haver, William. *The Body of This Death: Historicity and Sociality in the Time of AIDS.* Stanford, Calif.: Stanford University Press, 1996.

Heisig, James, et al., eds. *Sourcebook in Japanese Philosophy.* Nagoya: Nanzan Institute for Religion and Culture, forthcoming.

Heisig, James W., and John C. Maraldo, eds. *Rude Awakenings: Zen, the Kyoto School, and the Question of Nationalism.* Honolulu: University of Hawaiʻi Press, 1995.

Henricks, Robert G., trans. *Lao-Tzu Te-Tao Ching.* New York: Ballantine Books, 1989.

Herder, Johann Gottfried von. *Reflections on the Philosophy of the History of Mankind.* Translated by T. O. Churchill. Chicago and London: University of Chicago Press, 1968.

Hirai, Atsuko. "Self-Realization and Common Good: T. H. Green in Meiji Ethical Thought." *Journal of Japanese Studies* 5(1) (Winter 1979): 107–136.

Hirano, Katsuya. "Spaces of Dissent: Cultural Politics in Late Tokugawa Japan." Ph.D. dissertation, University of Chicago, 2003.

Hofstadter, Richard. *Social Darwinism in American Thought.* Boston: Beacon Press, 1992.

Horio, Teruhisa. *Educational Thought and Ideology in Modern Japan: State Authority and Intellectual Freedom.* Translated by Steven Platzer. Tokyo: University of Tokyo Press, 1989.

Howland, Douglas. *Borders of Chinese Civilization: Geography and History at Empire's End.* Durham, N.C., and London: Duke University Press, 1996.

———. *Personal Liberty and Public Good: The Introduction of John Stuart Mill to Japan and China.* Toronto: University of Toronto Press, 2005.

———. *Translating the West: Language and Political Reason in Nineteenth-Century Japan.* Honolulu: University of Hawaiʻi Press, 2002.

Ienaga, Saburō. *The Pacific War, 1931–1945: A Critical Perspective on Japan's Role in World War II.* New York: Pantheon Books, 1978.

Ike, Nobutaka. *The Beginnings of Political Democracy in Japan.* Baltimore: The Johns Hopkins University Press, 1950.

Inoue, Kyoko. *Individual Dignity in Modern Japanese Thought: The Evolution of the Concept of Jinkaku in Moral and Educational Discourse.* Ann Arbor: Center for Japanese Studies, University of Michigan, 2001.

Inoue, Tetsujirō. "An Outline of National Morality, excerpt." Translated by Richard Reitan. In *From Japan's Modernity: A Reader,* ed. University of Chicago Center for East Asian Studies. Chicago: CEAS, 2002, 57–63.

Irokawa, Daikichi. *The Culture of the Meiji Period.* Translated by Marius Jansen. Princeton, N.J.: Princeton University Press, 1985.

Ishida, Ichirō. "The Spirit of Meiji." *Philosophical Studies of Japan* 9 (1969): 1–40.

Jameson, Fredric. *The Political Unconscious: Narrative as a Socially Symbolic Act*. Ithaca, N.Y.: Cornell University Press, 1981.

Jansen, Marius B. *Cambridge History of Japan*, vol. 5: *The Nineteenth Century*. New York: Cambridge University Press, 1989.

———. *Changing Japanese Attitudes toward Modernization*. Princeton, N.J.: Princeton University Press, 1965.

Japanese Society for History Textbook Reform, ed. *The Restoration of a National History*. Tokyo: Society for History Textbook Reform, 1998.

Katō, Hiroyuki. "A Reconsideration of Human Rights." Translated by J. Victor Koschmann. In *From Japan's Modernity*, ed. University of Chicago Center for East Asian Studies. Chicago: CEAS, 2002, 1–43.

Keene, Donald. *Dawn to the West: Japanese Literature in the Modern Era*. New York: Holt, Rinehart and Winston, 1989.

———. *Modern Japanese Literature*. New York: Grove Press Inc., 1956.

Ketelaar, James Edward. *Of Heretics and Martyrs in Meiji Japan: Buddhism and Its Persecution*. Princeton, N.J.: Princeton University Press, 1990.

Kōsaka, Masaaki. *Japanese Thought in the Meiji Era*. Translated by David Abosch. Tokyo: Pan-Pacific Press, 1958.

———. "The World and Meiji Japan." *Philosophical Studies of Japan* 3 (1961): 57–78.

Kropotkin, Petr. "Anarchist Morality." In *Kropotkin's Revolutionary Pamphlets*, ed. Roger N. Baldwin. New York: Dover Publications, Inc., 1970, 80–113.

Lande, Aasulv. *Meiji Protestantism in History and Historiography: A Comparative Study of Japanese and Western Interpretations of Early Protestantism in Japan*. Frankfurt: Verlag Peter Lang, 1989.

Lincicome, Mark E. *Principle, Praxis, and the Politics of Educational Reform in Meiji Japan*. Honolulu: University of Hawai'i Press, 1995.

Lowell, Percival. *The Soul of the Far East*. Boston and New York: Houghton, Mifflin and Company, 1888.

MacIntyre, Alasdair. *A Short History of Ethics*. New York: Simon and Schuster, 1996.

Mackie, J. L. *Ethics: Inventing Right and Wrong*. New York: Penguin Books, 1990.

Maruyma, Masao. *Studies in the Intellectual History of Tokugawa Japan*. Translated by Mikiso Hane. Tokyo: University of Tokyo Press, 1974.

Marx, Karl, and Frederick Engels. *The German Ideology, Part One*, ed. C. J. Arthur. New York: International Publishers, 1970.

Matsumoto, Sannosuke. "The Idea of Heaven: A Tokugawa Foundation for Natural Rights Theory." In Tetsuo Najita et al., eds., *Japanese Thought in the Tokugawa Period 1600–1868*. Chicago: University of Chicago Press, 1978, 181–199.

———. "Society and the State in the Thought of Kuga Katsunan." *Journal of Pacific Asia* 1 (1994): 126–141.

Mill, J. S. "On Liberty." In *Utilitarianism, Liberty and Representative Government*. London: J. M. Dent and Sons, 1922.

Motora, Yujirō. *An Essay on Eastern Philosophy.* Leipzig: R. Voigtlanders Verlag, 1905.

Nagai, Michio. "Herbert Spencer in Early Meiji Japan." *Far Eastern Quarterly* 14 (1954): 55–64.

Najita, Tetsuo. *Japan: The Intellectual Foundations of Modern Japanese Politics.* Chicago and London: University of Chicago Press, 1974.

———. "Some Reflections on Idealism in the Political Thought of Yoshino Sakuzō." In *Japan in Crisis: Essays on Taishō Democracy,* ed. Bernard S. Silberman and Harry D. Harootunian. Princeton, N.J.: Princeton University Press, 1974, 29–66.

———. *Visions of Virtue in Tokugawa Japan: The Kaitokudō Merchant Academy of Osaka.* Honolulu: University of Hawai'i Press, 1987.

Najita, Tetsuo, and H. D. Harootunian. "Japan's Revolt against the West." In *Modern Japanese Thought,* ed. Bob Tadashi Wakabayashi. Cambridge: Cambridge University Press, 1998, 207–272.

Najita, Tetsuo, and Irwin Scheiner, eds. *Japanese Thought in the Tokugawa Period: Methods and Metaphors.* Chicago: University of Chicago Press, 1978.

Najita, Tetsuo, and J. Victor Koschmann, eds. *Conflict in Modern Japanese History.* Princeton, N.J.: Princeton University Press, 1982.

Nakashima, Rikizō. "Kant's Doctrine of the 'Thing-in-Itself.'" Ph.D. dissertation, Yale University. New Haven: Price, Lee and Adkins Co., 1889.

———. "Mr. Percival Lowell's Misconception of the Character of the Japanese." *New Englander and Yale Review* 14(2), New Series (February 1889): 97–102.

Natsume, Soseki. *Kokoro: A Novel, and Selected Essays.* Translated by Edwin McClellan. New York: Madison Books, 1992.

Nimura, Kazuo. *The Ashio Riot of 1907: A Social History of Mining in Japan.* Translated by Terry Boardman and Andrew Gordon. Durham, N.C., and London: Duke University Press, 1997.

Nishida, Kitarō. *An Inquiry into the Good.* Translated by Abe Masao and Christopher Ives. New Haven, Conn.: Yale University Press, 1987.

Nitobe, Inazō, ed. *Western Influences in Modern Japan.* Chicago: University of Chicago Press, 1931.

Nivison, David S., ed. *Confucianism in Action.* Stanford, Calif.: Stanford University Press, 1959.

Nolte, Sharon H. "National Morality and Universal Ethics: Ōnishi Hajime and the Imperial Rescript on Education." *Monumenta Nipponica* 38(3) (Autumn 1983): 289–294.

Okakura, Kakuzō. *The Book of Tea.* New York: Dover Publications, Inc., 1964.

Ōnishi, Hajime. "Questioning Moral Foundations." Translated by Richard Reitan. In *Sourcebook in Japanese Philosophy,* ed. James Heisig et al. Nagoya: Nanzan Institute for Religion and Culture, forthcoming.

Passin, Herbert. *Society and Education in Japan.* New York: Teachers College, Columbia University, 1965.

Piovesana, G. K. *Recent Japanese Philosophical Thought, 1862–1912.* Tokyo: Enderle Bookstore, 1963.

Pyle, Kenneth. *The New Generation in Meiji Japan: Problems of Cultural Identity, 1885–1895.* Stanford, Calif.: Stanford University Press, 1969.

Reitan, Richard M. "Claiming Personality: Reassessing the Dangers of the 'New Woman' in early Taishō Japan." *positions: east asia cultures critique* (forthcoming).

———. "Ethics and Natural Right Theory: Competing Conceptions of Nature during the Meiji Period." *Nempō Nihon shisōshi* 8 (March 2009): 1–28.

———. "National Morality, the State, and 'Dangerous Thought': Approaching the Moral Ideal in late Meiji Japan." *Japan Studies Review* 9 (2005): 23–58.

Rorty, Richard. *Philosophy and the Mirror of Nature.* Princeton, N.J.: Princeton University Press, 1979.

Rousseau, Jean-Jacques. *The Social Contract,* ed. Lester G. Crocker. New York: Washington Square Press, 1967.

Rubin, Jay. *Injurious to Public Morals: Writers and the Meiji State.* Seattle: University of Washington Press, 1984.

Sagara, Tōru. "How the Japanese Take the Moral Laws: Japanese Thinkers in Modern Times." *Philosophical Studies of Japan* 11 (1975): 1–16.

Sakai, Naoki. *Translation and Subjectivity: On "Japan" and Cultural Nationalism.* Minneapolis and London: University of Minnesota Press, 1997.

Sansom, G. B. *The Western World and Japan.* New York: Vintage Books, 1973.

Scheiner, Irwin. *Christian Converts and Social Protest in Meiji Japan.* Berkeley and Los Angeles: University of California Press, 1970.

Schwantes, Robert S. "Religion and Modernization in the Far East: A Symposium. I. Christianity versus Science: A Conflict of Ideas in Meiji Japan." *The Far Eastern Quarterly* 12:2 (1953): 123–132.

Shaku, Sōen. "The Law of Cause and Effect, as Taught by Buddha." In *The World's Parliament of Religions,* vol. 2, ed. John Henry Barrows. Chicago: Parliament Publishing Company, 1893, 829–831.

Shimomura, Toratarō. "The Modernization of Japan, with Special Reference to Philosophy." In *The Modernization of Japan: A Special Edition in the Philosophical Studies of Japan,* vol. 7. Compiled by Japanese National Commission for Unesco. Tokyo: Japan Society for the Promotion of Science, 1966, 1–28.

Shively, Donald H. "Motoda Eifu: Confucian Lecturer to the Meiji Emperor." In *Confucianism in Action,* ed. David S. Nivison. Stanford, Calif.: Stanford University Press, 1959, 302–333.

———."Nishimura Shigeki: A Confucian View of Modernization." In *Changing Japanese Attitudes toward Modernization,* ed. Marius B. Jansen. Princeton, N.J.: Princeton University Press, 1965, 193–241.

Sidgwick, Henry. *The Methods of Ethics,* 7th ed. Indianapolis: Hackett Publishing Company, 1981.

Silberman, Bernard S., and Harry D. Harootunian. *Japan in Crisis: Essays on Taishō Democracy.* Princeton, N.J.: Princeton University Press, 1974.

Stephen, James Fitzjames. *Liberty, Equality, Fraternity.* Cambridge: Cambridge University Press, 1967.

Tanaka, Stefen. *Japan's Orient: Rendering Pasts into History.* Berkeley and Los Angeles: University of California Press, 1993.

Taylor, Charles. *Human Agency and Language: Philosophical Papers I.* Cambridge: Cambridge University Press, 1985.

Thelle, Notto R. *Buddhism and Christianity in Japan: From Conflict to Dialogue, 1854–1899.* Honolulu: University of Hawai'i Press, 1987.

Thomas, Julia Adeney. *Reconfiguring Modernity: Concepts of Nature in Japanese Political Ideology.* Berkeley and Los Angeles: University of California Press, 2001.

Tsunoda, Ryūsaku, et al., eds. *Sources of Japanese Tradition,* vol. 2. New York: Columbia University Press, 1964.

Uchimura, Kanzō. "Ninomiya Sontoku: A Peasant Saint." In *Ninomiya Sontoku: His Life and "Evening Talks,"* ed. Ishiguro Tadaatsu. Tokyo: Kenkyūsha, 1955.

Volosinov, V. N. *Marxism and the Philosophy of Language.* Translated by Ladislav Matejka and I. R. Titunik. Cambridge, Mass.: Harvard University Press, 1996.

Wakabayashi, Bob Tadashi, ed. *Modern Japanese Thought.* Cambridge: Cambridge University Press, 1998.

Watsuji, Tetsurō. *Watsuji Tetsurō's Rinrigaku: Ethics in Japan.* Translated by Yamamoto Seisaku and Robert E. Carter. Albany: State University of New York Press, 1996.

Yamasaki, Taikō. *Shingon: Japanese Esoteric Buddhism.* Boston and London: Shambhala, 1988.

Yamazaki, Masakazu, and Tōru Miyakawa. "Inoue Tetsujirō: The Man and his Works." *Philosophical Studies of Japan* 7 (1966): 111–126.

Žižek, Slavoj. *The Sublime Object of Ideology.* London and New York: Verso, 1989.

Index

Abe Jirō, 146, 160
Admonition to Soldiers and Sailors, 4
alterity (otherness): Fredric Jameson on,
167n.3; and Hiratsuka Raichō, 159;
and national morality, 125, 140, 151,
200n.112; of religion, 73, 74; and
violence, 116, 128, 151, 192n.3
anarchism, xiii, 102, 120, 153; as
contested term, 114, 142; as
dangerous thought, 115–116, 126,
128–129, 150–151; and "other"
moral communities, 151; and
Red Flag Incident, 128, 142; and
resistance to national morality,
134–135. *See also* dangerous thought
ancestor worship: and Hozumi Yatsuka,
120, 194n.8; in moral training
textbooks, 132, 136; and national
morality, 118–119
Ancient Studies School. *See* Kogaku
Anesaki Masaharu, 141
Arahata Kanson, 128, 135, 143–144
Aristotle, 43, 44
Ashio copper mine, 128, 135, 195n.33,
197n.57
authority theories of ethics, 139–140

Boshin Edict (Boshin shōsho), 134, 147,
196n.52
Boxer War, 98–99
British idealism, 112. *See also* Green, T. H.
Buckle, Henry Thomas, 11, 170n.30,
186n.1

Buddhism, 7, 9; esoteric, 16; as
intellectual religion, 63–64; and
karma *(ingasetsu)*, 60–61, 70,
108–109; and King of Immovable
Wisdom, 16–17; morality of,
60–62, 67–68, 108, 182n.2; and
no-self doctrine *(muga ron)*, 55–56,
68, 108–109, 188n.22; as "otherworldly" teaching, 42; *samsara*,
61; and *satori*, 108; social utility
of, 65–68. *See also* Christianity,
Buddhist critique of; Confucianism,
Buddhist critique of; evolution, and
Buddhism
bunka. See culture
bunmei: Arahata Kanson on, 144; and
Charter Oath, 12; and violence,
99–100; vs. *wénmíng*, 99–100. See
also *bunmeikaika*; civilization
bunmeikaika, 2; defined, xiii; Douglas
Howland on, 168n.1, Nishimura
Shigeki on, 169n.14, 170n.22. See
also *bunmei*; civilization
bushidō, 98
Butler, Judith, 21, 173n.63

capitalism: as immoral, 126, 135,
140, 149; Katayama Sen on, 136;
Sakamoto Seima on, 142
causality, doctrine of, xiv, 9, 57, 64, 68;
ingasetsu/karma as, 60–61, 70,
108–109; Inoue Tetsujirō on, 35,
60; Katō Hiroyuki on, 59; Kozaki

Hiromichi on, 72; Nishimura
Shigeki on, 44
Charter Oath, 12
China, 28, 77, 105, 192n.1; and Boxer
War, 98; and family system, 130;
Hegel on, 187n.9; and national
character, 82, 84, 86, 130, 156,
193n.4; and *rinri,* 47; and Sino-
Japanese War, 99–100; and *wénmíng,*
99–100
Christianity: Buddhist critique of,
58–62, 64, 68, 78; collision between
education and religion, 79; and
evolution, xiv, 59–60, 70; Inoue
Tetsujirō's critique of, 59–60, 65,
66–67, 74, 78; and interiority, 74,
77–79; as irrational, 58, 64, 73,
182n.4; "new spirit" of, 69, 79; as
"otherworldly" teaching, 42, 64,
65, 120; as revelatory religion, 74;
as socially divisive, xiv, 65–67, 74,
78; social utility of, 68–70; and
transcendent moral authority, 78.
See also God; Kozaki Hiromichi;
Uchimura Kanzō; Uemura Masahisa
Chu Hsi Confucianism. *See*
Confucianism; Shushigaku
civilization: contesting hierarchies of,
81–83, 86, 90, 92, 97, 100–101,
103, 111; defined, xiii; hierarchies
of, xv, 8, 44, 85, 87, 146; and
progress, 8, 11, 85. *See also bunmei;
bunmeikaika;* civilizing; ethics, of
civilization
civilizing, 7, 25; critique of, 9, 16–17;
of the "foolish," xiii, 2, 12; and
legislation, xi, 10–13, 15, 99;
as social control, 2. *See also
bunmeikaika;* civilization
civil society, 163–165
Comte, Auguste, 23, 34; and three stages
of social development, 73
Confucianism: Buddhist critique of,
62–63; and Chu Hsi, 23; and five
relations, 47, 180n.87; as form
of ethics, 103; heaven-human
unity, 109; Inoue Tetsujirō on,

97–99, 101–106; Motoda Eifu
on, 66; as natural religion, 74;
Neo-Confucianism, 1, 6, 23–24,
25, 54, 169n.10, 173n.2, 174n.5;
Nishi Amane's critique of, 24–26;
Nishimura Shigeki on, 42–44, 53,
63, 64, 120; as outmoded thought,
9–10, 28, 29; as practical studies,
23–24, 28–29; Thomas Havens on,
54. *See also* Kogaku; Shushigaku;
Yōmeigaku
cosmopolitanism, 157; and nationalism,
96–97
creationism: critique of, 59–60; defense
of, 60
culture, x, 46, 93, 127, 193n.4;
Christianity as wellspring of, 69;
essentialized attributes of, 131; and
1930s discourse on, 157, 201n.11;
and spiritual culture, 112. See also
Kulturkampf

dangerous thought, xi, xv, xvi, 114;
Fukasaku Yasubumi on, 127–128;
Inoue Tetsujirō on, 126; national
morality as, 151; as obstacle to
the ideal, 128; suppression of,
114–118, 120, 121, 125, 129–131;
Yamagata Aritomo on, 127. *See also*
anarchism; individualism; literary
naturalism; new woman; socialism
de Certeau, 80, 186n.80
dictionaries: and codification of terms,
45, 47–49, 163; *Explanation of Terms
for Education, Psychology and Logic,*
22, 45, 47, 49, 50, 180n.90. *See
also* Inoue Tetsujirō, *Dictionary of
Philosophy (Tetsugaku jii)*
Doak, Kevin, 193n.4, 200n.2
dōtoku. See morality

economics: as basis for morality,
136–137; as determinant of morality,
148; as inseparable from morality,
145–146, 198n.94
education, 162, 164; and civilizing, xii,
2; and knowledge acquisition,

10–11, 13, 15; Motoda Eifu on, 14,
53, 66; Nakashima Rikizō on, 91;
ordinances and codes, 10, 11–12,
14, 15; and Teachers' Colleges, 91,
126, 131, 132, 195n.40; of women,
158–159. *See also* Imperial Rescript
on Education; moral training; moral
training textbooks
egoism, 97, 101, 124, 177n.46
emperor: divinity of, 142, 148–149; and
High Treason Incident, xii, 102,
125, 135–136; Kawakami Hajime
on, 145, 149; loyalty to, 52, 79, 118,
194n.8; and national morality, 118;
as national moral symbol, 116, 161;
and *tennōsei* ideology, 168n.4
enlightenment, 9, 13–14, 17, 18, 19; and
Christianity, 70; and Romanticism,
82; as *satori,* 108. See also
bunmeikaika; civilization
epistemology of representation, 32–33,
54–56, 80, 82; defined, xiv, xv,
30–31; destabilization of, 81–82, 89,
103–104, 111; and *A New Theory of
Ethics,* 38; and Nishimura Shigeki,
44; and religion, 57–58, 72, 80; and
rinrigaku, 54–55; and subject-object
opposition, 38, 48–49, 54–55, 72, 87,
88; vocabulary of, 44, 48. *See also*
hylomorphic epistemology
ethics: authority theories of, 139;
Christianity as disruptive of, 67;
of civilization, xi–xii, 2, 17, 21, 87,
111, 167n.4; Confucian, 53, 62–63,
97, 103, 109; as corrective to social
failings, 15; "decline" of, 6, 12–14,
94, 98, 109, 161–164; dissemination
of, 51–54, 131–134; early Meiji
theories of, 31–44; and epistemology
of representation, 54–56, 80, 82; of
the family-state, 131, 132, 196n.45;
foundations for, xiii, 2–3, 31–41, 58,
63, 88, 95–97, 109, 111, 137, 162;
of humanism, 153, 158, 165; and
hylomorphic epistemology, 108, 113;
and interiority, 57; Japanese *(Nihon
rinri),* 97, 105–107, 111, 189n.33;

legitimization of, 57, 154; methods
of, 79; of national particularism,
158; Occidental, 97, 101, 104, 107,
153, 155, 165; Oriental, 38, 92,
97, 101, 107, 155; of personalism,
89–90, 92; and practical studies,
29–30, 176n.31; resistance to, xiii;
of self-realization, 88–89, 158; of
spirit, xi–xii, xv, 80, 82, 86–92, 113,
167n.4; of state-ism, 138–139, 149;
of the stronger, 146; and Taoism,
68; of terrorism, xv, 144–145;
of T. H. Green, 88, 146; and the
universal, xvi, 111; utilitarian, 22,
50, 81, 87. *See also* moral training;
rinrigaku
evolution: and Buddhism, 60–61, 108;
and Christianity, 59–60; and
Confucianism, 63; "god of," 190n.60;
Inoue Enryō on, 46, 179nn.82–83;
Inoue Tetsujirō on, 33–37, 39;
Japanese translations for, 45; Katō
Hiroyuki on, 40–41; and progress,
xiv, 40; and religion *(shūkyō),* 73. *See
also* Social Darwinism; survival of
the fittest

family-state: as "element" of national
morality, 115, 118–119, 150; Hozumi
Yatsuka on, 131, 194n.8; Karasawa
Tomitarō on, 134; in moral training
textbooks, 132, 136–137
family system, 119, 130–131
filial piety, 14, 62, 137; and Imperial
Rescript on Education, 93, 162; and
Inoue Tetsujirō's "Commentary,"
93–94; loyalty-as-filiality, 130–131,
132, 136, 194n.8; and national
morality, 115, 116, 118–121, 134,
150; Ōnishi Hajime on, 94–96. *See
also* loyalty
folk spirit. See *minzoku,* folk spirit;
Volksgeist
foolishness, xi, xiii; of civilization,
16–21; Fukuzawa Yukichi on,
1, 2, 10–11; and *gumin* (foolish
masses), 2, 19; as immoral, 7; Inoue

Enryō on, 68; Inoue Tetsujirō
on, 4, 15, 21, 153; and J. S. Mill,
87; and Kanagaki Robun, 18–21,
172nn.59–60; and legislation, xi, 7,
12; as other of civilization, 2, 20–21,
173n.65; Sakatani Shiroshi on, 9;
Tsuda Mamichi on, 9–10. *See also*
Kanagaki Robun; Kawanabe Kyōsai;
Mantei Ōga
Fujishima Ryō-on, 64, 78
Fukasaku Yasubumi, xi, 95, 163, 193n.4;
on dangerous thought, 127–128; on
Japanese moral character, 130–131;
on origins of national morality,
119; on state personalism, 123–124,
154–155. *See also* national morality
Fukuzawa Yukichi, 6, 18, 30, 73; *An
Encouragement of Learning,* 10, 29;
on foolishness, 2, 11; on knowledge
acquisition, 10–11; on levels of
civilization, 7; on meat eating, 16;
Outline of a Theory of Civilization,
11, 81; on Sino-Japanese War,
99–100, 190n.58
Funayama Shinichi, 119

German Romanticism, xii, 82, 112, 141.
See also Herder, J. G.
gesaku (literature of play), xiii, 2, 18, 20,
21. *See also* Kanagaki Robun; Mantei
Ōga
Gluck, Carol, 167n.4, 194n.9, 195n.33
God, xiv, xv, 55, 79; as absolute spirit,
111, 112, 187n.14; emperor as,
149; and evolution, 35, 59, 60, 70,
190n.60; and Kozaki Hiromichi,
72; and *rinrigaku,* 57, 58, 72; and
Uemura Masahisa, 71, 77–78. *See
also* Christianity
good. *See* ethics; moral training; *rinrigaku*
good wife/wise mother, 158–159. *See also*
new woman
government: based on the people, 159–
160; and Charter Oath, 12; critiques
of, 135, 141–142; Fukuzawa Yukichi
on, 11; and interiority, 76–77; Katō
Hiroyuki on, 40; and relation to

Shintō, 65. *See also* Boshin Edict;
Imperial Rescript on Education
great ultimate *(taikyoku),* 24, 55–56, 109,
177n.48
Green, T. H., 83; and Confucian ethics,
105, 109; and Ninomiya Sontoku,
146; and personalism, 121–122, 138,
146; and spiritual principle, 88–89,
187n.14. *See also* personalism
group-oriented principle *(dantaishugi),*
130–131
gumin (foolish masses). *See* foolishness

Harootunian, H. D., 156, 157, 173n.2,
174n.3
Haver, William: on integration, 73
healthy thought, 162, 165; and good wife/
wise mother discourse, 158; Inoue
Tetsujirō on, 114, 126; vs. Western
thought, 129; as wholesome *(kenzen
na)* thought, 127, 128, 140–141. *See
also* dangerous thought
hedonism, 34, 62, 177n.46
Hegel, G. W. F., 34, 72, 83, 86, 106, 107,
187n.9
Herder, J. G., 82–83, 84
Hibiya Riot, 128, 195n.32
High Treason Incident, xv, 149; and
dangerous thought, 126–129;
and Kōtoku Shūsui, 102. *See also*
anarchism; dangerous thought
Hiratsuka Raichō, 158–159
Hōtoku (repaying virtue) movement, 145
Howland, Douglas, 77, 167n.4, 168n.1
Hozumi Yatsuka, 149, 195n.41; and
ancestor worship, 120, 194n.8; and
moral training textbooks, 132;
and national morality, 119–120,
131–132; on socialism, 127, 155
humanism: as critique of moral
particularism, 165; and ethics of
personalism, 153, 157–158, 160, 165;
and Nishibe Susumu, 163
hylomorphic epistemology, 108–110,
113, 156; characteristics of, 108,
191n.81; and heaven-human unity,
109; and subject-object identity, 88,

26, 50, 83; relocation of, 111–112;
and universal existence, 34–36,
38; and virtue of the human heart
(shintoku), 100–103; and Watsuji
Tetsurō, 160–161, 202n.27; and
Yoshino Sakuzō, 159–160
universalization, 72, 96, 117, 173n.65;
of civilized practice, 13, 19; of
Occidental ethics, 92, 97, 101, 106;
and suppression, 3, 115, 125, 131,
150, 153, 165
utilitarianism, xv, 22, 27, 50, 81, 86–87;
Fukasaku Yasubumi on, 131;
and hedonism, 34, 62, 177n.46,
183n.20; Inoue Enryō on, 59; Inoue
Tetsujirō's critique of, 97–98, 101,
103, 104–105, 106, 189n.50; in Inoue
Tetsujirō's *New Theory of Ethics,*
33–34; J. S. Mill's "Utilitarianism," 87,
187n.11; Murakami Senshō on, 62;
and Nishi Amane, 31; and reason
(risei), 50

violence: of civilization, 99–100, 190n.60;
concealment of, 154; discursive,
192n.3; and national morality, 116,
117; and pursuit of the ideal, xi, xvi,
117, 125, 128, 151, 200n.112
Volksgeist (folk spirit), xi–xii, 82, 83, 84,
112, 193n.4. See also *minzoku*

Wang Yang-ming, 127, 191n.69. *See also*
Yōmeigaku
Watanabe Kazan, 28
Watsuji Tetsurō, 157, 164; and national
morality, 160–161, 165, 194n.9,
202n.27; on the state, 202n.26; and
subject-object unity, 188n.24
way of humanity *(jindō),* 25; as contested
term, 143–144

wénmíng, 99–100, 190n.59. See also
bunmei
West, 8, 10, 99; and civilizational
hierarchies, 111, 112, 146, 170n.22,
174n.3; civilization of, xi, 7, 13,
18, 81; differentiating Japan from,
82, 130–131, 137–138, 145, 156,
190n.62, 197n.70; emulation of, 14;
expansion into East Asia, 5, 85; as
ill, 155; as imagined space, xiii, 7;
Inoue Tetsujirō on, 93, 98, 101, 104,
117, 130; Japan's cultural struggle
with, 157, 163; knowledge and
skills of, 7, 24, 26, 28–29, 48, 59, 69;
materialistic values of, 155; moral
and religious teachings of, 25, 42, 67,
69–70; Nakashima Rikizō on, 85, 90,
92; Okakura Kakuzō on, 112–113;
poisonous thought of, 126, 142,
154–155, 189n.50; power of, 1, 5, 31,
101; satirization of, 18–19. *See also*
ethics, Occidental

Yamagata Aritomo: and dangers of
socialism, 127, 155; and legalism,
14–15
Yanaka Village, 135
Yōmeigaku, 29; identity of knowledge and
action *(chikō goitsu),* 108, 192n.82;
Inoue Tetsujirō's study of, 81, 97–99,
101–106, 108, 111, 191n.69; journal
Yōmeigaku, 103, 106, 109–110.
See also Confucianism; Kogaku;
Shushigaku
Yoshida Kumaji, 95, 119, 135, 160, 163
Yoshida Seiichi, 122, 129, 140, 157
Yoshino Sakuzō, 159–160, 165

Zen no kenkyū, 89, 139–140, 188n.23
Žižek, Slavoj, 129

About the Author

Richard Reitan received his doctorate in history from the University of Chicago in 2002. His research centers on issues of ethics, gender, and identity in modern Japanese intellectual history. He has published a number of articles on related topics, among them "National Morality, the State, and 'Dangerous Thought': Approaching the Moral Ideal in Late Meiji Japan" (*Japan Studies Review,* 2005) and "Claiming Personality: Reassessing the Dangers of the 'New Woman' in early Taishō Japan" (*positions: east asia cultures critique,* forthcoming). Professor Reitan is currently on the history faculty at Franklin and Marshall College.

Production Notes for Reitan / MAKING A MORAL SOCIETY

Interior designed by University of Hawai'i Press Production Department with text in Minion Pro and display in ITC Clearface Heavy.

Composition by Lucille C. Aono

Printing and binding by The Maple-Vail Book Manufacturing Group